China's Strategic Interests in the South China Sea

This book explores China's strategic interests in the South China Sea, with specific emphasis on power projection and resource security. China's regional actions and reactions are reshaping power dynamics in East and South-East Asia, while economic and geopolitical futures depend on the variegated outcomes of these complex and iterative relationships with neighbouring countries and the USA.

The Introduction assesses China's external and internal dynamics and influences, examines China's search for energy and resources, and looks at China's oil security through the lenses of diplomacy and economics. The Country Case Studies explore China's relationships with Japan, the Philippines, the USA and Vietnam with regards to claims, disputes, conflicts and strategic interests in the South China Sea. The Conclusion incorporates insights and builds on a number of factors and issues to produce a better understanding of the incentives, motivations and rationales that propel China to project power and secure resources in the South China Sea.

Key features:

- offers an in-depth analysis of China's strategic interests in the South China Sea;
- assists scholars and students in understanding Chinese relationships with neighbouring countries;
- explains China's power projection and its implications on US economic and security pacts;
- explores the links between peace, prosperity and security, and the acts supporting these goals.

Sigfrido Burgos Cáceres is a consultant specializing in international development, political economy and foreign affairs. From 2007–12 he was based in Rome, Italy, at the Food and Agriculture Organization of the United Nations. He has published peer-reviewed journal articles on China's natural resource quests in Africa, South-East Asia, South America and globally. Together with Sophal Ear he co-authored *The Hungry Dragon: How China's Resource Quest Is Reshaping the World* (Routledge, 2013). He lives in Mobile, Alabama, with his wife.

China's Strategic Interests in the South China Sea

Power and resources

Sigfrido Burgos Cáceres

LONDON AND NEW YORK

First edition published 2014
by Routledge
2 Park Square, Milton Park, Abingdon, Oxfordshire OX14 4RN

and by Routledge
711 Third Avenue, New York, NY 10017

First issued in paperback 2015

Routledge is an imprint of the Taylor & Francis Group, an informa business

© 2014 Sigfrido Burgos Cáceres

The right of Sigfrido Burgos Cáceres to be identified as the author of this work has been asserted by them in accordance with the Copyright, Designs and Patents Act 1988.

All rights reserved. No part of this book may be reprinted or reproduced or utilised in any form or by any electronic, mechanical, or other means, now known or hereafter invented, including photocopying and recording, or in any information storage or retrieval system, without permission in writing from the publishers.

Trademark notice: Product or corporate names may be trademarks or registered trademarks, and are used only for identification and explanation without intent to infringe.

British Library Cataloguing in Publication Data
A catalogue record for this book is available from the British Library

Library of Congress Cataloging in Publication Data
Burgos Caceres, Sigfrido, author.
   China's strategic interests in the South China Sea : power and resources / Sigfrido Burgos Cáceres. – First edition.
      pages cm
   Includes bibliographical references and index.
Summary: "Explores China's strategic interests in the South China Sea, with a specific emphasis on power projection and resource security. Contains sections on China's power and resources and case studies on Japan, Vietnam, the USA and the Philippines, and discusses how China's actions are reshaping the power dynamics in East and South-East Asia"– Provided by publisher.
   1. China–Strategic aspects. 2. South China Sea–Strategic aspects. 3. National security–China. 4. Sea-power–China. 5. China–Foreign relations–21st century. 6. Energy security–China. 7. Natural resources–China. 8. Natural resources–South China Sea. I. Title.
   UA835.B86 2013
   355'.033051–dc23
                          2013022046

ISBN13: 978-1-85743-823-9 (pbk)
ISBN13: 978-1-85743-709-6 (hbk)

Typeset in Times New Roman
by Taylor & Francis Books

Europa Commissioning Editor: Cathy Hartley
Editorial Assistant: Amy Welmers

Contents

Preface	vii
Acknowledgements	x
Acronyms and abbreviations	xi

PART I
Introduction 1

1 Assessing China's external and internal dynamics
and influences 3

2 Understanding China's global search for energy
and resources 24

3 China's oil security: diplomacy, economics and the prospects for
peaceful growth 45

PART II
Country case studies 57

4 Japan 59

5 The Philippines 74

6 The United States of America 81

7 Vietnam 104

PART III
Conclusion 119

8 Power projection 121

vi *Contents*

9 Resource security 132

Bibliography 143
Index 155

Preface

This book examines the People's Republic of China's strategic interests in the South China Sea, and focuses on power projection and resource security. Certainly, China pursues other strategic interests, but in order to make this book a manageable endeavour it discusses chiefly the topics of power and resources while making connections to economics, governance, national security, politics and society. It takes a close look at how dynamics in these multidimensional domains affect the drafting of strategies and policy-making, and the influence they have on state actions.

China is a large, populous country that is unique owing to its salient features: the Chinese Communist Party; accelerated economic growth resulting from low-cost labour; trade openness; domestic consumption and urbanization; rapid industrialization and strong support for exports; autocratic capitalism; one-party rule and political repression; one-child policy; censorships; and firm government control of a large number of aspects of Chinese socio-cultural life. The latter also extends to structural development, banking, finances, the economy and the military in the form of direct and indirect interventions. For instance, the Chinese Government has intervened proactively in economic affairs since the 1970s and managed entry into the World Trade Organization in 2001 following 15 years of negotiations. This meant a new impetus towards the development of trade, the fine-tuning of a motor for growth and prosperity, and liberalization.

The Government knew that looking outwards instead of inwards was the route to becoming a superpower. Throughout the country, and especially in coastal areas, domestic production and manufacturing plants were supported. Commercial and industrial output was directed towards internal and external markets. Internally, this meant that job creation resulted in rising incomes, which in turn were allocated to consumption and savings (or investments). Externally, output was exported not only to abutting countries in the region but also internationally, to the wealthy consumption-oriented countries in the West. The massive selling of outputs over 30 years meant that revenues increased exponentially. This occurred through the collection and accumulation of fees, capital gains, dividends from state-owned investments, interest income, remittances, taxes, and record profits in the private sector. As money

viii *Preface*

flowed into China, the Government devised a plan to spend the incoming funds strategically (in all sorts of monetary denominations)—a centrally planned economy figuring out how, when and where to put the money in order to reap the most benefits.

As expenditures were allocated, strategists in China reasoned that all successful states sit on three strong pillars: prosperity, power and security. In order to solidify China's foundations and pillars the Government decided to invest heavily in education and research, infrastructure, the strengthening of institutions, overseas business development via sovereign funds, state banks, joint ventures and so on, and by developing a mighty military (air force, army and navy). The short- and long-term rationale behind these expenditures was prosperity through economic growth, especially given that full employment lifts many out of poverty, ensures social stability and prolongs the continuity of a single-party state governed by a privileged few in the capital, Beijing. However, the linking of these dots is incomplete without the inclusion of essential contributions to production: energy sources, natural resources and raw materials. The absence of these essential inputs can bring the economic and industrial machinery to an abrupt stop, and the Chinese Government is fully aware of this reality. With this in mind, it is at this narrowed juncture that officials inform decision-making by understanding that there are prerequisites to keeping China buoyant and moving forward. And since it is believed that the South China Sea holds the promise of vast reserves of oil and gas, as well as an important sea conduit, it is not surprising that the Chinese Government is so assertively focused on controlling (or owning) the territories, resources and waters in the South China Sea.

The problem is that China is not the only country in the region that seeks to claim control or ownership of assets and shipping lanes in this location. Six other countries have expressed an interest in the South China Sea, all of which have overlapping territorial and maritime claims that are contested and disputed in bi- and multilateral settings. These countries include Brunei, Indonesia, the Philippines, Malaysia, Taiwan and Vietnam. Estimates of oil deposits vary greatly, ranging between 1,100m. metric tons to 17,700m. tons of crude oil, and similarly natural gas deposits are estimated at between 25,000,000m. cu m and 57,000,000m. cu m.

Owing to the number of claimants and the complexity of handling competing claims and recurrent disputes, as well as the potential windfalls from oil and gas revenues, the Chinese Government has designed an overarching strategy of power projection in the South China Sea, one that is aimed at securing critical resources and heralding the arrival of a powerful military force in East and South-East Asia. The Chinese Government is quite ready to show its new-found assertiveness, boldness and capacity to act as a regional leader, but neighbours are anxious that China will use its economic and military power to settle outstanding claims by force.

This book comprises three parts: Introduction, Country Case Studies and Conclusion. The Introduction assesses China's external and internal dynamics and influences, examines China's search for energy and resources and looks at China's oil security through the lenses of diplomacy and economics. The Country Case Studies explore China's relationships with Japan, the Philippines, the USA and Vietnam with regards to claims, disputes, conflicts and strategic interests in the South China Sea. While Japan and the USA are not claimants or disputants to territories or resources in the South China Sea, they are deeply vested in the area owing to interstate commerce, international trade, shipping routes, regional security and power balancing. The Conclusion incorporates insights derived from China's actions, behaviours, reactions and policies, and builds on a number of factors and issues identified in the Introduction to produce a better understanding of the incentives, motivations and rationales that propel China to project power and secure critical resources in the South China Sea.

Sigfrido Burgos Cáceres
Mobile, Alabama, USA
April 2013

Acknowledgements

This book is an attempt to capture a country's portrait at a time of momentous change: a freeze-frame snapshot of a fast-moving target. I could not have done this work without the scholarly input of academics, analysts and researchers around the world, as well as commentators and journalists covering China, South-East Asia and the South China Sea, who write and publish articles, books, chapters and essays. I am indebted to Cathy Hartley, Commissioning Editor, and Amy Welmers, Editorial Assistant, both in Academic Reference at Routledge. Also, many thanks to Alison Phillips for her truly exceptional copy-editing and for making this book conform to house style. Last, I want to thank my wife, Amy, for her devotion, encouragement, love, patience, support and understanding.

Chapter 2 is based on an article previously published in *Central European Journal of International Security Studies*, Vol. 7, No. 1, 2013.

Some of the material in Chapter 4 appeared in a peer-reviewed article published online by the *Georgetown Journal of International Affairs*, 2013.

Acronyms and abbreviations

ASEAN	Association of Southeast Asian Nations
CACF	The China-Africa Cooperation Forum
CCP	Chinese Communist Party
CFR	Council on Foreign Relations
CNOOC	China National Offshore Oil Corporation
CPDA	China Public Diplomacy Association
CPI	Consumer Price Index
CUES	Code for Unalerted Encounters at Sea
ECS	East China Sea
EEZ	Exclusive Economic Zone
EU	European Union
FDI	Foreign Direct Investment
FTA	Free Trade Agreement
GDP	Gross Domestic Product
ICJ	International Court of Justice
NEAC	National Energy Administration of China
NGO	Non-governmental Organization
OECD	Organisation for Economic Co-operation and Development
PAP	People's Armed Police
PLA	People's Liberation Army
PM	Prime Minister
SCS	South China Sea
UN	United Nations
UNCLOS	United Nations Convention on the Law of the Sea
UNCTAD	United Nations Conference on Trade and Development
USA	United States of America
USEIA	United States Energy Information Administration
USGS	United States Geological Survey
WTO	World Trade Organization

Map of South East Asia

Part I
Introduction

1 Assessing China's external and internal dynamics and influences

Background

Of critical importance to the Chinese Government is the maintenance of domestic security and stability, that is, the minimization of sparks that could ignite popular unrest or mass revolts. The leadership in Beijing paid close attention to the wave of demonstrations and protests that erupted in the Middle East and North Africa during 2011. They recognized the power of the people to take to the streets to complain about abuses, indifference, injustice, mistreatments, oppression and about national leaders holding on to their positions for decades. The Chinese Government perceived the Arab Spring as an expression of widespread dissatisfaction with governance and political parties, as well as with income disparity, sluggish growth, and unequal distribution of benefits among citizens. In short, the Government had a glimpse of what could happen in China were things to get out of control—a taste of techniques in civil resistance and the use of social media to bring about change.

As far as domestic security and stability are concerned, growth and prosperity move to the top of the list of influencing factors. During the period of trade openness and explosive growth in China in the 19th and 20th centuries the urban and coastal regions boomed, while the rural and interior highlands lagged behind.[1] In terms of household income, internal comparisons are dismal, while international comparisons are alarming. According to an article in *Forbes*, 'the average annual household income in China, converted to dollars, was $10,220, compared with $84,300 in the United States'.[2] A report based on data collected in 2009 revealed that approximately 66% of Chinese household incomes were 'lower than the average household income in Bolivia'.[3] These figures suggest that China is a rich–poor country: wealthy on the surface yet impoverished at its core. The income–wealth disparities between the coast and the highlands, and the urban and rural areas, have in the past created tensions within China, especially when prosperity is not felt in the remote hinterlands.[4] History teaches a lesson on the risks of inequality and divisiveness. In 1927, following the failed uprising in the city of Shanghai, Mao Zedong capitalized on these differences and gathered enough momentum to form a peasant army that eventually defeated the opposing forces and captured the

4   *Introduction*

coastal regions. In his attempt to create a more cohesive, equal and united country, Mao cut off China from the international trading system, and this ultimately resulted in protracted economic decline and a lengthy period of destitution, humiliation, shame, poverty and indigence.[5]

Current Chinese leaders, however, are smarter, incentivized and very quick learners. In March 2011 members of the Politburo Standing Committee of the Chinese Communist Party (CCP) crafted a more sensible plan to achieve domestic security and stability, one which involved securing popular trust and loyalty via economic growth, full employment, and rising incomes, and which published news of a grand and powerful China that is no longer bullied by foreign hegemons or regional imperial forces. This approach feeds on nationalistic sentiments, that is, it fuels the popular discourse with uplifting slogans such as the 'revival of the nation', thus signalling the intention of Chinese leaders to become reform-oriented nationalists. However, the purchase of loyalty via economic growth was bought hastily. For example, a report by *60 Minutes* in early March 2013 revealed that while China's economy is now the second largest in the world, the country's rapid growth may have created the largest housing bubble in history, especially since the Chinese Government backed and encouraged the construction of a large number of buildings, shopping malls, and infrastructure projects that are now sitting empty or underutilized, collecting dust and accruing financing costs. Moreover, the strategy for industrial expansion was executed too rapidly and poorly, with minimal consideration for markets, pricing or profit margins. Now, as then, the driving rationale is to create an economy with full employment, and the thinking behind it is that personal and household income will be spent wholly on consumption and savings. In fact, in order to finance a percentage of industrial and manufacturing expansion, the Chinese tapped into private domestic savings, and now depositors find themselves risking their savings at the hands of greedy industrialists or inept government planners. Also, as national capital is sucked into long-term projects, many fear that internal consumption will suffer in the short term (e.g. there will be insufficient money available to buy domestic outputs), which puts more pressure on exports to Western markets that since 2008 have been sadly depressed and are recovering far too slowly.[6]

In the paragraph above we touched upon nationalism and popular loyalty to the CCP. With that in mind, the reader might ask: who is pushing the Chinese Government to adopt such an approach? The answer lies in the composition of the CCP. It is now known that 'Chinese military men, who make up about 20 percent of the Central Committee, have become increasingly vocal about their desire to drive the United States' out of the East and South China Seas. The CCP meetings in Beijing are said to be abound with 'long-standing rhetoric about ending a century of humiliation at foreign hands', which makes such an approach conveniently justifiable and easy to pack into sound bites that ignite popular boldness, courage and pride. However, a firm approach to foreign policy is not always welcomed. Throughout

East and South-East Asia, considerable alarm is being expressed at the way in which the CCP has abandoned Deng Xiaoping's well-known pragmatic internationalism. Many regional actors have expressed hope that the General Secretary of the Communist Party of China, Xi Jinping, will be able tactfully to curb the military's increasing bellicosity.[7]

The Chinese Government's central economic and financial planning works by directing all major sectors of the economy and formulating decisions about the use of available resources. The Chinese industrial and manufacturing base intentionally produces more goods than it can consume; therefore, there is immense pressure on the Government to export these products to countries throughout the world. Thus, China has become a major exporter and importer of inputs, that is, the energy sources, raw materials and natural resources (such as diesel, petrol and oil) required to keep the economy running efficiently and at full speed. If these inputs are derived from nearby regions, it is likely that a large percentage arrive by air or land (which use even more inputs in order to run or operate), but if massive inputs are sourced from abroad, they definitely arrive by sea, that is, by ships carrying containers. These ships and vessels, almost without exception, have to pass through the East China Sea and the South China Sea, regardless of their port of origin. This being said, the safe passage of inputs through waters that are not totally controlled by China is taken as a 'strategic vulnerability', a weak point that can be 'intentionally troubled' so that China's growth is impaired. To be sure, the dynamic works in both ways: just as it needs to draw inputs in, China needs to get outputs out. The Chinese, in this trade-dependent scenario, have to work diligently to make sure that foreign demand for its goods are either maintained or increased, which explains why China has been playing banker to the USA and the European Union (EU).

Externally, China has a strong interest in either maintaining or increasing control over buffer territories, that is, land masses adjacent to the Chinese mainland which confer what is known as the first line of natural defence. The majority of people of the traditional Han Chinese core are grouped in the eastern part of the mainland. This area is characterized by much rainfall and humidity, which separates it from the arid and dryer central and western parts of the country. From the standpoint of threat mitigation and security, the Chinese mainland is dependent upon the reciprocity or outright control of four non-Han Chinese buffer territories that hug the country. These territories are Mongolia, Manchuria, Tibet and Xinjiang. The control of these buffer territories is critical to China because it provides layers of protection against India from the west, South-East Asian countries from the south-east, Russia from the north, or any attack across the western steppes. Think of it as an artificial and natural fencing for a property, an intentional delimitation that lets outsiders know that they have crossed the line and that moving forward could mean that they are perceived to be intruders. The presence of deserts, forests, jungles, mountain ranges, steppes and wastelands (in Siberia) provide the Chinese mainland with barriers or obstacles against attacks by foreign actors.

6   *Introduction*

However, to the east and south, China is open to vast bodies of water (e.g. shores, East China Sea, Sea of Japan and South China Sea), and there are a number of countries that for some time have been seeking partial or total control of these shared waters (e.g. Japan, South Korea, Taiwan, the Philippines and Vietnam). This exposure carries deep implications for national security, especially when related to the protection of borders, territories and strategic interests. To China, control of the critical South China Sea is a security imperative.[8]

Challenges, obstacles and setbacks

The EU and the USA form two of the world's largest economies. They are deeply interconnected not only between themselves but also with the rest of the world. As the world witnessed from 2008, their problems and struggles easily trickle down into global economies, especially those that depend heavily on exports to the West to support their economic growth. Hence, China is one such country to feel the impact of the continuing job crisis, declining prospects for economic recovery, sluggish growth of gross domestic product (GDP), and the delay of purchases owing to uncertainties. China's two most important customers are undoubtedly the EU and the USA. Decreased consumption in general and fewer high-value purchases in particular by consumers, private firms, multinationals and public sector entities, along with increased competition from vibrant developing-emerging countries, has shaken the Government's plans to achieve popular well-being and national prosperity. As China's economic engine decelerates (GDP growth targets for 2013 rested at 7.5%),[9] national job security has weakened and Chinese consumers have changed spending patterns to account for a world economy that is full of uncertainties and not yet on a stable footing. The amendment of domestic consumption levels has affected domestic demand for products and services, which puts further pressure on local firms to tighten belts in an effort to weather the storm. And, as if this is not enough, regional sea routes have been under closer scrutiny following a series of territorial spats in the islands and nearby waters of the South China Sea, which has 'soured' relations between China and its consumption-driven neighbours.[10]

The Chinese Government has come to understand that when the EU and the USA suffer from economic ills, a large number of countries are affected to an even greater degree. The economic and financial struggles of the West inevitably influence China, whether or not this consequence had been foreseen. The affluent and wealthy cities and towns in the coastal regions are particularly affected because they depend largely on exports and trade to keep their local economic engines running, and the marginalized and poor highlands in the interior are affected too because they are reliant upon aid, grants and subsidies that are difficult to secure from the central government in Beijing since priorities are reshuffled when national economic growth is compromised. The CCP, in order to tackle the main triggers for social unrest in the country, 'have announced record government spending in 2013 that will sustain growth and maintain the ruling Communist Party's grip on power through an enhanced budget for internal security'. The Chinese Government promised to raise the fiscal deficit target to 2% of GDP in 2013, its highest since 2010 and up from 1.6% in 2012.[11] Alongside this stimulus, the Government floated the news to media outlets of an increase of almost 9% in the 2013 domestic security budget, taking it to US $128,000m.—a boost to military expenditure for the third year in a row. However, this particular announcement gave considerable concern to East and South-East Asian leaders since it implied that China's military apparatus would gain more strength.[12]

With regard to buffer territories, the Chinese Government has to deal tactfully with stresses and strains. Actors and networks in Tibet and Xinjiang are not very keen on the idea of being occupied by Han Chinese. The Government is fully aware that losing buffer territories is risky and 'bad press', especially because it threatens national security and widens the opportunity for aggressors to further destabilize already unstable regions (e.g. through the encouragement and promotion of radical religious groups). In 2009, for example, unrest and violence in Xinjiang resulted in the deaths of nearly 200 people. This was followed by a forceful crackdown that produced numerous arrests of accused protesters and rioters, as well as a near-total shutdown of internet connections and overseas telephone services. Many non-governmental organizations (NGOs), such as Amnesty International, accused the Chinese Government of abusing its authority, using excessive force, and illegally torturing detainees. As a convenient solution, 'in both Buddhist Tibet and Muslim Xinjiang, China hopes that economic development, improved infrastructure, and steady demographic shifts will gradually ease the ethnic tensions that periodically erupt into violence'.[13] However, the quick-fix measures do not entirely address core grievances advanced by ethnic minorities, which include, but are not limited to, government interference in religious affairs, discrimination in economic opportunities, and a steady arrival of 'wild' Han Chinese that threatens to erode regional cultural identities.[14]

Tibet has emerged as a strategic interest to both China and India. Instability in Tibet is indeed a cause for concern since neither country could profit from its control. Obviously, a full-blown war between China and India is far-fetched in view of geographical limitations: the Himalayas. This great mountain system forms a barrier between the Plateau of Tibet to the north and the alluvial plains of the Indian subcontinent to the south, and its terrain is so treacherous and challenging that a large-scale armed conflict launched from either side is unfathomable. However, if China or India were to gain control of territories on each other's side of the Himalayas, it is believed that sustained threats could ensue via military bases or counterinsurgency outposts.[15] According to the Chinese Government, the perceived threat lies in Indian troops invading Tibet. To the Indian Government in Delhi, the perceived threat is the entry of the People's Liberation Army (PLA) into

8 Introduction

northern Pakistan from the southern mainland or accross India's far north-eastern frontier, bordering the state of Arunachal Pradesh. However, this cannot be entirely blamed on China or India given that, when 'the colonial power, Britain, withdrew from India, it left a dangerous legacy of carelessly or arbitrarily drawn borders'. As a result, tensions between China and India spark occasionally. Most contentious are the borders in Kashmir, where China, India and Pakistan have competing claims. To complicate matters, China has extended its control and influence over portions of Kashmir, largely with the support of Pakistan.[16] Today, without doubt, Sino–Indian rapprochement has progressed positively since the bitter war of 1962.

As noted earlier, China seeks domestic stability to prolong political continuity. Leaders of the CCP look out for the minimization of risks and threats, and the maximization of opportunities and strengths throughout the territory. They understand that the central and western parts of China are in need of attention, development assistance, provision of adequate education, improvement of health care delivery, and progressive inclusion into national well-being to avoid carving a deep rich-poor divide that runs the risk of igniting apathy, divisiveness, mistrust and the seeds of local revolutions.[17] This targeted aid to the interior of the country calls for trillions of dollars in public investments, which means that robust, sustained economic growth and constructive opportunism in the coastal regions is an absolute priority. The emphasis on trade promotion, the protection of sea routes, and the build-up of military power can be viewed through this lens: China is seeking to perfect and perpetuate a model of socialist market economy or autocratic capitalism that validates not only this system of governance but also justifies it by claiming that China acts thus nationally, regionally and internationally in order to spread the most benefits to the most people most of the time. Moreover, the CCP leaders realized early on that if inputs stop rolling in and outputs stop flowing out, the whole model will start to exhibit major flaws and show signs of crumbling and, not much later, as if by domino effect, economic transfers to the interior will start dropping, along with employment, incomes and consumption, which is politically risky since popular tensions and social unrest could invite strikes, protests, revolts and calls for change.[18]

Maintaining these inflows, outflows and internal transfers is a never-ending challenge for the Chinese Government. At the intersection of macroeconomics and strategic policy-making we find that China's economic model is tinkered from the cusp, meaning that regulation of indices and parameters such as building permits, business and housing start-ups, incomes and wages, employment, inflation, exchange rates, balance of trade, and profits, to name but a few, are cleverly manipulated to devise a particular economic-financial outcome. The problem with this tinker-as-we-go mechanism is that it frequently results in gross misallocations of resources that bring about productivity mishaps, and that these hiccups in market-regulating dynamics tend to further exacerbate the messy interplay between demand and supply, or, more simply, between inputs and outputs. Above all, one of the most pervasive alterations is that of inflation, which erodes the country's ability to compete with other low-cost producers of goods around the world and ends up raising the high costs of bailing out the other two-thirds in the Chinese mainland. In response, the Government decided to manage inflation rates more decisively by lowering the control target of annualized consumer price index to 3.5% for 2013, compared with 4% for 2012. However, some scholars argue that China's authoritarian market economy is a growth-oriented model in which 'central government leaders are intelligent designers of institutional change, provincial and local officials are potential predators, and private firms are potential prey ... and that reductions in discriminatory policies are the major institutional contributors to China's market miracle, whereas improvements in the rule of law and in the protection of private property rights are not needed for short-run economic growth'.[19] Of course, this argument assumes a purely money-driven approach that fails to consider the interplay of politics, power, security and status.

The obstacles and setbacks confronted by the leadership in Beijing are tremendous. Most of these complex issues have to be addressed internally while closely observing overseas activity. China's banking stability, economic activity, financial soundness and manufacturing might is so intertwined that a miscalculation in one area can precipitate disaster in another at lightning speed. More importantly, the Chinese Government can no longer rely on the paradigms of three decades ago. It must outgrow its emphasis on low value-added goods and gradually migrate to process and manufacture higher value-added items such as tractors, solar panels, communication and information technologies, machines that make machines, speed boats and vehicles, among others. The paradigm shift and strategic reorientation of efforts and resources (including humans) necessitates a more modern, knowledgeable workforce, that is, a well-educated and trained mass of workers willing to go further than competitors. This could, in part, explain China's renewed support for the arts, education, science, mathematics and engineering, as well as ambitious targets for building a green economy, one with a lower demand for hydrocarbons and reduced pollution levels. At the same time it means that China will have to come to grips with real high-stakes competition with established industrial nations such as France, Germany, Japan and the USA, all of which value aesthetics, quality, longevity and reliability. This is the new battleground upon which it must fight.

Power projection: understanding China's military build-up

China's military build-up and modernization encompasses the armed forces and national defence capabilities. Its progressive strengthening is grounded on the Government's desire to uphold national security, sovereignty, and maritime and territorial integrity. According to a report released in 2013 by the Ministry of Finance, China's official defence budget for that year was expected to be raised to 720,000m. yuan, representing an increase of approximately

10 *Introduction*

11% compared with 2012. The issue with defending maritime and territorial integrity is that there are numerous land and water delimitations that remain contested, that is, other countries have overlapping claims over the same land masses or seas. This is further complicated by the fact that China is resolutely dependent on the high seas to trade, prosper and survive—an input-intensive and export-led economic model that cannot ship its goods is doomed to fail. The open geographical layout of the East China Sea and the South China Sea exposes China to blockades, delays and interdictions. The East China Sea is touched by North and South Korea, Japan and Northern Taiwan, with an archipelago to the south. The South China Sea is touched by Southern Taiwan, the Philippines, Borneo, Vietnam, Malaysia and Singapore, with a grouping of islands in the middle (i.e. the Paracel and Spratly Islands). If one looks at this configuration from a naval standpoint, it becomes clear that the Government's security concerns emanate from the likelihood of aggressors or disputants to attack the mainland or invade the East and South China Seas through wide openings along the south-eastern shore. In particular, China fears that Japan or the USA could choke China by closing off maritime access points. More specifically, Japan or the USA could place naval fleets strategically not inside the string of islands but outside, thus diverting Chinese warships away from the mainland and into the wide open sea, which decreases the chance of successful retaliation and increases vulnerabilities.[20]

Against this background, the Chinese Government has few to zero options: China must defend the East and South China Seas and seek control of the disputed territories in order to minimize risks and threats. At play, the argument goes, is state survival in a vicious anarchical international system. According to Michael Wesley, 'it is in the South China Sea that the components of Asia's changing power dynamics are most concentrated and on display: China's growing strategic heft and paranoid sense of entitlement; its Southeast Asian neighbors' hopes and misgivings about China's regional dominance; and the United States' compulsion to meet China's strategic challenge'.[21] While it is true that China does not currently have the naval capability to challenge the USA in the high seas, this does not mean that it would not make it difficult for the USA to settle scores with ease and expediency. The Government is maintaining a low profile, while waiting patiently to complete its military build-up and modernization so that in the near future it could face any challenge in an authoritative manner. However, it would be irresponsibly misguided to assume that China's difficulties are only concerned with the delivery of aircraft carriers, submarines and warships. This assumption is dangerous because it misses the human component, that is, that admirals, naval officers, seamen and ratings require years of education and training to fully manoeuvre naval deployments and launch attacks on real aggressors. The development of naval commanders and their junior officers takes decades. Also, one can safely assume that a series of exercises in open waters will be closely examined by regional and foreign powers. Therefore, the difficulties that China faces are numerous: the expected naval build-up and military modernization will take many years to be completed. Put simply, in contemporary times China has never dictated military or naval orders to admirals or commanders leading a truly mighty fleet of warships in these seas—real experience is lacking. Chinese military officers have yet to demonstrate to the world the country's ability to deploy coherently a sequential, multilayered, and multi-armed defensive ring around its territorial waters.[22]

Of course, the Chinese Government understands its structural limitations and is aware of its shortcomings. The civilian and military leadership within the CCP have crafted a more tailored strategy to stave off a US or Japanese maritime intervention in the East and South China Seas: a tactical usage of anti-ship missiles launched from the coast and capable of destroying enemy warships, the more pronounced use of cyber warfare to decipher enemy plans before they become operational, and a very much increased presence of submarines and small military garrisons in controlled territories. It is likely that the US Administration and military officials, along with scholars and pundits, are not counting on an all-out war with China, but they are prepared to engage in mounting an attack should conditions or situations change in the near future. The philosophy on both sides of the Pacific is 'expect the best, prepare for the worst', while making it difficult for either party to claim victory.

Let's look closely at the tailored strategy. US military and warfare strategists posit that the land-based, anti-ship missile defence plan against naval invasions is flawed unless it is complemented with accurate maritime reconnaissance and effective positioning systems. These complementarities are evident at first sight: in order to fire missiles and destroy warships in the high seas the Chinese will need to know where these ships are. Both reconnaissance and ocean positioning are only possible if space-based hardware and accompanying systems work to pinpoint warships or submarines on the surface, coupled with a fire-control mechanism that is integrated intimately with land-based controls and chain of command safeguards. It has been well documented that the Chinese have launched a space programme led by the China National Space Administration, and that space exploration has been accompanied by satellite operations since the early 1970s. It is only reasonable to assume that China already has a functional maritime reconnaissance and positioning system in operation, but what is not known is if the USA has developed the anti-satellite functional capabilities that would render Chinese satellites useless and their land-based missile attack plans totally worthless. Additionally, while it may be true that the Chinese Government has approved plans to enhance its coast-based missile stations, these are still inherently vulnerable to sea-based targeting—and attacks—by fighter jets and helicopters departing from aircraft carriers, drones (i.e. unmanned aerial vehicles), submarine-launched missiles, and cruise missiles.[23]

The Chinese military is therefore confronted with the unfortunate situation of having to proceed with extreme caution. However, this awkward position breeds creativity, and the CCP and its military men decided on a counter-strategy: acquire, control, or own small plots of land or seaports in countries

12   *Introduction*

touching the Indian Ocean,[24] the East China Sea, and the South China Sea. During the last few years the Chinese Government has floated ideas and plans of building deep-water ports (with naval outfits) in Bangladesh, Cambodia, Myanmar (Burma), Pakistan and Sri Lanka. In fact, a number of these ports have already been designed and financed, and are operational to varying degrees. Alongside ports come roads and railways, that is, the essential infrastructure to move energy sources, raw materials and natural resources into the mainland, as well as the shipping of goods for export to countries around the globe. Again, the same logic applies here: in order to finance large-scale infrastructure projects to sustain economic growth, the Government needs to feed the self-realizing cycle of capital-intensive investments and protection of strategic interests.[25]

Politically, China is forced to enhance (or at least maintain) amicable rapprochement with rogue and unstable countries in order to gain access to or control of ports and plots of land. Over the years, Bangladesh, Cambodia, Myanmar, Pakistan and Sri Lanka have all undergone periods of instability and unrest, and China would be foolish to assume that co-operation and reciprocity with these countries can be sustained in the long term. Let's look at Pakistan, for example. For some time leaders in Islamabad have been catering to US and European interests in exchange for aid and technical assistance, so China remains cautious about forging close ties with a pliant government that takes money from the West. By late 2012, for example, Myanmar, a reliable Chinese ally, had hosted a visit by the US President, Barack Obama, and had shown itself to be receptive to democratic processes and the beginnings of the rule of law. The rapprochement with 'Myanmar fits into a larger effort by the Obama administration to reorient American foreign policy more toward Asia and to engage the countries on China's periphery at a time of nervousness in the region about Beijing's increasing assertiveness'.[26] The Chinese have figured out that Myanmar's shift into US orbit has in part to do with resentment of China's rapacious exploitation of natural resources in the country and with political manipulations.

The negotiation, financing and construction of airports, seaports, naval bases, railways and roads in other countries does not translate directly into 'absolute' securement of strategic interests. All foreign countries are subject to their own socio-political dynamics, and the Chinese Government, no matter how benevolent and generous it is, can still be subjected to blackmail, discrimination, marginalization or opportunism. Local communities can rebel against Chinese influence and assets, just as in the past countries have reacted angrily against the USA when it announced major settlements in distant regions (Latin America, Central Asia and the Middle East). The fact that these Chinese-backed infrastructures exist in these volatile countries does not necessarily mean that unimpeded access is secured in the long term. Additionally, as if this were not enough, these capital-intensive projects are vulnerable to local, regional or foreign attacks by vandals, guerillas forces, insurgency movements, national armies or international coalitions.

China's external and internal dynamics and influences   13

A number of infrastructure projects in the East and South China seashores run the risk of never getting started. Some will be shelved on account of rivalry and suspicion, while others will be dropped because they are not approved by national legislatures. As a whole, Chinese proposals are examined carefully and usually end up undergoing scrutiny by anti-China elements in countries that have competing territorial and maritime claims over the same seas. This means that Chinese control and influence of say, ports and trade-relevant highways, is limited to what other countries decide to grant to China; so the notion that open, unlimited and unrestricted access to these entry–exit points is given simply because China is asking for them is not at all true. Moreover, the type of control and influence that China seeks along the shorelines of the East and South China Seas lies at the heart of regional suspicions that the Government is bent on hegemony and forceful acquiescence to its whims. The majority of members of the Association of Southeast Asian Nations (ASEAN) have come up with the logical calculus that in order for China to guarantee free and open access to critical entry-exit points along these shores it will have to muster significant political and military power, which is exactly what ASEAN has feared since its inception. While facing mounting uncertainties in terms of threat perception and economic expectation, scholars argue that ASEAN member countries will choose either to work with or balance against China, while others believe that they will respond by 'hedging'. In considering these options, these countries have to take into consideration their individual interests within the economic, political and security structure of the South-East Asian region.[27]

It is worth noting that a collective 'let's-fear-China' situation is dangerous because it can become a self-fulfilling prophesy: as countries expect China to behave badly, any move that has a slightly negative connotation will be flagged as being detrimental to the region. Certainly, since the CCP came to power, China has infrequently engaged in offensive military procedures, and those few instances have led to undesirable outcomes. For instance, the Chinese offensive period of the Korean War, from 25 November 1950 to 25 January 1951, achieved a stalemate but at a terrible cost to China (in terms of casualties and physical losses). The Battle of Chamdo in 1950, also known as the Chinese invasion of Tibet, resulted in the incorporation of Tibet into the People's Republic of China, which was successful then but continues to attract international condemnation and irritation regarding the escalation of Tibetan self-immolations.[28] And finally, in 1979 China's 29-day incursion into Vietnam (considered to be a response to what the Government interpreted as a collection of provocative actions and policies on the part of Hanoi) is still haunting the CCP since Vietnamese elements believe that their neighbour is bent on waging a multifaceted war of sabotage.

All in all, the Chinese Government has managed to send out a loud message regionally and internationally, and this is that its neighbours must now learn to deal with a competent and powerful military force that is growing and improving as time goes by. China is projecting an image of having

14 *Introduction*

superpower capabilities: the world's second largest economy; international media coverage; a seat in the UN Security Council along with multi-party consultations in regional peace talks; a space programme and space explorations; the world's highest railway; the biggest dam; the longest bridge; the most ambitious hydro-engineering project in human history; hosting and dominating the Olympics for the first time; and a mighty military force that it is said will soon rival US interests and power in Asia.

Internal security targets and external projection of power

The Chinese Government has designed, developed and implemented an efficient, functional and well-funded internal security apparatus which is tasked with maintaining domestic stability. Domestic stability is a catch-all phrase denoting an internal balancing act between anti-China and pro-China elements, the eradication of radical ideological and religious spin-offs as well as nascent terrorist cells, the dismantling of criminal rings, human trafficking and drug fiefdoms, the incarceration of criminals, killers, drug dealers, transgressors and law offenders, and the monitoring of groups or social movements that may prove to be destabilizing to the country. The Chinese security apparatus comprises several entities and systems which include, but are not limited to,[29] the Ministry of State Security, the Ministry of Public Security, the People's Armed Police (PAP), the PLA, and the state judicial and penal systems. This large apparatus is justified because of China's large population, its extensive borders with a number of multi-ethnic countries, and its history of internal tensions and struggles. To CCP leaders, the issue is not about current domestic tensions or uprisings, it is the probability of an 'unfortunate event' that could provoke a series of further incidents that would be much harder to contain. As such, planning against probabilities and worst-case scenarios is the prudent approach to risk and threat mitigation, and the consequent instructions emanating from this planning is the coherent build-up of an internal security apparatus to tackle probability targets. The Chinese Government promised to increase spending on public security in 2013 by boosting support to central, local and provincial governments, including the PAP, courts, correction centres and gaols, surveillance, and other areas of domestic security. Public security expenditure was expected to increase by 8.7% from 2012 levels to 769,000m. yuan.[30] Against this background, domestic politics have been dominated by two interlocking rationales: having a single security apparatus that is supposed to be effective and useful for internal and external needs; that is, dealing with a wide portfolio of destabilizing incidents using relevant ministries alongside the assistance of the PAP and the PLA, which for some time have been taught to distance themselves from offensive operations.[31] To varying degrees, China is still undergoing an opaque transitional period of rapid economic growth, military repositioning and social development, and the way in which this transition is managed domestically will hold significant implications for the Chinese state concerning both its internal and external security. To be sure, the use of armed forces (that for decades have been taught and trained for internal security actions) as a tool for offensive and belligerent operations could result, at best, in a stalemate or, at worst, a truly resolute defeat.

It is thus important to direct our attention to considering the complexity and magnitude of China's internal concerns and issues, as well as the challenges of simultaneously having to deal with external threats or foreign operation (i.e. a Sino–Japanese war, conflagration in the South China Sea, or occupying a neighbour such as Myanmar, for example), and the fact that counting on an inexperienced and untested security apparatus could lead to strategic overreach: a bundling of negative events might not outstrip China's ability and willingness to deal with chaos but would in all likelihood outstrip its logistical, operational and organizational capabilities. In sum, the evolving security apparatus was initially conceived to maintain stability within China and not as a tool to project power outwards. This implies that the crocheted strategy of utilizing a combination of army, navy, air force, civilian and military police, secret intelligence and thematic agencies for the purpose of projecting power externally is risky and not entirely grounded on bankable assets, experienced personnel, and the resource-intensive capacity of embarking on sustained warfare. However, despite some scepticism, a scholar at the Strategic and Defence Studies Centre argues that 'the People's Liberation Army's maritime denial strategy is quietly maturing, leaving the United States facing some difficult choices. As submarines and precision-guided strike capabilities accumulate in Chinese arsenals—and are woven into war plans—the US capacity for sea control and power projection in the Western Pacific, long taken for granted, is steadily being eroded'.[32]

Conveniently, in the 1980s the Chinese Government started to transfer responsibility for domestic security to the PAP. Similarly, border patrol and some elements of the PLA have retained some responsibility for the maintenance of internal peace and social stability. Nowadays, the PLA routinely besieges the information technology networks of foreign companies and governments in order to gain access to the systems of US defence contractors, as well as stealing 'technology blueprints, negotiating strategies and manufacturing processes from more than 100, mainly American, companies in a score of industries'.[33] More broadly, the PLA has shifted its attention away from domestic affairs and is now focusing more intently on regional and international issues, such as power projection in the East China Sea, the South China Sea, the Indian Ocean, and by showcasing its troops and equipment on holidays and special events. Also, the Chinese have been focusing on aerospace since it represents the latest frontier in creative and technological know-how. China's military is seeking investments in 'parts manufacturers, materials producers, leasing businesses, cargo airlines and airport operators'. Today, China 'rivals the United States as a market for civilian airliners, which China hopes to start supplying from domestic production'. This focus is not surprising given that the new CCP leaders have 'publicly

16   Introduction

emphasized long-range missiles and other aerospace programs in its push for military modernization'.[34] However, despite this reorganization of responsibilities and increased budgets for internal and external security, it remains obvious that China is still suffering from structural limitations, many of which 'undermine its ability to project power and make credible threats'.[35]

As the world tries to make sense of China in terms of prosperity, power and security, there is confusion or misperception about the degree of military power the Government says it can deploy theoretically and what it can deploy in reality. As facts stand, China has proved it has the power to deal with its people (both critics and supporters) and control its internal dynamics, but its capacity to coerce or manipulate its neighbours and other regional actors through sheer military strength is very limited. The media coverage of Taiwan's oft-quoted fear of an invasion has been overplayed, and the potential naval attack on Vietnamese or Japanese fishing vessels on the high seas to claim a few barren islands is frequently used to highlight China's regional 'feistiness'. The projection of Chinese power is real, but slow and systematic. The Chinese Government is clever enough to mix hard and soft power to achieve its objectives. Some say that in consideration of China's state of transition from regional backwater into a major player in international affairs, that hard power is preponderant and instrumental, while others argue that the key aspect of soft power is 'power'.[36] At times, commentators tend to overestimate the influence of popular culture, political events or military exercises on national attitude and foreign policies, but ultimately power-seeking is there.

National policy-making versus international politics

As one reads this and the following chapters, make no mistake that the rise of China is widely understood around the globe as the growing economic, military and political influence of China in world affairs, specifically on the effect that this so-called peaceful and non-intrusive rise will have on East and South-East Asia. However, China's rise has also been a major issue in US and European policy discourse. Politicians on both side of the Atlantic are routinely trying to figure out what the rise of China means to their countries and what implication it will have on commerce, finance, trade, power dynamics and the maintenance of global peace.[37]

In terms of national security and policy-making, the Chinese Government appears to adjust its actions and reactions according to what Europe, Japan and the USA are willing to do jointly, and not on what China plans to do at any given time. These calculations and corrections are based on realistic and practical considerations that relate to economic, political and military power,[38] and the likely outcomes of decisions in the short, medium and long term. As of 2013 China would be unable to win a war on the high seas against the USA. A naval showdown would inevitably embarrass China and confirm regional suspicions. The Government's plan of establishing ports along the shores of the East and South China Seas seems workable, but it will be fraught with costs, dangers, doubts, suspicion and uncertainties. At the moment, the political conditions are not favouring China, and it is likely that as the global economy recovers, some of the ASEAN member countries will firmly align themselves with the USA instead of colluding with China and India in an attempt to fall on the right side.

From an international perspective, major powers know and understand that the financial and physical demands of rapidly building up a Chinese force strong enough to secure territorial and maritime sovereignty will in all likelihood drain resources away from more economically important sectors (i.e. the renewable and non-renewable energy industries), and that the Chinese Government is dealing with a number of delicate internal issues that include rural protests, Tibetan unrest, and infighting within the CCP, among many others issues. The international community continues to hold on to the belief that as long as the USA keeps on dumping money into defence, national security and naval power build-up, the Government will be left with few options: one of these being to neutralize US influence within the region. In this case, the risk to the Government is of bothering or pestering the USA too soon, which could precipitate China's fears of blockades, interdictions or strategic encirclements. The real magnitude of these risks partly explains why China chose to enmesh itself so intricately in the US economy, so much so that the Obama Administration will pause before acting against China. In parallel, the new Chinese President, Xi Jinping, on his first trip abroad, chose to promote deeper co-operation with Russia[39] while the USA continues to tighten ties with its own allies across the Asia-Pacific region.[40]

China's emergence as a major power is evident in its growing influence and engagement in world political issues. For example, China was against Western intervention in the Syrian turmoil (ongoing in 2013), which can be seen as a form of 'soft balancing'.[41] However, Europe and the USA do not necessarily view China's foreign policy activities and pronouncements as being beneficial, especially because they erode the confidence of other nation states in the peace-making process that the West has perfected over time in unstable regions. Also, major powers in the West understand that China is using 'cheap options' to rally against traditional hegemonies: vociferous rhetoric, allying with former foes, insinuations, criticism, and a hard-line stance are used by members of the CCP to foster nationalist support among citizens for China's plans.

Despite the contestable interpretation of the rise of China, Western perspectives tend to fall into a wide landscape with 'positive-sum view on the one end and zero-sum view on the other end'.[42] The Chinese Government's assertiveness in the East and South China Seas is interpreted as an operation in which China wins and everyone else loses, while China's quest to secure energy and resources (away from the mainland) is perceived as Chinese annexation of the oil and gas that other world economies need to function and survive. In studying the way in which China's actions are interpreted,

18 *Introduction*

scrutinized and analysed, many scholars fail to realize that the Chinese Government is still struggling to find lasting solutions to fundamental strategic challenges and problems, and that any degree of contestation against traditional powers is in its infancy.[43] The regional tensions that Chinese civilian and military vessels can cause by patrolling areas that are disputed by neighbours is a truly debilitating situation that diverts energy and efforts from other more important national matters, but it is not a situation that could sink any country into protracted chaos. At present, all of the options on the table for the new Chinese leaders are weak and have serious limitations. In the near future, China's path will be one that will avoid making risky decisions or becoming trapped in 'lose-lose scenarios' that would lead to unfortunate outcomes. During the past 20–30 years China has proved that it has the ability to make its own way, but the new factor is that the Government lacks the tools to mould circumstances in its favour so that decision-making is easier, more certain and more predictable.

In the end, to signal strong alternatives, the Chinese Government's flourishing relationships with small and medium-sized powers around the globe sends the clear and unambiguous message that China can turn to its very own sources of support, to counterbalance Europe, Japan and the USA when necessary.

Concluding remarks

China's assertiveness in the South China Sea arises from decades of economic growth and the consequent build-up of its military power, its heightened nationalism that feeds from a strong cultural identity, and its triumphalism in the wake of European and US financial crises. South-East Asian countries have been concerned by this testy assertiveness and troubled by the opacity of Chinese politics, particularly with the poorly understood processes of military decision-making amid a proliferation of apparently separately controlled maritime forces. China, on the other hand, is anxious about the more active and reassuring role being played by the USA in the region, partly in response to Chinese activism. Most of the ASEAN member countries have welcomed the USA as a counterbalance against a steadily increasing Chinese power, yet their economies have become increasingly dependent upon China's economic growth. As a whole, South-East Asia does not want to be a party to or witness any potential armed conflict between China and the USA, or China and Japan. The problem is that there is no apparent resolution to what the Chinese Government calls, in practice, these 'indisputable disputes'.[44]

China exhibits two modes of diplomacy when dealing with crises: passive and behind-the-scenes diplomacy, and proactive and stage-managing diplomacy. Most studies that examine the second mode tend to rely on Chinese strategic and security interests in explaining China's foreign behaviours. However, government interests have not changed much. In fact, they remain largely the same, but different behaviours have been witnessed over time. This calculated demeanour should be explained not by China's estimations and strategic interests but rather by internal changes within the country itself. Since the beginning of the 21st century China has undergone an evolutionary change of state identity—from a careful accommodator to a very tactful designer.

China and its allies have been resolutely supporting each other in efforts to uphold sovereignty, protect national security[45] and to promote development and strategic interests. Nonetheless, these actions are perceived by the West as alignments and bulwarking against US and European interests that ultimately run counter to their traditional hegemonic tendencies. One could argue that US and European commentators are slowly amending their views to incorporate the conceptualizations of increasingly independent Chinese international relations scholars that have taken the delicate task to portray their motherland's rising status in international politics and to identify Chinese national interests more holistically, while emphasizing socialist concepts such as anti-hegemony. The result is a form of morphed international relations scholarship that combines the language of Western foreign affairs with a unified world view that emphasizes a modern China within the context of traditional socialist foreign policy directives.

A large number of reformists within China hope that the new CCP leadership will exhibit a greater commitment to the drafting and enacting of a modern Chinese constitution, as well as the promotion of a more independent judiciary. More urgently, though, reform voices have called for an end to the country's notoriously abusive and antiquated system of re-education through labour—a harsh approach to behavioural reform that allows the police to imprison drugs dealers, political offenders, prostitutes and narcotics addicts for up to three years without a hint of a trial. Above all, level-headed and sensible Chinese thinkers continue to insist that an increasingly militaristic China runs the risk of being perceived as another Iraq, Iran or North Korea, and that the EU and the USA will not hesitate to counterbalance China ever more strongly if this trend continues.

China's sophisticated thinking about its future appears as a multidimensional and well-crafted 'Grand Strategy' that addresses and incorporates challenges and opportunities on both national and international fronts, with the fundamental goal of advancing (or at the very least protecting) China's strategic national interests without being blocked or constrained by other great powers. The all-pervasive distrust issue that arises in international relations signifies that China is shifting its belief that the only world superpower is not at all ready to accommodate a rising China, one that is more assertive and defensive towards upholding its core strategic interests. Xi Jinping will face the task of guiding China to a more sustainable model of growth, one that is less dependent on external inputs and which relies more on domestic sources, while also keeping the country moving forward without becoming involved in conflicts or irreconcilable differences: mounting tensions in the East and South China Seas add to the difficulty of this task.

20   *Introduction*

Fitting the pieces together

This chapter assessed China's external and internal dynamics and influences to give readers a sense of the complexity of the issues that the country's leadership has to deal with. China is a big country with a large population. Its challenges and problems require careful analysis because actions, reactions, policies and policy instruments need to be examined through several lenses, many of which are unique to a government led by a Communist party and a nation which is redefining its position on the world stage. The sections above provide a brief and superficial overview to many of the issues that have emerged in recent years, and a number of themes are tightly connected to critical prerequisites that undergird economic growth. Three of these prerequisites (or critical inputs) are energy sources, raw materials and natural resources—all of which are truly essential to force the economic machine to advance forward. In the next chapter I will go a little deeper in trying to explain China's global search for energy and resources.

Notes

1 Most of China's despondent poor and marginalized live west of the more affluent and wealthier coastal regions.
2 In the interest of clarification, the median US income is $47,300 and one of the few similarities was average household assets: in both China and the USA the average family's assets were about eight times its average income. See: Robert O. Weagley, 'One Big Difference between Chinese and American Households: Debt', *Forbes*, 24 June 2010. Available at: www.forbes.com/sites/moneybuilder/2010/06/24/one-big-differen ce-between-chinese-and-american-households-debt/.
3 George Friedman, 'The State of the World: Assessing China's Strategy', *Stratfor: Global Intelligence*, 6 March 2012. Available at: www.stratfor.com/weekly/state-world-assessing-chinas-strategy.
4 On taking office former Prime Minister Wen Jiabao and former President Hu Jintao repeatedly pledged to narrow income inequality and spread China's expanding wealth more evenly in an effort to stave off mass revolts.
5 For an extensive examination of this issue, see: William A. Callahan, 'National Insecurities: Humiliation, Salvation, and Chinese Nationalism', *Alternatives: Global, Local, Political,* Vol. 29, No. 2, 2004, 199–218.
6 For related arguments, see: Dong He and Wenlang Zhang, 'How Dependent Is the Chinese Economy on Exports and in what Sense Has its Growth Been Export-Led?' *Journal of Asian Economics*, Vol. 21, No. 1, 2010, 87–104.
7 'China's Nationalist Wave: Beijing's Naval Aggression Is a Threat to Peace in the Pacific', *Wall Street Journal,* 10 December 2012.
8 Ji Guoxing, 'China versus South China Sea Security', *Security Dialogue*, Vol. 29, No. 1, 1998, 101–12.
9 'China Keeps 2013 GDP Growth Target Unchanged at 7.5%', *Xinhua*, 5 March 2013. Available at: http://news.xinhuanet.com/english/china/2013–03/05/c_132207941.htm.
10 Zhao Hong, 'The South China Sea Dispute and China-ASEAN Relations', *Asian Affairs*, Vol. 44, No. 1, 2013, 27–43. This author describes how external actors, principally the USA, but also India and Japan, have been drawn in as a counterweight to China, in a co-ordinated power-balancing act. Zhao Hong assesses the possible impact of this political (and geographical) dispute on the essentially economic relationship between China and ASEAN.

China's external and internal dynamics and influences 21

11 Kevin Yao and Aileen Wang, 'China Bets on Consumer-led Growth to Cure Social Ills', *Reuters*, 5 March 2013.

12 Prime Minister Wen Jiabao said that China 'should accelerate modernization of national defense and the armed forces so as to strengthen China's defense and military capabilities ... should resolutely uphold China's sovereignty, security and territorial integrity, and ensure its peaceful development'. Andrew Jacobs and Chris Buckley, 'China's Wen Warns of Inequality and Vows to Continue Military Buildup', *New York Times*, 4 March 2013. Available at: www.nytimes.com/2013/03/05/world/asia/on-eve-of-chinas-party-congress-vows-of-change.html?_r=0.

13 'Tibet and Xinjiang: Marking Time at the Fringes', *The Economist*, 8 July 2010. Available at: www.economist.com/node/16539510.

14 Ibid.

15 J. Mohan Malik, 'China-India Relations in the Post-Soviet Era: The Continuing Rivalry', *China Quarterly*, Vol. 142, June 1995, 317–55; Keshav Mishra, *Rapprochement Across the Himalayas: Emerging India-China Relations in Post-Cold War Period* (Delhi, India: Kalpaz Publications, 2004).

16 'Indian, Pakistani and Chinese Border Disputes: Fantasy Frontiers', *The Economist*, 8 February 2012.

17 In particular, Xi Jinping, the new Chinese president, noted unbalanced economic development, income disparity, and inequalities dividing urban and rural residents, all of which increase social strains.

18 For related arguments, see: Ming Tsui and Xiao Li, 'Attitudes Regarding the Market Economy in Urban China', *Sociology Today*, Vol. 2, No. 2, 2012, 185–90.

19 Yongjing (Eugene) Zhang, 'China's Evolution Toward an Authoritarian Market Economy—A Predator–Prey Evolutionary Model with Intelligent Design', *Public Choice*, Vol. 151, No. 1–2, 2012, 271–87.

20 China's territorial claims over the South China Sea are in part driven by beliefs among Chinese policy-makers that it could be a second Persian Gulf. 'Beijing Pushes the Diplomatic Envelop on South China Sea Dispute', Natural Security Blog: Post (Washington, DC: Center for a New American Security, November 2012). Available at: www.cnas.org/blogs/naturalsecurity/2012/11/beijing-pushes-diplomatic-envelop-south-china-sea-dispute.html.

21 Michael Wesley, 'What's at Stake in the South China Sea?' Snapshot 11 (Sydney, Australia: Lowy Institute for International Policy, July 2012). Available at: www.lowyinstitute.org/publications/whats-stake-south-china-sea. This author argues that 'the territorial disputes in the South China Sea get much less attention than other crisis points in the Taiwan Straits and the Korean Peninsula, but are arguably more unpredictable and dangerous'.

22 'China's Three-Point Naval Strategy', IISS Strategic Comments, Vol. 16, Comment 37 (London: International Institute for Strategic Studies, October 2010). Available at: www.iiss.org/publications/strategic-comments/past-issues/volume-16–2010/october/chinas-three-point-naval-strategy/.

23 X. Yan, *Ancient Chinese Thought, Modern Chinese Power*, trans. D. Bell, Z. Sun and E. Ryden (Princeton, NJ: Princeton University Press, 2011).

24 Robert D. Kaplan, 'Center Stage for the Twenty-first Century: Power Plays in the Indian Ocean', *Foreign Affairs*, Vol. 88, No. 2, 2009, 16–32.

25 Andrew Erickson and Gabe Collins, 'Beijing's Energy Security Strategy: The Significance of a Chinese State-Owned Tanker Fleet', *Orbis*, Vol. 51, No. 4, 2007, 665–84. The authors posit that 'the global oil shipping system transports oil from some of the world's most unstable areas ... as Chinese naval power and oil import dependency rise, security-minded factions in China's leadership may use the country's resource needs to justify further pursuit of blue water naval capabilities ... the majority of new tankers being built for Chinese shipping firms will fly China's flag, which helps set a legal basis for militarily protecting these vessels'.

22 Introduction

26 Peter Baker, 'Obama, in an Emerging Myanmar, Vows Support', *New York Times*, 18 November 2012. Available at: www.nytimes.com/2012/11/19/world/asia/obama-heads-to-myanmar-as-it-promises-more-reforms.html.

27 Ian Tsung-Yen Chen and Alan Hao Yang, '"A Harmonized Southeast Asia?" Explanatory Typologies of ASEAN Countries' Strategies to the Rise of China', *Pacific Review*. Version of record first published on 26 February 2013.

28 Andrew Jacobs, 'Tibetan Self-Immolations Rise as China Tightens Grip', *New York Times*, 22 March 2012. Available at: www.nytimes.com/2012/03/23/world/asia/in-self-immolations-signs-of-new-turmoil-in-tibet.html. The author of this article notes that 'spasms of unrest have coursed through modern Tibetan history with some regularity since 1959, when the Dalai Lama fled to India after a failed uprising. Between 1987 and 1989, the region was rocked by protests that were brutally crushed. The most recent crackdown began in March 2008, when rioting in Lhasa, the Tibetan capital, led to the death of at least 19 people, most of them Han Chinese'.

29 For obvious reasons, there is little coverage and reporting devoted to China's contemporary intelligence capabilities, which one could argue is focused on both external and internal targets. For more information on this subject, see: Nigel Inkster, 'Chinese Intelligence in the Cyber Age', *Survival*, Vol. 55, No. 1, 2013, 45–66.

30 Andrew Jacobs and Chris Buckley, 'China's Wen Warns of Inequality and Vows to Continue Military Buildup', *New York Times*, 4 March 2013.

31 Paris H. Chang, 'The Rise of Wang Tung-Hsing: Head of China's Security Apparatus', *China Quarterly*, Vol. 73, 1978, 122–37; Jerome Alan Cohen, 'Chinese Law: At the Crossroads', *China Quarterly*, Vol. 53, 1973, 139–43; Chris Ogden, 'Beyond Succession: China's Internal Security Challenges', *Strategic Analysis*, Vol. 37, No. 2, 2013, 193–202. Ogden emphasizes the 'multitude of (mounting) social and economic issues—particularly outside of the political realm—that China's new leaders will have to face ... three themes central to this transition—a search for internal stability; China's multiple, interlocking internal issues; and the longevity, resilience and adaptability of the CCP—in order to assess their impact on China's domestic and, critically, external politics'.

32 Raoul Heinrichs, 'America's Dangerous Battle Plan', *The Diplomat*, 17 August 2011. Available at: http://thediplomat.com/2011/08/17/america%E2%80%99s-dangerous-battle-plan/.

33 'China's Cyber-Hacking: Getting Ugly', *The Economist*, 23 February 2013.

34 Keith Bradsher, 'China's Focus on Aerospace Raises Security Questions', *New York Times*, 21 January 2013. Available at: http://dealbook.nytimes.com/2013/01/21/china-looks-to-aerospace-in-a-bid-for-growth/.

35 Michael D. Swaine, *The Role of the Chinese Military in National Security Policy-making* (Santa Monica, CA: RAND Corporation, 1998).

36 David C. Kang, 'Soft Power and Leadership in East Asia', *Asia Policy*, Vol. 15, 2013, 134–37.

37 Lian Ma, 'Thinking of China's Grand Strategy: Chinese Perspectives', *International Relations of the Asia-Pacific*, Vol. 13, No. 1, 2013, 155–68.

38 J. Wang, 'China's Search for a Grand Strategy: A Rising Great Power Finds Its Way', *Foreign Affairs*, Vol. 90, No. 2, 2011, 68–79.

39 President Putin has distanced Russia from the West while putting a new focus on Asia, particularly relations with China—a point stressed when Russia played host to the Asia-Pacific Economic Cooperation summit meeting in Vladivostok in September 2012.

40 David M. Herszenhorn and Chris Buckley, 'China's New Leader, Visiting Russia, Promotes Nations' Economic and Military Ties', *New York Times*, 22 March 2013. Available at: www.nytimes.com/2013/03/23/world/asia/xi-jinping-visits-russia-on-first-trip-abroad.html.

41 R. A. Pape, 'Soft Balancing Against the United States', *International Security*, Vol. 30, No. 1, 2005, 7–45.

42 T. J. Christensen, 'Fostering Stability or Creating a Monster? The Rise of China and U.S. Policy Toward East Asia', *International Security*, Vol. 31, No. 1, 2006, 81–126.

43 K. G. Lieberthal and J. Wang, 'Addressing U.S.–China Strategic Distrust', John L. Thornton China Center, Monograph Series 4 (Washington, DC: The Brookings Institution, 2012).

44 RAND Corporation, 'Asian Perceptions of a Rising China', Chapter 4 of Institutional Report No. MR1170. Available at: www.rand.org/content/dam/rand/pubs/monograph_reports/MR1170/MR1170.ch4.pdf.

45 China expressed misgivings about US plans to deploy 14 new missile interceptors in Alaska, where 26 of the existing 30 are already in place, in response to threats from North Korea in 2013.

2 Understanding China's global search for energy and resources[1]

Background

The most traded commodity in the world is oil. The reason for this is that oil and its derivatives make the world move. It is used to fly jets and planes, run motors of boats, motorcycles, vehicles and ships, and to drive factory equipment and machines.[2] In the absence of alternative energy sources, oil will remain the substrate of choice in global manufacturing and production. Moreover, world-wide societal aspirations to attain Western lifestyles is fuelling an unprecedented competition for gas, forest products, minerals, oil and water, as rising and rapidly growing nations like Brazil, Chile, India, Indonesia, Russia, South Africa, Turkey and Vietnam pursue comfort, prosperity and economic security for more and more of their people.[3] In all truth, energy is the essence of modern civilization, and as societies and economies around the globe grow faster, so too do their energy consumptions.

As world audiences witness the growth of China (and other emerging economies), a key question emerges: is there enough oil left in the world to welcome market economies into the elite club of the First World? There is no certain answer. However, statisticians and resource experts claim that the world has already hit peak oil.[4] As demand meets supplies (resulting in varying oil prices) energy analysts and oil geologists expect the output of conventional petroleum to peak at about 1.25m. barrels per day (b/d) in 2015 and then to begin an irreversible and steady decline that could constitute a trigger for bitter competition for the oil that is left underground. To sum up, the global reserves of crude oil are dwindling as more countries fuel their economic engines.

Introduction

From 2011 the spate of tensions between China, Japan, the Philippines and Vietnam exhibited in stark terms the race in the South China Sea for what petroleum geologists argue are sizeable deposits of oil and gas. Chinese energy analysts and oil experts believe that the South China Sea presents a critical new energy frontier that lies close to the mainland and that, if properly exploited, could make China less dependent on oil imports from Africa and the Middle East. Currently, China is locked into importing oil in order to grow and survive. The dynamic economic growth rates experienced during the last 20–30 years, coupled with increased manufacturing levels, rising exports of low-cost goods, rapid urbanization, and higher demands for air travel and land transport, among many other factors, are whetting China's appetite for crude oil, natural gas, rubber, timber and critical minerals.[5] The need for massive amounts of energy sources, raw materials and natural resources is in part driving the Chinese Government's defence (military), energy and foreign policies. To give an idea of China's accelerated economic dynamism, one has to look at exports. China's exports increased from $184,000m. in 1998 to $2,050,000m. in 2012 (imports amounted to $1,820,000m. in 2012). As a result, China's trade surplus increased from $44,000m. in 1998 to $231,000m. in 2012. Figures for 2012/13 showed that China's economy performed quite strongly despite a protracted world economic recovery, weak international market demand for products and services, and heavy downwards pressure on the domestic economy. This performance has attracted increasing pressure from both the USA and the European Union (EU) for China to upwardly revalue its currency.[6]

During the past 23 years, the Chinese economy has grown at an annual rate of around 8%, a pace that stands out in 2013 especially as the global economy recovers from the financial meltdowns in the EU and the USA. A 8% yearly growth rate is indeed impressive, but experts note that there are three potential scenarios that could derail China from its undisputed track record of consistent economic throughput: (1) the bursting of a property bubble; (2) unbalanced rebalancing; and (3) rising political unrest.[7] Even under temporary duress created by a widespread economic slowdown, China's phenomenal hunger for aluminum, cement, copper, gold, iron, platinum, silver and steel have in part caused its crude oil and gas consumption to rise. In fact, in no short measure, this accelerated usage of resources turned it into the world's second largest oil importer after the USA.[8] This surge in imports of energy sources, natural resources and raw materials can partly explain why the National Energy Administration of China (NEAC) classified the South China Sea as one of the most important offshore sites for crude oil extraction and natural gas production. By 2015 the Chinese Government's goal is to produce 150,000m. cu m of natural gas from deposits beneath the seabed, representing a significant increase from 20,000m. cu m of natural gas produced during the 2011–12 period.

In recognition of much-heralded resource depletion and discussion concerning climatic changes, China has set out to replace some of the coal, oil and gas it consumes with alternative forms of energy such as geothermal, nuclear, solar and wind energy while addressing shortcomings that have interfered with a more successful expansion of renewable energy.[9] In the mean time, while China continues to buy oil from traditional oil-producing countries, it is also seeking its own sources of oil and gas abroad. These sources

26 *Introduction*

are found in distant locations, which are frequently, by common standards, not idyllic destinations for foreign visitors. Africa, Central Asia, South America and South-East Asia all have underground oil deposits. China, however, is also interested in minerals such as bauxite, copper, iron ore, gold and silver, as well as natural resources such as timber and rubber.[10] David Zweig and Bi Jianhai note that China has been courting resource-rich states through 'building goodwill by strengthening bilateral trade relations, awarding aids, forgiving national debts, and helping build roads, bridges, stadiums, and harbors. In return, China has won access to key resources, from gold in Bolivia and coal in the Philippines to oil in Ecuador and natural gas in Australia'.[11] Furthermore, as China consolidates its position in Africa as a major player in oil and gas, it gains leverage to block other international oil companies from entering upstream operations such as crude oil exploration and production by locking in generous concession agreements with many resource-rich states, as well as by financing the long lead times required for designing, funding and developing oil sites in territories that so far remain unclaimed or in areas too logistically complicated to propose profitable business endeavours.[12]

China's world-wide search for energy and resources is devoid of moral considerations. Given that sought-after energy sources and natural resources are often found in nation states with weak governance and oppressive leaders, the Chinese Government has struck accords, agreements, deals and pacts with other governments that have little to no respect for, or interest in, international norms of conduct. These ways of conducting business put China at odds with US and European government officials because it undermines long-stipulated objectives in sensitive regions such as isolating obstreperous and undisciplined governments or punishing them for not respecting civil and human rights, seeking nuclear proliferation, hosting religious radicals and terrorists, non-compliance with international law, and failing to promote freedoms and democracy.[13] The Chinese Government is clearly focused on what it wants: critical inputs to run its economy and spread prosperity. Owing to China's visible presence and stellar ascendancy, the tectonic plates of the international political system are shifting for a second time since the end of the Cold War.[14] As a result, Europe and the USA follow closely China's assertiveness and new-found confidence in foreign affairs, as well as attempting to bring China, other major emerging economies, and the developing world under a collaborative framework to address climate change, international terrorism and resource depletion. The latter is particularly critical given that developing countries will generate nearly 80% of growth in world energy demand by 2020, with the Middle East representing 10% and China representing approximately 30%, according to predictions by the McKinsey Global Institute.[15]

Approach and research to write this chapter

Through an extensive literature review that covered a selection of hardcover and paperback books, backgrounders, briefs, reports, working papers, essays, scholarly articles, magazines and media sources, this chapter aims to understand China's global search for energy and resources. A number of keywords such as Beijing, China, Energy, Energy Sources, Gas, Natural Resources, South China Sea, and Oil were typed into Google Scholar and JSTOR to identify and select the most pertinent writings on the subject matter by reputable academics, commentators, doyens, experts, journalists, observers, practitioners and scholars.

This chapter asks: how, where and why is China searching for energy and resources globally? This question guides the discussion throughout, and connects to economic, environmental, geopolitical and strategic dimensions. This research contributes to an increasing body of work on China's demand for crude oil, gas, minerals and timber by authors such as Shawn Breslin, Bobo Lo, Heinrich Kreft, David Zweig, Erica Downs, Chris Ogden, Amy Jaffe, M. Koo, Ian Taylor, Andrew Monaghan, Sam Bateman and Ralf Emmers.

Economics: Western growth with an Eastern style

The first 13 years of the 21st century have witnessed rapid economic growth and massive consumption of energy and resources by large, vibrant countries such as China, Brazil, India, Russia and South Africa. This has resulted in major increases in global demand for oil, gas and minerals. In fact, in terms of fossil fuels, since 2004 global supply has been unable to keep up with global demand, thus leading to a major increase in the price of oil.[16] The US Energy Information Administration, in a report released on 12 March 2013, estimated that in 2013 total world consumption of oil (90.13m. b/d) would continue to be higher than total world production (89.84m. b/d). The rapidly rising cost of energy and resources may be hurting oil-importing countries, but it is helping oil-exporting states to fill up their national coffers. In fact, it seems prudent to mention that China's annual imports of energy and resources from developing countries are assisting these states to offset the increased costs of non-oil goods that are heavily reliant on oil and gas for their production and transport. Additionally, the oil-producing states, especially large producers such as Angola, Kuwait, Nigeria and Saudi Arabia, to name but a few, increase their fiscal revenues as oil prices rise. Over the years, these countries have accumulated significant foreign exchange reserves that in some instances have been used to advance personal agendas and interests.[17]

China's rapid economic growth and massive consumption of energy and resources is brought about the manufacturing of low-cost and little value-added goods for export to many Western countries. The overall contribution of domestic Chinese consumption of products and services is comparatively lower. For instance, between 2008 and 2012 consumption accounted for 42% of China's gross domestic product (GDP), compared with 68% for the USA, 64% for India, 58% for Europe, and 55% for Japan. One could say that China has opted to implement a resource mobilization model to fast economic growth instead of a consumption-led approach. Certainly, this is changing quickly as Chinese incomes rise. High-ranking government officials are starting to recognize that over-reliance on exporting to high-income countries may prove to be extremely risky. However, change is difficult, especially for a country guided by one-party rule. To be sure, the business world has noticed this heavy complexity and warn that China is slow to effect change. Gurcharan Das, the former Chief Executive Officer of Procter & Gamble in India, noted that 'Beijing remains highly suspicious of fast-talking capitalists and entrepreneurs. Also, only about ten percent of credit goes to the private sector in China, even though the private sector employs 40 percent of Chinese workforce'.[18]

In terms of economic benchmarking, copper—a ductile metal with high thermal and electrical conductivity—is closely watched by analysts, governments and traders. It is called 'Dr Copper' because it is a proven bellwether for the overall health of the global economy. Copper is used by many industries. A strong demand for the metal often indicates that the overall economy is in the process of expansion. By March 2013 the three-month copper price on the London Metal Exchange hovered at US $7,772 per metric ton, up from 2012 prices which averaged $7,350 per ton, thus continuing the Chinese recovery that should help to support metal prices in the future. This price volatility is largely driven by the belief that China, by far the world's largest user of copper (accounting for 40% of global copper consumption), has an insatiable need for the metal.[19] For example, in 2012 China's copper consumption reached 7.8m. tons.[20] Rising commodity prices from 2012 to 2013 can be partly explained by companies and individuals hoarding commodities of all types—from cooking oil and cotton to copper—and gambling that prices will increase. However, experts agree that successive rounds of interest rate increases and moves to mitigate speculation by greedy traders will have a somewhat negative impact on commodities and other critical markets in the short term. Generally, China's long-term demand for commodities remains robust owing to the economy's size and rapid growth.[21]

If copper wires the Chinese economy, then oil usage is the economic lubricant that keeps the manufacturing and industrial sectors going at full speed. China is becoming increasingly dependent on national and international oil, especially from Africa, Central Asia and the Middle East. This creates interstate competition, and the threat of investment protectionism is growing as a result. The control of natural resources by sovereign wealth funds and state-owned enterprises is a primary concern. Many resource-rich countries are becoming increasingly anxious about China's thirst for direct and unimpeded control of natural resources, particularly gas, minerals, timber and oil. As developed and developing countries experience an expansion in the deployment of foreign direct investments from China—most of these occur in the natural gas, mining and oil industries—there is a growing tendency to examine transactions more closely. In fact, transactions that involve government-controlled entities, oil-for-infrastructure deals, and natural resources are being subjected to intense scrutiny in countries where these transactions occur.[22] A study by the Council on Foreign Relations notes that in recent years at least 11 powerful economies, together responsible for 40% of all foreign direct investment in 2006, have passed new laws that would restrict certain types of foreign investment or would expand government oversight.[23] This said, in early 2012 the third largest energy company in China, the government-owned China National Offshore Oil Corporation (CNOOC), began drilling with a modern rig in deep waters in non-disputed areas off the southern coast of China. Actions such as this provoke criticism from neighbours as China sparks new disputes over oil, gas and mineral exploration in the South China Sea, which signals that the CCP plans to maintain its hard line on the high seas.

Tellingly, one of the major attractions of the oil industry is its highly inelastic demand, that is, price increases do not greatly decrease the demand for oil in the short run. This being the case, if oil companies can maintain a higher price for oil, they will not lose sales volumes and thus will reap high profits. This is the reason why the Middle East has enjoyed amicable relations with China, Europe and the USA. For example, the USA's oil imports bill accounts for over two-fifths of the total US trade deficit. Another source to the US trade deficit is the protectionist and mercantilist policies of major trading partners, especially China. China accounted for about one-quarter of global growth between 2000 and 2010, outstripping the USA in the race for the lead position as trade-maker.[24] This evolving oil competition is due to the fact that the CCP's legitimacy and power, as well as the social stability of the whole country, heavily depends on the Chinese Government's ability to ensure sustained economic growth above 8%, in order to generate employment for thousands of young people joining the labour force, and to provide improving living standards for its citizenry.

As the Chinese Government has linked economics with stability and political continuity, senior government officials are not only busy handling international affairs (i.e. involvement with Syria and North Korea, and building relationships with Australia, Russia and Brazil) but they also pay close attention to the evolving domestic dynamics that could very easily derail economic, military and political plans (i.e. social unrest, popular revolt, labour strikes and rural upheaval).

China, as well as Europe and North and South America, has a healthy appetite for natural gas, which is considered to be a relatively benign fossil fuel. For example, Peru, in South America, has reserves of several trillion cu ft of natural gas in its remote south-eastern jungle. The development of this resource is beneficial for the world's energy security, air quality and the Peruvian economy. China is fully aware that exploiting its natural gas reserves could transform Peru from a net importer of energy into a net exporter. Furthermore, Peru is cognizant that this transition can translate into boosting growth, job creation and fiscal revenues.[25] In fact, a shift from oil to gas may lower energy prices. In general terms, when energy costs fall, it brings food prices crashing down as well because the cost of producing foods is closely tied to the price of crude oil and natural gas, given that hydrocarbons (i.e. fuel

30 *Introduction*

and petrochemicals) are so widely and heavily utilized in the cultivation of cereals, grains and vegetables.[26] This is important owing to rising demand for animal and non-animal foods in China. The Earth Policy Institute estimates that if China keeps on growing at a baseline level of 8% per year, by 2030 the per caput income of 1,500m. Chinese will be the same as that of the USA during the mid-2000s.[27]

Meanwhile, the CCP and its advisers believe that there have been attempts to stymie China's growth. With the help of European allies, the USA has stepped up its pressure on China to revalue its currency, the yuan. This is easier said than done. If the CCP allows the yuan to appreciate rapidly—not just to please critics but also to reduce inflation—it will generate a contraction in exports which will become more expensive in foreign markets and less competitive when compared with other offerings in the marketplace. As a result, unemployment will increase also. Moreover, if inflation continues to accelerate, widespread dissatisfaction could spread rapidly. Evidently, China embraces free and open trade expansion because it recognizes that if a country wants to be a world power then it has no choice but to abide by the dictum of the World Trade Organization. To this effect, China's growing commitment to economic liberalization as well as to global commercial etiquette and trade rules has resulted in increased foreign investment, savings and trade.

China's problems are not limited to the economy. During 2013 the Chinese Government was expected to confront continuing international concern regarding its cyberspace policy and its handling of North Korea; effect a delicate balancing act of prioritizing foreign policy against a number of domestic concerns; provide smart responses to international calls for greater political openness; and contend with internal challenges regarding health care access and affordability. There are also environmental, legal and social conflicts. For instance, William Nobrega notes that 'between 1992 and 2005, 20 million farmers were evicted from agriculture due to land acquisition, and from 1996 to 2005, more than 21% of arable land in China has been put to non-agricultural use'.[28] According to Edward Wong of the *New York Times*, in March 2013 more than 16,000 dead pigs were found floating in creeks and rivers providing drinking (potable) water to Shanghai. To make matters worse, in the same month a dense haze similar to volcanic fumes engulfed the capital, causing convulsive coughing fits and other respiratory difficulties for the people, and obscured the portrait of Mao Zedong on the gates to the Forbidden City. In fact, so severe are China's environmental woes, especially the heavily noxious air, that senior CCP officials have been forced openly to acknowledge many of these problems. However, even as officials call for restrictions on pollutants, state-owned entities—such as China's energy and oil firms—have been putting profits ahead of health in order to bypass new regulations. In raw environmental terms, there is a large number of polluted cities in China.

The following section examines some of the most pressing environmental issues.

Environment: prosperity and wealth at any cost?

From the 1800s until the present day, the world has witnessed an exponential growth of money and commerce, economic development, the expansion of trade, urbanization, a boom in residential and commercial construction, an explosion of manufacturing and industries, and an irresponsible use of world's limited energy sources. Why did it happen? One might profitably ask why not! During this time frame, all the coal, biofuels, oil and gas required to fuel the money market economic model seemed relatively harmless, extremely cheap, and seemingly inexhaustible. Indeed, it was this paradigm that facilitated the acceleration of petroleum usage and our inability to stop consuming it, to the point that some Western countries are now termed 'oil addicts'.[29] Regrettably, this carries a collective burden: environmental problems. People say that one can manage risk only when it can be measured—this is China's dilemma regarding carbon dioxide. It is an invisible, odourless, tasteless gas that is known to cause global warming. However, at present it does not appear significantly to harm any of China's inhabitants, so the perception is that managing this gas (and other pollutants) is not only costly but that there are also negligible economic pay-offs.

A World Bank study estimated that pollution annually costs China between 8% and 12% of GDP owing to escalating medical bills, lost workdays due to illness, damage to animals and crops, and money spent on disaster relief.[30] Similarly, China's National Bureau of Statistics estimated that health problems, environmental degradation, and lost workdays resulting from pollution cost China anywhere from 4% to 9% of its total economic output.[31] It is often said that in terms of the amount of pollution produced without regulations China has the edge in comparison to industries in the USA that face the highest compliance costs. Companies such as Dow Chemical and U.S. Steel spend about 3% of their revenues on environment-related expenses. By comparison, Chinese competitors such as Sinopec and Bao Steel spend only about one-tenth as much. Unfortunately, this polluting largesse comes at a steep price to Chinese citizens. Sixteen of the world's 20 most polluted cities are located in China. In fact, China has close to 100 cities, each with a population of over 1m., and 66% of these cities fail to meet World Health Organization air quality standards.[32] In the end, it all comes back full circle: whatever China's pollution-based competitiveness and environmental cost advantages are at the individual enterprise level, they are probably being completely offset by the aggregate social costs (i.e. health care) of heavy pollution.

Let's look at agriculture. In terms of energy utilization for food production, it takes 35 calories of fossil fuel to make one calorie of beef in confinement and 68 calories of fossil fuels to make one calorie of pork.[33] China, with a population of 1,300m., is adopting a richer meat-based diet that will need to be supplemented from abroad. If this is indeed the case, the intensification of livestock production systems will demand more energy and resources that are already dwindling. No wonder people often ask: will it be food or fuel? To avoid reaching a carbon dioxide level of 560 parts per million, world leaders

32 *Introduction*

will require a massive global energy project aimed at conservation, emission mitigation and oil substitution. This initiative will have to leave some room for developed countries to grow, using fewer fossil fuels, and for countries like Brazil, China, India, and others to move ahead under a progressive pollution cutback programme, until they fully climb out of poverty and are able to become more energy efficient.[34] These are all ambitious ideas that merit consideration given these declining resources.

However, when it comes to fossil fuel consumption for the production of all manner of items, from foodstuffs to objects, sceptics ask: how does the world know whether oil usage has peaked? In order to answer this question one has to look at indicators. The first is that many of the important oil- and gasfields that have supplied our insatiable demand for natural gas and crude oil for so many years are now experiencing diminished outputs—in other words, they are being emptied. For example, some of the world's largest oil- and gasfields—including Burgan in Kuwait, Cantarell in Mexico, Ghawar in Saudi Arabia, and Samotlor in Russia—are in decline or about to reach exhaustion. The second is that, year after year, major oil producers are spending more resources to discover new oil and natural gas reserves but they are finding less oil and gas. In fact, according to studies, 1980–1990 was the last decade during which new discoveries exceeded the rate of extraction from existing fields. In the past 25 years, only two major oil- and gasfields have been discovered: the Kashagan field in Kazakhstan's sector of the Caspian Sea and the Tupi field some 150 miles off the coast of Rio de Janeiro, Brazil.[35] The solution to declining oil supplies will involve a clever combination of renewable, eco-friendly, domestically produced energy supplies, including biofuels, geothermal, solar, oceanic waves and wind energy generation.

In the interest of reasonable comparisons, 2,500m. of 7,000m. people currently depend on wood and other biomass fuels that cause even more deforestation and air pollution. As an energy source, coal replaced wood because—pound for pound—it contains twice as much energy as wood does. During the 1850s crude oil emerged as an alternative energy source and this was burned in the form of kerosene to light lamps in households and streets. Today, for many countries, the preferred energy sources are natural gas or methane, which burns cleanly and has the added advantage of giving off relatively small emissions of carbon dioxide and even smaller emissions of other noxious pollutants (such as those which officials are trying to reduce over China's cities). Regrettably, it has not been widely adopted because most natural gas supplies are located far from end users, so transportation costs are very high. However, industrial engineers, systems designers and energy experts have considered and proposed importing natural gas from distant suppliers by transporting it, in liquefied form, by sea in ships fitted with high-pressure containers. The only problem with this proposal is that special terminals need to be designed, built, fitted and equipped to receive liquefied gas which adds extra layers of upfront costs that create a disincentive to investment in infrastructure projects of this magnitude.[36]

With the above in mind, China, Europe, Japan and the USA should embrace the unique challenge of developing—as far as possible—green economies as decidedly, wholeheartedly, and with the same creativity, dedication, entrepreneurship, investment and intelligence they previously employed to accelerate economic growth at any cost. Comparatively speaking, this is a minor challenge when compared to the major setbacks that the world has experienced and learned to overcome during the last 500 years. In fact, such large-scale projects that move forward as public-private partnerships enjoy strong government and corporate commitment, and effective engineering, industrial and university leadership across many countries, along with an internationally binding climate change mitigation framework designed to engage in sustainable and sustained economic growth that aims to maintain and protect the environment.[37] Commentators have directed our attention to China's evolving water crisis. In other parts of the world this is not a new phenomenon. William Finnegan, reporting from Cochabamba, Bolivia, stated: 'the world is running out of fresh water, at a time when demand is rapidly increasing … with protestors fighting the water privatization that has taken place'.[38]

With regard to international climate negotiations, it has been observed that if China is pushed too hard, some of its poorest yet most populous provinces—with low per caput emissions and relatively high levels of energy inefficiency—may ask to negotiate for themselves with intergovernmental organizations in the hope of achieving more favourable terms and greater leniency than the Government would impose on them.[39] In addition, the success of Chinese solar panel manufacturers has opened up this sub-sector as an industry that could be profitably developed. And if it were successful, increasing supplies and investments in research and development would force prices down so far that businesses and households would be able to afford solar cells to reduce coal-burning and greenhouse gas emissions. However, environmental concerns are overshadowed by China's emergence as both a military and an economic rival—heralding a profound shift in the distribution of global power. As China becomes ever more powerful, two thing are likely to happen internationally: one, states will begin to perceive China as a growing security threat; two, China will try to use its growing influence to reform the rules and institutions of the international system to better serve its strategic interests. The next section examines this.

Geopolitics: borders, sovereignty and the thirst for power

Control of oil and gas brings power. Power provides a complete sense of security. Security, both from external and internal threats, is a prerequisite to prosperity and stability. China seeks all of these things.

Let's examine oil and power. Between 1970 and 1990 a small group of oil-producing and -exporting countries managed to seize control of the international oil and gas system. These countries were able severely to restrict supply in order to reap the benefits of much higher prices. The USA, in large part

34   *Introduction*

motivated by concerns about control of oil and gas reserves in the Middle East, engaged in the Gulf War in 1991, the invasion of Iraq in 2003, and the subsequent occupation of Iraqi territories. Currently, the overriding US fear-driven belief—which is exacerbated by intense media coverage—is that the Chinese Government's discourse about 'peaceful development' in the region may be a ruse to deceive Asian leaders and the international community about China's long-term aims, including the replacement of the USA in East Asia and to challenge its global dominance. State power is based on sustained economic growth and government officials are well aware that no major emerging economy can do this without securing energy supplies and integrating itself into the globalized capitalist system.[40]

Several commentators have theorized that China may be maintaining a low profile for now until it is fully capable of challenging the USA in Asia and elsewhere, although China's push into Africa, Central and South-East Asia, and Latin America in search of energy sources, raw materials, and natural resources seems to suggest that the long-expected global contest for the world's remaining crude oil has already begun.[41] In recognition of its energy and market development needs, China has influenced and lobbied its South-East Asian neighbours to focus their attention on regional economic integration, and it has generally succeeded in overcoming ASEAN's recurrent historical suspicions because renewed regional vitality offers protection from the insalubrious effects of globalization at the hands of Western traditional powers. Cambodia, for example, is pivotal to China's strategies to project greater influence in South-East Asia, buffer long-standing rivals, and potentially tame the USA's hegemony.[42]

To compete with this, in 2000 China established the China-Africa Cooperation Forum (CACF)[43] to incentivize commerce, promote trade and foster investments with more African nations. Unintentionally, however, China's energy and resource needs can have deleterious impacts on some African states. It is now well documented that increasing dependence upon natural resource exports powerfully escalates the risk of conflicts.[44] This is particularly worrisome in countries where the cost of a typical civil war is $50,000m.[45] Additionally, unrestricted access to resource rents has significantly worsened governance in the African continent.[46] China's relations with Iran, Myanmar, North Korea and Sudan, which are considered pariah states by Europe and the USA, are cause for concern. China is also strengthening its ties with Nicaragua and Venezuela, which enjoy lambasting the USA's foreign policies in Latin America. Meanwhile, Australia has been a beneficiary of China's insatiable quest for coal, gas, minerals (e.g. copper, iron ore, tin and zinc) and oil. The Australian capital, Sydney, is exploring the prospect of establishing preferential trade agreements with China, as well as with ASEAN.

In 1991 the Soviet Union disintegrated into 15 separate countries. After nearly a decade devoted to making the transition to capitalism the new Russian Federation became a key player in world oil and gas markets. China is seeking a relatively stable relationship with Russia, which hinges on strategic collaboration and pragmatic utilitarianism as both countries not only counterbalance the USA but also depend on oil and gas to sustain their economic growth. Meanwhile, China and India continue to hold talks on energy cooperation, the success of which would greatly ease competitive frictions between the two Asian titans as their economies grow and expand, and as demand for oil and gas increases.[47] Additionally, both countries have initiated efforts to resolve tense border claims that led to war in 1962, as well as opening dialogues on topics such as climate change, security, water scarcity, terrorism, globalization, radicalism, non-proliferation and reforms to the UN.[48]

More importantly, world leaders need to consider how the magnitude of China's energy and resource needs affects the international oil market. As India and Brazil start to consolidate their positions in foreign markets, and China's demands continue to grow, global prices and supplies are affected. China, Europe and the USA share an interest in achieving stable oil prices in the marketplace, safe and protected shipping routes, and a secure international environment that fosters investments and capital flows, all of which can help to sustain their economic prosperity and that of the rest of the world. In the end, all large oil consumers, be they traditional powers (e.g. the EU and the USA) or emerging ones (e.g. Brazil, China, India, Russia and South Africa) share an interest in an open energy market that lacks artificial restrictions on supplies. If such a market were achieved, Brazil, China, India and others would be less tempted to secure supply sources through costly bilateral deals.[49]

China's clash in December 2012 with Japan and Vietnam over fishing stocks and navigation rights has drawn attention to the dissonance between rhetoric and actions, that is, the loud marketing of China's peaceful rise and a barrage of accusations and protests from the country's neighbours. For example, Vietnamese officials accused Chinese fishing vessels of severing a cable attached to one if its ships exploring for oil and gas along the Gulf of Tonkin. Vietnam interpreted this action as an attempt by China to prevent any other South-East Asian country from pursuing oil deposits. As expected, China argued that it is too heavily dependent on international sea lanes to bring oil and inputs from Africa and the Middle East, and expressed concern about its strategic vulnerabilities.

The following section connects some thoughts and examines the strategic dimension.

Strategic: what should China do to get what it wants?

Throughout recorded history, countries have sought to gain control of energy sources, raw materials and critical natural resources, and to manage the use of these inputs for their own economic, military, political and social benefit. Few would disagree that oil and geopolitics are tightly interconnected. It is no secret that the global politics of energy is shaping economic and diplomatic intercourses around the world. In relation to Asia, a report for the US Congress notes that the thirst for oil and gas is sending China and others in an all-out search for energy sources to the point that these states are prospecting

36   *Introduction*

in parts of the world where they have not been seen before.[50] China emerged relatively unscathed following the financial crisis of 2008–11, which provided the country with a clear opportunity to harness its strategic advantages while the EU and the USA struggled to recover from the downturn. In terms of natural resource acquisition, China has cleverly crafted a niche position to assist other nation-states financially through key tactical investments or direct monetary transfers while they are suffering from deficits on the balance of payment at a time when the West cannot come through as it has done in the recent past.[51] For example, China has undertaken numerous negotiations in Central Asia for a multi-million-dollar pipeline to transport Caspian Sea oil into mainland China.

The economic growth of China is a critical element of the transformation of the global order that is under way, and the Chinese Government is testing its ability to influence global decision-making by working together with regional and international actors which embrace its style of governance. In early 2013 China held a $3,400,000m. portfolio of foreign exchange reserves, and was expected to continue to make concerted tactical overtures and strategic investments through its sovereign wealth funds, state-owned firms and state-controlled financial institutions. When one considers China's hunger for oil, gas, coal and other natural resources, these emerge as likely candidates of interest. International scholar Marc Lanteigne notes that what separates China from other states, and indeed previous global powers, is that not only is it 'growing up' within a milieu of international institutions that are far more developed than ever before, but more importantly, it is doing so while making active use of these institutions to promote the country's development of global power status.[52] Finally, China has been using 'soft power' in its neighbourhood while raising few hegemonic suspicions.[53]

China's economic diplomacy has superseded that of the USA's since China's neighbours now clearly understand that China is their guaranteed engine for growth.[54] Through economic diplomacy China has markedly improved its relations with Australia, one of the USA's most faithful allies in the Asia-Pacific region. Certainly, China's regional integration in Asia will make it easier for high-ranking CCP officials to manipulate economic power in support of geostrategic ambitions that could pose a threat to US and European interests in the future. The Chinese Government's participation in a number of regional bodies has paid handsomely in terms of acceptance, prestige and image-building. It is easy to perceive that prosperity-driven cosmopolitanism is superseding the biased attitude of one-party ideologues who distrust regional organizations as tools to constrain China's influence, interests and power.[55] However, despite these successful rapprochements, uncertainties about the availability of supplies and increased demand from emerging countries such as Brazil, China, India and others have attracted fears about energy insecurity.

Although many commentators and observers welcome China's economic growth and international assertiveness, foreign diplomats and government officials are concerned about the prospect of the country significantly increasing its military (army and naval) power. Again, it is important here to underscore that China's dependence on foreign oil—especially from Africa and the Middle East—will make it more concerned about and engaged with the South China Sea routes used by its oil and gas tankers, as well as sea lanes in the Indian Ocean, the Strait of Malacca, and the Taiwan Strait. CCP officials believe that China could face an energy and economic crisis if its oil and gas supply lines are blocked. For some time a rumour has circulated that China is building up its navy in order to protect its commercial ships and oil tankers, and to oversee shared shipping routes. The new naval strategy comprises defensive and offensive approaches. Furthermore, China is forging a number of strategic relationships along sea lanes running from the Middle East to the East and South China Seas so that it can protect its commercial and energy interests. Also, it has closely liaised with Pakistan regarding infrastructure projects, with Myanmar in order to establish radar systems and to build airstrips, and with Bangladesh concerning naval facilities. Clearly, China wishes to build its own capacity to secure critically important sea lanes, but it also seeks to continue to co-operate with Europe, Indonesia, Japan, Malaysia, Singapore and the USA to keep the straits open. In the end, it seems that CCP officials will have to engage in a range of diplomatic, economic and political measures to ensure a steady supply of energy sources, raw materials and natural resources.[56]

However, the widespread use of renewable energy sources would not only reduce dependence on oil suppliers located in volatile regions (e.g. North Africa and the Middle East) but also the potential terrorist threats that nuclear plants and liquefied gas terminals might attract. To avoid sinking into a debilitating energy crisis, China must cut its need for new energy generation plants via aggressive investments in efficiency. To this end, the impact of setting standards, of fiscal incentives and of generous subsidies should not be underestimated. For instance, countries like Denmark, Germany, Norway and Spain imposed manageable standards on their utilities, alongside tax deductions and subsidies for wind power, thus creating a market in the 1980s and 1990s for wind turbine manufacturers in Europe and the USA. Commentators insist that rich countries should invest heavily in research and development in all energy sectors, promote conservation, develop inexpensive, feasible and viable forms of renewable energy, and test a number of possibilities to significantly reduce greenhouse gases through large-scale geologic carbon sequestration.[57]Additionally, a geostrategic imperative for developed and emerging market economies is the recognition that intentionally conserving natural gas and crude oil puts less money in the hands of autocratic regimes and hostile forces. Conservation also mitigates and slows climatic changes. In the end, leaders around the globe need to be reminded that the precipitous descent of some of the world's poorest countries into food insecurity, instability and poverty raises the risks of potentially detrimental spillover effects, ranging from a increase in illegal migration to organized crime.[58]

38 *Introduction*

Analysis: reflections from afar

At the heart of a dramatic upsurge in the usage of energy and resources lies the Industrial Revolution of the 1800s. This is usually dated to the very early experiments with the successful powering of industrial machinery and steam locomotives. Today, new waves of energy and resource usage surge through China. And a fact that should not be so easily dismissed is that, as time passes, China will build up a powerful mix of cheap skilled labour, flexible manufacturing and industrial capacity, investment-friendly central government, and massive domestic markets. However, audiences need to recognize that China's importation of oil, gas, minerals and timber from the developing world can cause a series of unintended problems. There is a propensity for armed conflicts to take place in countries that depend heavily on energy sources, raw materials and natural resources for their export earnings partly because belligerent groups can extort the economic gains from this trade to finance their subversive operations. Also, conflicts of interest over energy and resources can make secession more likely.[59]

To this end, China must develop ties that do not flout international standards of good governance and human dignity, or threaten US or European security. Under its energy- and resources-based defence, energy and foreign policies, the Chinese Government has become quite assertive and bold in seeking what it needs in international markets to keep its economic machinery running at full speed. The USA and the EU should contemplate the construction of a stable Asian balance of power that will certainly be in the collective interest of China, its neighbours and competitors. While keeping China's actions in sight, the world sees a need for balanced, patient and far-sighted leaders who adapt easily to rapid changes in the global distribution of commercial, economic, political and military powers, without allowing the temptation of raw combativeness to override their peaceful rhetoric and common goals of peace and prosperity. In other words, China's ascendancy need not be chaotic and violent.

China faces a host of challenges that could have significant destabilizing effects on regional growth and the global economy if not handled smoothly. For example, one of the most frequent scenarios advanced is that if China's growth slows and unemployment rises, the country could face uncontrollable political unrest from those who lose their jobs and the hundreds of millions of peasants still living in the countryside.[60] Journalists and foreign commentators have noted that the authoritarian wall in China has for some time revealed fissures. This is partly explained by the up- and downstream effects of the economic slowdown, which, inevitably, affected China given that much of its exports flow to the USA and EU members. As these countries could not boost consumption by flooding the system with new money, China started to decelerate its manufacturing and industrial engines, and that immediately resulted in lay-offs, unemployment, insecurity, uncertainty and reduced confidence in the current governing system of one-party rule. The Chinese

Government is adept at handling popular revolt in distant locations, in capturing and imprisoning artists, at managing its economic dealings, and at attracting foreign capital, but it remains to be seen if officials can stamp out the waves of dissatisfaction that might swiftly form if China were to encounter an insurmountable roadblock or misstep. Private sector strategists and investment bankers are not convinced that sustained growth will occur and that stable business will flourish in China, not least because basic property rights protection and the rule of law are lacking. Some pundits believe that India's differentiating advantage comes in the form of an 'entrenched and vibrant democracy that will ultimately drive India to outperform China socially and economically'.[61] In fact, the world needs to start asking more pertinent questions: will global affairs continue to be heavily influenced by the USA's free market democracy or will it start gathering some intense momentum via China's authoritarian state capitalism? Indeed, by 2013 the Chinese model of growth had come under attack in view of declining GDP, rising unemployment and volatile exports (more in Chapter 3).

China has gone to great lengths to keep democratic waves of political modernization from infiltrating Chinese territories. For instance, it has shut down internet sites, stymied communications, banned political art and harangued against Nobel Prize nominations. Through the implementation of these measures, in the near term at least, the Chinese Government hopes successfully to stifle demonstrations and thwart protests. Undeniably, the surge of democratization that has swept through North Africa has sent shockwaves to the parts of the world where authoritarian regimes are still in place. China has not been immune to these incendiary popular movements. However, it is important to highlight that authoritarianism in China is of a far higher quality and of a deeper breadth than in the Middle East. This does not mean that China is protected from the possibility of violent revolutions—far from it. If revolution does indeed become a reality, it will not come from the disenchanted poor but from an upwardly mobile middle class dissatisfied with anachronistic government that prevents the productive social classes from achieving their true potential. This is the starting-point for revolution, which could ignite other groups to join forces to bring democracy to a land ripe with opportunity. Once the one-party rule becomes stagnant or very much unable to pacify the masses, then change is sure to result, one way or another. For China, the problem will be that political unrest will surely produce economic decline or complete stagnation.[62]

Kevin Rudd, who served as Australia's prime minister from 2007–10, stated that the Obama Administration's 'pivot to Asia' made strategic sense because Chinese officials were starting to doubt US staying power and its commitment to the region. However, Robert S. Ross argued that the US Administration has responded to Chinese assertiveness by reinforcing US military and diplomatic links to the Asia-Pacific region, but that the 'pivot' is based on a serious misreading of its target, that is, China remains far weaker than the USA and is deeply insecure; so, in order to make the Chinese Government more

40   *Introduction*

co-operative, the US Administration should work to assuage China's anxieties, not exploit them[63] (see Chapter 6).

Commentators, the media and observers have been somewhat optimistic on the subject of fierce resource competition—primarily owing to China's talk of peaceful development and neighbourliness. However, there is much money to be made out of conflict and war, and the race to secure those remaining pockets of energy sources, raw materials and natural resources is the ideal catalyst for the US and European military-industrial complexes to lobby their respective governments to find any excuse to leverage friction, difficulties and tensions that could precipitate yet another war of giants. The military deployments of powerful Western states to the Middle East and Central Asia can be partly explained by this internecine geopolitical contest of setting strongholds in existing and potential oil- and gasfields. With this in mind, Chinese officials are not afraid to be assertive when it comes to protecting and overseeing the critical strategic interests that lie in its backyard, and to dilute some of the influence that the USA has on the Asian region.

A series of recent retaliations highlight how China, Japan, several South-East Asian nations and the USA remain far apart in resolving what has become a volatile flashpoint. For many years now, China has resented US involvement in disputes regarding maritime and territorial delimitations. High-ranking CCP officials insist that interstate differences and issues should be settled peacefully between China and the individual countries involved, without the USA acting as an unsolicited broker. In short, China disputes most of the locations in the East China Sea and the South China Sea (including the Paracel, Senkaku, and Spratly Islands, the Reed Bank and the Scarborough Shoal) that are known to be rich fishing grounds and which potentially contain reserves of oil and natural gas. Other locations have been claimed according to historical records but are not officially disputed through formal complaints.

Concluding remarks

China's transformation from regional backwater into influential global actor and international powerhouse has increased its demand for essential productive inputs. Automobiles, construction, industrial production and manufacturing influence China's global search for energy sources, raw materials and natural resources. This global search has extended to distant locations where the remaining reserves are thought to be found, and has been informing the Chinese Government's foreign, energy and military policy-making. However, other emerging economies and developed countries are also in need of the same inputs, which increases the potential for contestation and conflict. As critical resources dwindle, bitter competitions ensue. China's economic, military and political actions and initiatives are designed and geared to protect nationally critical interests, but government officials are strategic and tactful in doing so without raising hegemonic suspicions. To understand

China's global search for energy and resources one has to remember where the country stood following the Second World War, where it stands today, and where is it going to be in the future. China, like any other nation state in the international system, wishes to create opportunities, prosperity and well-being for its citizens. The question that remains to be answered is whether there are sufficient inputs for all actors to move ahead at the same speed.

Notes

1 This chapter is based on an article previously published in *Central European Journal of International Security Studies*, Vol. 7, No. 1, 2013.
2 Robert Looney, *Handbook of Oil Politics* (New York: Routledge, 2011); 'Oil Markets Explained', *BBC News*, 18 October 2007.
3 Thomas L. Friedman, *Hot, Flat, and Crowded: Why We Need a Green Revolution—And How It Can Renew America* (New York: Farrar, Straus and Giroux, 2008).
4 Ugo Bardi, 'Peak Oil: The Four Stages of a New Idea', *Energy*, Vol. 34, No. 3, 2009, 323–26.
5 Sigfrido Burgos Cáceres and Sophal Ear, 'The Geopolitics of China's Global Resources Quest', *Geopolitics*, Vol. 17, No. 1, 2012, 47–79; Eugene Gholz and Daryl G. Press, 'Enduring Resilience: How Oil Markets Handle Disruptions', *Security Studies*, Vol. 22, No. 1, 2013.
6 Joan E. Spero and Jeffrey A. Hart, *The Politics of International Economic Relations* (Boston, MA: Wadsworth, 2010); Michael Yahuda, *The International Politics of the Asia Pacific* (New York: Routledge, 2012).
7 Bob Davis, 'In Fast-Growing China, Dangers Threaten to Hamper its Success', *Wall Street Journal*, 11 April 2011.
8 S. Julio Friedmann and Thomas Homer-Dixon, 'Out of the Energy Box', *Foreign Affairs*, Vol. 83, No. 6, November/December 2004, 72–83.
9 Judith A. Cherni and Joanna Kentish, 'Renewable Energy Policy and Electricity Market Reforms in China', *Energy Policy*, Vol. 35, No. 7, June 2007, 3616–29.
10 Sigfrido Burgos Cáceres and Sophal Ear, 'China's Natural Resource Appetite in Brazil', *Asian Journal of Latin American Studies*, Vol. 24, No. 2, 2011, 71–92.
11 David Zweig and Bi Jianhai, 'China's Global Hunt for Energy', *Foreign Affairs*, Vol. 84, No. 5, September/October 2005, 25–38.
12 Sigfrido Burgos Cáceres and Sophal Ear, 'China's Oil Hunger in Angola: History and Perspective', *Journal of Contemporary China*, Vol. 21, No. 74, 2012, 351–67.
13 See: Burgos and Ear, 'The Geopolitics of China's Global Resources Quest'; Burgos and Ear 'China's Natural Resource Appetite in Brazil'.
14 Samuel S. Kim, *China and the World: Chinese Foreign Relations in the Post-Cold War Era* (New York: Perseus Books, 1998).
15 McKinsey Global Institute, 'Curbing Global Energy Demand Growth: The Energy Productivity Opportunity', May 2007.
16 Christine Hauser, 'Rising Gas and Food Prices Push U.S. Inflation Higher', *New York Times*, 13 May 2011.
17 Nathan Jensen and Leonard Wantchekon, 'Resource Wealth and Political Regimes in Africa', *Comparative Political Studies*, Vol. 37, No. 7, September 2004, 816–41; Burgos and Ear, 'China's Oil Hunger in Angola: History and Perspective'.
18 Gurcharan Das, 'The India Model', *Foreign Affairs*, Vol. 85, No. 4, 2006, 2–16.
19 Carolyn Cui and Tatyana Shumsky, 'China's Warning Signs for "Dr. Copper"', *Wall Street Journal*, 11 April 2011.
20 Wei Tian, 'Copper Giant Seeks Investment', *China Daily–Asia Pacific*, 15 March 2013.

42 *Introduction*

21 In particular, demand for copper remains strong owing to solid growth in industrial production, electricity usage and fixed-asset investments. The same could be said of other minerals critical to manufacturing industries.
22 'Special Report: Beyond Doha', *The Economist*, Vol. 389, No. 8601, 2008, 30–33.
23 Francis E. Warnock, 'Doubts About Capital Controls' (New York: Council on Foreign Relations Press, 2011).
24 Glenn R. Hubbard and Peter Navarro, *Seeds of Destruction: Why the Path to Economic Ruin Runs through Washington and How to Reclaim American Prosperity* (New York: Pearson Education Ltd., 2011).
25 Sebastian Mallaby, 'NGOs: Fighting Poverty, Hurting the Poor', *Foreign Policy*, September/October 2004, 50–58.
26 Michael Klare, 'We're On the Brink of Disaster', *Salon.com*, 26 February 2009.
27 Lester R. Brown, *Eco-Economy: Building an Economy for the Earth* (Washington, DC: Earth Policy Institute, 2001).
28 William Nobrega, 'Why India Will Beat China', *Business Week,* 22 July 2008.
29 D. Sandalow, *Freedom from Oil: How the President Can End the United States' Oil Addiction* (New York: McGraw-Hill, 2008).
30 The World Bank, 'Clear Skies, Blue Water: China's Environment in the New Century' (Washington, DC: The World Bank, 1997).
31 National Bureau of Statistics of China. Available at: www.stats.gov.cn/english/. accessed April 2011.
32 See: Friedman, *Hot, Flat, and Crowded.*
33 Richard Manning, 'The Oil We Eat: Following the Food Chain Back to Iraq', *Harper's*, Vol. 308, No. 1845, February 2004, 39–45.
34 Thomas L. Friedman, 'The Power of Green', *New York Times Magazine*, 15 April 2007.
35 Michael Klare, 'End of the Petroleum Age?', *Foreign Policy in Focus*, 26 June 2008.
36 Gerald B. Greenwald, *Liquefied Natural Gas: Developing and Financing International Energy Projects* (Alphen aan den Rijn: Kluwer Law International, October 1998), p. 386.
37 Joel Makower and Cara Pike, *Strategies for the Green Economy: Opportunities and Challenges in the New World of Business* (New York: McGraw-Hill, 2009).
38 William Finnegan, 'Leasing the Rain: The World Is Running Out of Fresh Water, and the Fight to Control it Has Begun', *New Yorker*, Vol. 78, No. 7, April 2002, 43–52.
39 Doaa Abdel Motaal, 'Negotiating with Only One China on Climate Change: On Counting Ourselves Lucky', *Yale Journal of International Affairs*, Vol. 6, No. 1, winter 2011, 74–84.
40 For an excellent examination on the perceptions of China's ascendancy, see: G. John Ikenberry, 'The Rise of China and the Future of the West,' *Foreign Affairs*, Vol. 87, No. 1, 2008, 23–37.
41 Paul Godwin, *China's Defense Modernization: Aspirations and Capabilities* (Alexandria, VA: CNA Corporation, April 2001); Bernard D. Cole, *The Great Wall at Sea: China's Navy Enters the 21st Century* (Annapolis, MD: Naval Institute Press, 2001); Larry Rohter, 'China Widens Economic Role in Latin America', *Washington Post*, 20 November 2004; Korby Leggett, 'China Flexes Economic Muscle throughout Burgeoning Africa', *Wall Street Journal*, 29 March 2005.
42 Sigfrido Burgos Cáceres and Sophal Ear, 'China's Strategic Interests in Cambodia: Influence and Resources', *Asian Survey*, Vol. 50, No. 3, 2010, 615–39; Sigfrido Burgos Cáceres and Sophal Ear, *The Hungry Dragon: How China's Resource Quest Is Reshaping the World* (New York: Routledge, 2013).
43 The China-Africa Cooperation Forum (CACF) is a Beijing-based initiative headed by the China Internet Information Center (see: www.china.org.cn/english/features/China-Africa/81869.htm). CACF was establised in 2000 to promote Chinese investments in China.

44 Paul Collier and Anke Hoeffler, 'Greed and Grievance in Civil War', *Oxford Economic Papers*, Vol. 56, No. 4, 2004, 563–95.

45 Paul Collier and Anke Hoeffler, 'Violent Conflict', in *Global Problems: Global Solutions*, ed. B. Lomberg (Cambridge: Cambridge University Press, 2004).

46 The new Extractive Industries Transparency Initiative is designed to improve governance in countries with large natural resource rents by establishing a set of codes, norms and standards to determine how natural resource export revenues should be accounted for, both by companies making the payments and by governments receiving them.

47 Fang Zhou, 'China, India Forming Strategic Ties', *China Daily*, 18 February 2005; Manjeet Kripalani, Dexter Roberts, and Jason Bush, 'India and China: Oil Patch Partners?' *Business Week*, 7 February 2005.

48 David M. Herszenhorn and Chris Buckley, 'China's Leader Argues for Cooperation with Russia', *New York Times*, 23 March 2013; Hari Kumar, 'India and China Deepen Economic Ties', *New York Times*, 27 November 2012; Bobo Lo, *Axis of Convenience: Moscow, Beijing, and the New Geopolitics* (Washington, DC: Brookings Institution Press, 2008).

49 Aaditya Mattoo and Arvind Subramanian, 'From Doha to the Next Bretton Woods: A New Multilateral Trade Agenda', *Foreign Affairs*, Vol. 88, No. 1, 2009, 15–26.

50 Kerry Dumbaugh, 'China–U.S. Relations: Current Issues and Implications for U.S. Policy', CRS Report for Congress No. RL33877 (Washington, DC: Congressional Research Service, March 2008).

51 Roger C. Altman, 'The Great Crash, 2008: A Geopolitical Setback for the West', *Foreign Affairs*, Vol. 88, No. 1, January/February 2009, 2–14.

52 Marc Lanteigne, *Chinese Foreign Policy: An Introduction* (New York: Routledge, 2009). Foreign policy instruments are launched on many fronts. For instance, to mobilize and co-ordinate social resources and civilian efforts towards the goal of promoting China's soft power, in 2013 the CCP established the China Public Diplomacy Association. To support this overall objective, the Chinese Government has adopted various measures to enhance Chinese soft power, such as establishing global news services and Confucius Institutes across the world, as well as launching English-based scientific journals and hosting a large number of conferences.

53 Zachary Keck, 'Destined To Fail: China's Soft Power Push', *The Diplomat*, 7 January 2012; Joshua Kurlantzick, *Charm Offensive: How China's Soft Power Is Transforming the World* (New Haven, CT: Yale University Press, 2007); Brian Spegele, 'New Tensions Rise on South China Sea', *New York Times*, 5 August 2012. Available at: http://online.wsj.com/article/SB10000872396390443659204577570514282930558.html.

54 Jeffrey D. Sachs, 'Welcome to the Asian Century', *Fortune*, Vol. 149, No. 1, 2004, 53–54.

55 Hugh De Santis, 'The Dragon and the Tigers: China and Asian Regionalism', *World Policy Journal*, summer 2005, 23–36; Burgos and Ear, *The Hungry Dragon: How China's Resource Quest Is Reshaping the World*.

56 Kevin Rudd, 'Beyond the Pivot: A New Road Map for U.S.–Chinese Relations', *Foreign Affairs*, March/April 2013; Robert S. Ross, 'The Problem With the Pivot: Obama's New Asia Policy Is Unnecessary and Counterproductive', *Foreign Affairs*, November/December 2012; 'China Military Build-Up Seems U.S.-Focused: Mullen', *Reuters*, 4 May 2009; Joshua Norman, 'WikiLeaks: China Hiding Military Buildup, Intentions', *CBS News*, 6 January 2011.

57 See: Friedmann and Homer-Dixon, 'Out of the Energy Box'; Burgos and Ear, *The Hungry Dragon*.

58 Sigfrido Burgos Cáceres and Joachim Otte, 'Linking Animal Health and International Affairs: Trade, Food, Security, and Global Health', *Yale Journal of International Affairs*, Vol. 6, No. 1, 2011, 108–09.

44 *Introduction*

59 Paul Collier, 'The Market for Civil War', *Foreign Policy*, May/June 2003, 38–45.
60 'What America Must Do to Compete with China and India', *Business Week*, 22 August 2005.
61 See: Nobrega, 'Why India Will Beat China'; Looney, *Handbook of Oil Politics*.
62 Andrew Bast, 'The Beginning of History', *Newsweek*, 18 April 2011.
63 See: Rudd, 'Beyond the Pivot: A New Road Map for U.S.–Chinese Relations'; Ross, 'The Problem with the Pivot: Obama's New Asia Policy Is Unnecessary and Counterproductive'.

3 China's oil security

Diplomacy, economics and the prospects for peaceful growth

Introduction

China's oil security is tightly linked to economic and foreign policies, as well as military strategy. Rapid economic growth requires resources, and China has been prowling international markets for oil, gas, minerals and timber. The Chinese Government has worked relentlessly to establish new supply relationships in every continent. Among its partners are the governments of Angola, Iran, Libya, Myanmar, Sudan and Venezuela—none of which are good examples of liberal democracy.[1]

Governments in all six continents—autocratic, authoritarian or democratic—view oil security as an inherent component of their national interests. China's quest to confidently secure foreign oil supplies support the dominant rationale behind its energy security policy largely because the country's increasing dependence on foreign oil is perceived by the Government as a weak spot—a strategic vulnerability. China has decided on a geostrategic and politically driven approach to oil security that is based on (1) a pragmatic participation in the international oil market, while at the same time attempting to hedge against price volatility and supply disruptions; and (2) strong reliance on state-owned entities to attain national strategic interests and advantageous decision-making that take place within a tactical framework designed to deepen the dominance of the Chinese Communist Party (CCP) and Chinese energy companies.[2]

To ensure political legitimacy and social stability, China must keep annual gross domestic product (GDP) growth at about 8% and inflation below 5%.[3] To sustain this rate of economic growth, CCP officials need to ensure that oil supply disruptions are either eliminated or kept at a minimum. The Chinese Government has responded to the challenge of potential oil shortages by undertaking a state-led effort to reduce its perceived vulnerabilities. It has relied mostly upon government agencies, the People's Liberation Army (PLA), and state-controlled oil companies to mitigate risks or threats. As a result, China's offshore and onshore operations in the oil sector are dominated by state-owned oil enterprises.[4]

Attempts to control foreign oil operations are facilitated by unimpeded access to national oil blocks and distribution pipelines. Chinese state-owned

46   *Introduction*

oil companies leverage comparative advantages to do so. They enjoy financing arrangements with state-owned financial institutions that offer them open access to abundant and inexpensive credit lines. China's goal to achieve privileged access to or extraction rights in existing oil reserves for its oil companies motivates senior CCP officials to sign accords and agreements in overseas locations with a combination of economic, commercial and diplomatic incentives. Also, in order to secure oil supplies even when Chinese oil companies do not actually own substantial stakes of productive oil assets in foreign countries, the Government has agreed with Iran, Kazakhstan, Russia, Sudan, Brazil and Venezuela to engage in credit-for-oil and infrastructure-for-oil deals. On the other side of the spectrum, commentators have expressed unease about 'energy insecurity' in other regions, but despite legitimate concern about the uncompromising China-first energy security mindset, the actual capacity for the Chinese Government to deliberately or inadvertently exacerbate the energy insecurity of other countries is limited.[5]

At present, a large proportion of China's oil demand is met through commercial transactions in international oil markets, so the most urgent threat to Chinese oil security are provincial, national and regional disruptions in major oil-producing areas, which is why the Chinese Government (along with Russia) is so sensitive to UN Security Council resolutions against Iran or military interventions in the Middle East. Tellingly, almost four-fifths of China's oil imports come from Africa and the Middle East, all of which are shipped by foreign-owned tankers passing through the Indian Ocean into the Straits of Malacca and, then, across the South China Sea until they reach Chinese seaports. The fact that high-ranking CCP officials are also senior executives of state-owned oil companies lends further evidence to the intimate link between the public and private sectors, and more so between energy and military policies: these are critical linkages that forcefully ensure that oil security forms a part of an overarching national security programme.[6]

It is no surprise to CCP officials in Beijing that the world's pattern of progress is unsustainable. The way in which many countries produce and use energy and deplete natural resources is causing climate change, ecological imbalances and other environmental problems. However, they also know that short of a world-wide collapse, there is no real need to curb the wave of prosperity that is sweeping over China, especially if Western countries are not willing emphatically to convert their orthodox growth models to more sustainable ones. Additionally, they are swift to acknowledge that the world is becoming more unstable, as evidenced by the rapid spread of financial crises around the globe, political upheavals, economic insecurity, and a shared vulnerability to radicalism and terrorism.

Furthermore, China has recognized that there is too much inequality in the modern world in the distribution of incomes and wealth, and in access to education, health, jobs and markets. Although China takes these factors into account, the country continues to push forward with its national priorities: pursuing oil security; lifting millions of its citizens out of poverty; becoming the prime locomotive of growth in Asia; enabling businesses and individuals to fulfil their aspirations via an alternative growth model; and carefully selecting the foreign affairs it wants to deal with—not as a global leader, but as a passive participant which calculates its potential gains and losses before inserting moral and sentimental considerations. China's leaders have been selectively incorporating the economic practices and dubious behaviours which brought success to the old powers. They have been forced to concede that they are becoming more enmeshed in an interdependent world, one with greater powers and more widely dispersed political influence. In short, China is conveniently utilitarian and evaluative, and the world is witnessing every step that the country takes.

Oil: what, who, where and how much?

As China rises economically, the likelihood of future conflict over existing oilfields will increase. The explanation of this correlation is very simple. Oil is a non-renewable resource, and as emerging market economies continue to grow they will demand greater quantities of a scarce critical commodity, thus creating a scramble for what is left underground.[7]

Even with phenomenal advances in exploration technology, no one has made a profitable oil discovery during the past 40 years. This is not owing to a lack of interest or effort. International oil companies have traversed the globe in search of oil at an incalculable cost. It would appear that the oil that was easily available just beneath the surface of the Earth has already been extracted.

When an oilfield is exhausted, no new oil materializes to take its place; that is to say, there is no renewal process. Since the 1960s the rate at which the world has consumed oil has outpaced the rate at which it has discovered new oilfields. Today, a country finds only about one new barrel of oil for roughly every four it uses. This is called discovery deficit. Meanwhile, it is estimated that the world's population will consume 120m. barrels of oil per day by 2025, over 50% more than it consumed in 2001. All countries are now forced to confront a bitter reality: the world is fast approaching the point at which conventional sources of oil will decline until they are gone forever. This is the rationale that informs China's oil security and its determined efforts to uncover renewable energy sources—the Chinese Government knows it will need all essential inputs in order to move the country forward.

World-wide, extraction of conventional oil has reached or is nearing its peak. As conventional oil becomes harder to find, unconventional oil has emerged as a solution, but it can only be found in small quantities deeply embedded within other components such as clay, mud, rock, sand and tar. Before it can be used in its liquid form, it must first be separated from these binding elements. Yet, oil extraction in the Middle East is not expected to peak until 2025. This means that a large percentage of the world's remaining oil will be concentrated in a few Middle Eastern countries, many of which

48   *Introduction*

embrace authoritarianism, like China. More than 50% of the world's remaining conventional oil is found in five countries: Kuwait, Iraq, Iran, Saudi Arabia and the United Arab Emirates. The remainder of the oil is found in comparatively small quantities in 14 other countries: Algeria, Angola, Azerbaijan, Brazil, China, Kazakhstan, Libya, Mexico, Nigeria, Norway, Qatar, Russia, the USA and Venezuela. This rapidly dwindling conventional oil has the added inconvenience that is found offshore beneath the world's oceans, making extraction complex, risky, environmentally harmful and detrimental to coastal communities and aquatic life. As if this were not enough, outside of the volatile Middle East, the oil that is left (i.e. the unconventional oil) is said to be much more expensive, environmentally destructive and technologically difficult to extract. Among the largest unconventional sources of oil are the tar sands of Canada and the shale regions of the US Midwest. In addition to the problems listed above, the process of excavating the tar and shale from the earth, extracting the oil, converting it into liquid form, and refining it into petroleum is far more energy-intensive and ozone-depleting than traditional methods of oil production, thus contributing to climate change, pollution, health issues and ecosystem deterioration.[8]

Within approximately five to 10 years, major international oil companies will have exhausted their own reserves unless major changes take place. In 2004 the Federal Trade Commission estimated that ExxonMobil and ConocoPhillips would run out of oil by 2017, Chevron by 2016, and Shell and British Petroleum by 2015.[9] Unfortunately for big oil companies, all of the world's remaining oil is more or less spoken for. Governments own the vast majority of what is left in terms of accessible reserves. In addition to the paucity of sites to drill, there is new and growing competition for the oil that is left, from the rising powers of Brazil, Russia, China and India, which are increasing both their consumption and their pursuit of oil abroad.[10]

As already noted, China offers significant economic and political incentives to its state-owned oil companies to search for offshore oil in countries with questionable records, or by facilitating deals to secure guaranteed supplies from new oilfields. However, Western commentators posit that the Chinese Government's oil security targets could be better served by active participation in global commodity markets, while others suggest that China's economic diplomacy is bringing it closer to belligerent, undemocratic states—a move that may prove detrimental in the long run.[11]

Diplomatic overtures, calculated outcomes

China's economic transformation has altered its geopolitical landscape and foreign policy options: an efficient, reliable, secure and stable mechanism to attain oil security is not possible unless all diplomatic tools are fully utilized. The Chinese Government is now placing greater importance on transnational co-operation and intergovernmental co-ordination. Owing to the perception of oil as a critical-strategic input, it has evolved into a kind of pseudo-weapon in international politics (and in the resolution of diplomatic conflicts), which leaves military interventions a little further behind in achieving peace and stability.[12]

In China, oil security is a driver for its foreign policy, diplomatic overtures and military strategy adjustments. However, it must not be forgotten that China's foreign policies are based on the principles of sovereignty and non-intervention in other countries' internal affairs, which explains why its oil companies prowl for oil overseas without requiring reforms of freedoms or governance. Also, the decline in the USA's world-wide reputation has reduced pressures on China to improve its record. As China's foreign policies have exhibited diverse and contradictory stances, the country is perceived as a deeply conflicted rising power with a series of different international identities.[13]

Around the world, the Chinese system of authoritarian growth (as opposed to democratic growth) is admired by leaders who seek a niche in the world economy for their countries, but who do not want to risk losing their own power. As already noted, this alternative model for growth is supported by Chinese finance, which assists governments in Africa, for example, to undertake capital projects without the kind of accountability and transparency that is required by international banks.

In China, the CCP is credited with advancing the people's economic prospects and this is considered by the poor and destitute to be more important than the right to vote or speak freely (criticizing the Government is not part of the birthright of every Chinese person). The lesson that China has learned from a volatile world is very clear: stability is the ultimate goal. It is for these reasons that dissident movements in China are crushed, religious liberties circumscribed, artists critical of national policies are imprisoned, political organizations prohibited, the internet is monitored and censored, and foreign criticism is prevented from jeopardizing internal order.

Diplomatically, South-East Asian leaders have voiced their security misgivings particularly in view of the fact that the gap in international stature that has existed between the USA and China has narrowed consistently during the last three decades. Following the Second World War, most Asian nations felt closer to a benevolent and powerful USA than to an impoverished and turbulent China. Today, however, China is associated with vibrant dynamism and economic success, to the point that is has been attracting a growing number of highly educated immigrants who perceive it as the next land of opportunity—similarly to perceptions of the USA in the 1960s and 1970s. To put this in context, the Chinese Government demonstrates its assertiveness and independence by organizing regional events from which the US Administration is excluded: an African summit; an East Asian conference; military exercises; and the Shanghai Cooperation Organization.

In order to gain a better understanding of Chinese diplomacy, I will briefly examine two situations: (1) China wants to recover Taiwan because it formed part of China from the mid-17th century until the end of the 19th century. The fact that the island was lost to the Japanese only strengthens China's

50   *Introduction*

determination to recover it, even though the Japanese left many years ago. The USA is not formally committed to rescuing Taiwan in the event of an attack directed by China because the USA does not want Taiwan to be so sure of US protection that it provokes China. Similarly, the USA does not want China to believe that it can attack Taiwan without incurring recriminations. Either way, a regional conflict initiated by China will only validate suspicions by neighbours of a non-peaceful rise to power; (2) China shields North Korea from Western vituperations given that the North Korean leadership is more likely to remain belligerent and dangerous if it feels threatened, while more likely to become a law-abiding state if engaged collaboratively and respectfully. Clearly, the ultimate rationale for keeping US military forces deployed in the Asia-Pacific region is to deter potential aggressions. This presence became all the more necessary when the USA became aware of the strong domestic pressures that could cause China to behave belligerently. The conceptual construct is that, should a crisis arise, China's leaders will look out to the Pacific and be confronted by a mighty US military force with the ability, capacity and determination to defend its national interests, as well as those of Japan, Taiwan, South Korea and other Asian allies.[14]

Throughout history, the rise of a new power has often led to war, whether caused by the desire of that power to spread its wings or attempts by rivals to smother it. Neither China nor Japan seem possessed of imperial ambitions, yet neither will appreciate being perceived as a junior partner or a lesser state. China's rise need not lead to wars, but this does not mean that contention or violent clashes will not happen. China's oil security will partly depend on tactful approaches and calculated outcomes—a juggling of commitments, proposals and solutions. The world will remain stable provided one country does not try to bully or intimidate another into doing something it does not want to do. China's relationship with the rest of the world will be based on a careful balancing of interests that sees the need for modest assurances, but not for oversensitivity.[15]

Broken economic models and what the world can learn from China

As the world witnesses the continuing woes of the US and European economies, and the potentially catastrophic consequences of the dissolution of the eurozone, it has become evident that we are living in a world of broken economic models. The conventional pathways that China, Europe and the USA have used to achieve rapid economic success no longer seem to work. For instance, the vaunted US model of consumer-led growth has now been demolished by the constant stream of reports suggesting stagnant wages, widening inequalities and declining household net worth.[16]

By early 2013 it had become clear that the US economy could no longer rely on lavish borrowing and spending to deliver growth and prosperity, particularly so because there was no clear sense of what could replace consumer spending as the engine of the global economy. Europe and the USA cannot export their way to rapid economic expansion given that weak economies abroad lack demand for Western products and services. Additionally, Europe and the USA cannot turn to greater government spending, as that would result in even larger, politically unsavory deficits—with the added disadvantage that it would not bring relief to the problems of long-term debt. Politicians in the USA refuse to jumpstart the economy with a massive fiscal stimulus because that might ignite inflation and pose a threat to retirement savings. In the case of the European Union countries, the traditionalist approach of managing a fragile equilibrium between slow economic growth and expensive welfare states has, finally, completely unravelled. This leaves persistent uncertainty about what may be next in terms of growth models.[17]

Even China, with its much-heralded investment-driven, export-dependent growth model that propelled it from impoverished backwater to the world's second largest economy in only three decades, is running out of steam. The new goal, as set out by the Chinese Government, is to shift growth away from investment in polluting, energy-intensive, unsustainable industries and towards domestic consumption,[18] particularly of services and green goods, such as energy-efficient vehicles, electricity-saving appliances, and environmentally friendly building materials. In terms of collateral damage, as China's reliance on export industries and investment-intensive capital goods is reduced, countries such as Japan and Germany will probably be substantially hurt because they have specialized in selling machinery and the equipment needed to build Chinese factories and heavy industry.[19] Today, world citizens keep asking this question: how did China lift more than 600m people out of poverty? The answer is simple: by quadrupling its carbon emissions. However, that approach will not be sustainable for long.

Overall, the world's traditional models of growth and prosperity are under assault on all fronts. While the wrecked models of growth differ from region to region, the breakdowns are occurring simultaneously and feed on each other (i.e. there is an umbilical connection between the sovereign debt crisis hovering over Europe and the economic recovery of the USA). At its climax, the abrupt erosion of wages and wealth has impoverished the global middle class, which is the main reason for the huge inequality gaps that have opened up. National leaders face a painful and, possibly, inconclusive economic stalemate ahead—or the emergence of novel ideas.

While not really novel, some ideas that have been modified from traditional models already exist in North America. In Canada, for instance, stringent banking regulations helped to insulate the country from the worst effects of the global financial crisis. Sound policy-making allowed it to preserve the sacred trust on its publicly funded education and health care systems. The record number of Americans heading to Canada between 2010 and 2012 in search of work and better living conditions is proof that the Canadian system of governance is working for its citizenry.[20]

Moreover, the world can learn some valuable lessons from China. First, the Chinese Government will not declare how it invests its foreign exchange

52 *Introduction*

reserves—which have grown rapidly during the past decade—but it is known that China spends 9% of GDP on infrastructure development, compared with 4% for Canada and only 1.7% for the USA—thus providing a long-term boost to jobs and development prospects. These investments partly explain why Chinese industrial centres have become irresistible to foreign investors. Second, the CCP has used its control over the exchange rate as a key plank of its economic development strategy and has built up immense trade surpluses. Third, it is important to understand that China's success is not merely due to its plentiful supply of low-wage labour. Today, China is producing an increasing number of academics, engineers, scientists and technicians. In 2003 it became the third country to launch a human into space. Fourth, its research and development budgets are growing; it is experimenting with new designs, techniques and procedures in such fields as bioengineering, civilian nuclear power and environmental technology.

Finally, China's global search for energy and resources and its desire for oil security may inevitably continue to raise the living standards of its people and to cut poverty rates in rural areas. However, the widening income gap between the upper and lower classes in China clashes acutely with socialist values, which for a long time have emphasized egalitarianism—inequality breeds resentment, especially when people start to suspect that the rich obtained their wealth not through diligent hard work, but through corruption and cronyism. In addition, the Chinese are concerned about pollution, bitter about industrial projects that force them off their land, and anxious about uncontrolled outbreaks of disease.

Concluding remarks

China needs to ensure its economic growth, political stability and socio-cultural development in the more competitive, complex, fragmented and fast-changing world of the 21st century. Chinese leaders recognize their ever-rising resources needs. They assiduously seek to secure foreign oil deliveries by proactively pursuing strategic bilateral relations with key energy producers and resource-rich countries. This approach, while not at all different from those being pursued by other emerging market economies, can prove to be problematic in a world of finite resources and an increasing number of actors pursuing them.[21] In essence, the aim of China's oil security is to lock up critical supplies to sustain growth, stimulate jobs and reduce vulnerabilities.

Whether global citizens like it or not, because the world is still organized around nation states, the decisions that leaders make and those supported by citizens today determine the possibilities of tomorrow. If this is indeed so, the CCP could easily claim that its formula for prosperity, peace and security is a combination of a strong, effective private sector and an assertive, coherent public sector (i.e. government) that work together to promote a vibrant economy that includes job creation, rising incomes, low inflation, increasing exports, and greater energy and resource (e.g. oil) supplies. For example, the prosperous Chinese cities of Guangzhou and Shanghai have been, for some time, deeply committed to building networks of co-operation involving the public, private and civil society sectors, and are now creating economic opportunities and advancing into the future with confidence.

Similarly to other governments in Europe and the USA, the Chinese Government aspires to sustained economic growth and social progress—new businesses, well-paid jobs, affordable education and health care, and progressive leadership in new industries, like biotechnology, microprocessors and clean energy. As China advances, the country's South-East Asian neighbours can reap benefits too. For example, some countries are increasing their presence in Myanmar, with China and Thailand taking a lead position owing to their possession of an infrastructure and the requisite business connections, as well as being on the ground already.[22] Additionally, for economic aid and technical aid developing countries can now turn to China, a generous donor that despite its superpower status appears to treat its partners fairly and with respect, and never asks sensitive questions.[23]

It is noteworthy that although the Chinese Government is aware of the constraints and limitations that it faces, it has identified five ways of creating new, well-paid jobs: increasing exports; improving the country's manufacturing base; leading the world in the production of renewable energy and energy conservation technologies; building a 21st-century infrastructure; and boosting its military capacity by upgrading the country's army and navy. With regard to renewables, China has installed more wind capacity that the USA; has captured approximately one-half of the global market in solar cells, and is racing ahead with tens of billions of dollars in new investments and incentives, in a determined effort to lead the world in both the installation and the export of clean technology products. In tandem with this, Chinese cities are independently tinkering with grants, incentives and loans to increase the manufacture of new clean energy products and more energy-efficient technologies.

It is clear that China—boosted by its economic performance and military build-up—is currently reshaping its strategic priorities and, for the first time since the Sino-Soviet rupture in 1956, is actively seeking to extend its influence through the construction of a stable alliance network and has been closely observing Russia, an oil-rich country, for that purpose.[24] Ultimately, the CCP will recognize that it must support a stronger focus on green technology, which will change the way in which China produces and consumes energy, and is the strategy most likely to fuel a fast-growing economy while strengthening its national security and vital strategic interests.

As former US President Bill Clinton noted, 'We live in the most interdependent age in history. People are increasingly likely to be affected by actions beyond their borders, and their borders are increasingly open to both positive and negative crossings: travelers, immigrants, money, goods, services, information, communication, and culture; disease, trafficking of drugs, weapons, and people, and acts of terrorism and violent crime.'[25] This said, China is acutely aware that pursuing a multi-pronged approach to oil security with

54 *Introduction*

rogue, undemocratic states, along with producing incessant carbon emissions, is not only largely unsustainable but is unpalatable in international forums.

To summarize, China is set to begin presenting forward-looking policies that incorporate modern conceptualizations regarding growth, politics and the environment. Studies on economic and social mobility have demonstrated that nations owe their success to government policies that equalize opportunities and prepare people to seize them. The Chinese Government, with its focus on oil security, education, research and development, entrepreneurship and job creation, is giving its youth the opportunity to take advantage of existing prospects and structural strengths.

Notes

1 Sigfrido Burgos Cáceres and Sophal Ear, 'The Geopolitics of China's Global Resources Quest', *Geopolitics*, Vol. 17, No. 1, 2012, 47–79; Brian Spegele, 'China Shops Around for Oil, Wary of Iran, Arab Spring', *Wall Street Journal*, 20 January 2012.

2 John Lee, 'China's Geostrategic Search for Oil', *Washington Quarterly*, Vol. 35, No. 3, 2012, 75–92.

3 'China's Premier Wen Jiabao Targets Social Stability', *British Broadcasting Corporation*, London, 5 March 2011.

4 Suisheng Zhao, 'China's Global Search for Energy Security: Cooperation and Competition in the Asia-Pacific', *Journal of Contemporary China*, Vol. 17, No. 55, 2008, 207–27.

5 Sigfrido Burgos Cáceres and Sophal Ear, 'China's Natural Resource Appetite in Brazil', *Asian Journal of Latin American Studies*, Vol. 24, No. 2, 2011, 71–92; John Lee, 'The "Tragedy" of China's Energy Policy', *The Diplomat*, 4 October 2012. Available at: http://thediplomat.com/china-power/the-tragedy-of-chinas-energy-policy/.

6 Yasheng Huang, *Capitalism with Chinese Characteristics: Entrepreneurship and the State* (New York: Cambridge University Press, 2008).

7 Robert Manning, 'The Asian Energy Predicament', *Survival*, Vol. 42, No. 3, 2000, 73–88.

8 Antonia Juhasz, *The Tyranny of Oil: The World's Most Powerful Industry—And What We Must Do to Stop It* (New York: HarperCollins, 2008).

9 Federal Trade Commission Bureau of Economics, 'The Petroleum Industry: Mergers, Structural Change, and Antitrust Enforcement', FTC Staff Study, August 2004, p. 68.

10 For comparisons, and based on values from the US Census Bureau, US Department of Energy, Energy Information Administration (EIA), 'World Oil Balance Chart 2003–7', the USA is the largest consumer of oil. With just 5% of the world's population, it uses almost 25% of the world's oil every year, with nearly 70% used for transport alone (this includes cars, trucks, farm machinery, trains, commercial airplanes, boats, motorcycles and private jets). Also, according to the EIA, 'Top World Oil Consumers, 2006 Table', the USA consumes as much oil every year as the combined total for the next five countries: China, Germany, India, Japan and Russia.

11 Andrew Kennedy, 'China's New Energy-Security Debate', *Survival*, Vol. 52, No. 3, 2010, 137–58.

12 Zhang Jianxin, 'Oil Security Reshapes China's Foreign Policy', Center on China's Transnational Relations, Working Paper No. 9. Available at: www.marshallfoundati on.org/documents/ChinaForeignPolicyEnergy.pdf.

13 David Shambaugh, 'Coping with a Conflicted China', *Washington Quarterly*, Vol. 34, No. 1, 2011, 7–27.

14 Madeleine Albright, *Memo to the President Elect* (New York: HarperCollins, 2008).
15 Gregory Chin and Ramesh Thakur, 'Will China Change the Rules of the Global Order?' *Washington Quarterly*, Vol. 33, No. 4, 2010.
16 According to the US Federal Reserve, between 2007 and 2010 US household net worth fell by 39%.
17 Robert Samuelson, 'The Sources of the Global Economic Stalemate', *Washington Post*, 24 June 2012.
18 Since mid-2012 the share of private consumption in China's GDP has been unusually low, at about 33%, compared with most economies in which the consumption ratio is higher than 50%.
19 Jamil Anderlini, 'China's Growth Model Running out of Steam', *Financial Times*, 5 March 2012.
20 'Canada: Beating the U.S. at Its Own Game', *The Week*, 3 August 2012, p. 16.
21 Sigfrido Burgos Cáceres and Sophal Ear, 'China's Oil Hunger in Angola: History and Perspective', *Journal of Contemporary China*, Vol. 21, No. 74, 2012, 351–67.
22 Thanaporn Promyamyai, 'Myanmar President Visits Thailand', *Agence France-Presse*, 23 July 2012.
23 Sigfrido Burgos Cáceres and Sophal Ear, 'China's Strategic Interests in Cambodia: Influence and Resources', *Asian Survey*, Vol. 50, No. 3, 2010, 615–39.
24 Mitchell Belfer, 'Editor's Policy Analysis: A Blueprint for EU Energy Security', *Central European Journal of International and Security Studies*, Vol. 6, No. 1, 2012. Available at: http://cejiss.org/category/issue/2012-volume-6-issue-1.
25 Bill Clinton, *Back to Work: Why We Need Smart Government for a Strong Economy* (New York: Alfred A. Knopf, 2011).

Part II
Country case studies

4 Japan[1]

Introduction

During 2012 global security concerns centred on developments in North Africa and the Middle East as the situation in these regions grew ominously volatile. By 2013, however, the peace and security environment in East Asia had also become increasingly unstable and was causing mounting concern. This trepidation over potential instability in East and South-East Asia is evident from the United States' strategic rebalancing toward the region. Specifically, in East Asia, the two main actors are China and Japan. China's territorial disputes with many of its neighbours have been well documented: India (concerning the state of Arunachal Pradesh, which China claims as part of Tibet), Japan, the Philippines, Taiwan (which China seeks to reclaim), and Vietnam. Whether the potential geopolitical turmoil in East Asia comes about depends entirely on the outcomes of these tense disputes.

One of the biggest threats to East Asian harmony and stability in 2013 was the ongoing dispute between Japan and China over five islets situated in the East China Sea, which Japan controls and calls the Senkakus but which China lays claim to and calls the Diaoyus. Little more than rocky outcrops in shark-infested waters, Japan won the islands as a victory prize in the Sino–Japanese War in 1895. Much later, the USA took over the administration of the islands at the end of the Second World War. Following the signing of the San Francisco Peace Treaty in 1951 China expected that Japan would be forced to relinquish the islands, and that they would be returned to China by right, but this did not prove to be the case. In 1972 the USA returned the disputed islands to Japan, which has administered them since. When China and Japan restored diplomatic relations in the 1970s, the leaders of the two countries decided to postpone the question of sovereignty of the islands until a future date.[2] The issue remains highly complex.

The Chinese Government considers the San Francisco Peace Treaty to be illegal and void. China enacted a Law on the Territorial Sea and the Contiguous Zone in 1992 that treats the Diaoyu/Senkaku Islands as Chinese possessions, thus trying unilaterally to change the status of the islands as defined by the Treaty.[3] Japan has accepted the jurisdiction of the International Court of

60 *Country case studies*

Justice (ICJ) as compulsory. Since China is undertaking various campaigns to promote their assertions in international forums, it would make sense for China to seek a solution based on international law. One only has to wonder why China has not referred the issue to the ICJ for resolution. Would not an international court settle this matter definitively?

In late 2012 the Japanese Government announced that it was to purchase several of the Diaoyu/Senkaku Islands from a family which had owned them privately for some years. China denounced the purchase and declared that the islands were being nationalized. As the islands were to be transferred from one Japanese entity to another, Japan's Government maintained that the status quo had not changed, and that therefore there was no need to open negotiations with China over the issue. The measure taken by the Japanese Government was simply a transfer of title under Japanese domestic law and merely stated that the ownership of the islands was returned from a private citizen to the Government. The objective was to minimize any adverse impact on the China–Japan relationship. In other words, purchasing the islands was considered to be the best option available to the Japanese Government in order to protect bilateral relations. It is noteworthy that in 2008, at a point when Sino–Japanese relations were stable, a joint communiqué issued on the occasion of a visit to Japan by the former Chinese President, Hu Jintao, stated in endearing terms: 'The Chinese side expressed its positive evaluation of Japan's consistent pursuit of the path of a peaceful country and Japan's contribution to the peace and stability of the world through peaceful means over more than 60 years since World War II'.[4]

Japan, its neighbours and the USA consider issues and options

In many quarters there is a growing opinion that China is now seriously contesting the Japanese ownership of the Diaoyu/Senkaku Islands owing to its new-found economic and military might, and that the Chinese Government is willing to cut off diplomatic relations in order to stress that its maritime and territorial claims should be considered seriously and thoroughly. In addition, it is believed that China is testing the reactions of the West to a variety of regional clashes and skirmishes, and that it is also calibrating countermeasures and evaluating the extent of international diplomatic support the country receives. As expected by senior Chinese officials, the US Administration has criticized the Chinese Government for its rash decision to set up municipalities and military garrisons on remote islands in the South China Sea more aggressively to secure its territorial claims. Moreover, US intervention in territorial disputes in the South China Sea—where China has been at odds with another US ally, the Philippines—has been interpreted in some Chinese quarters as a way for the United States to extend its influence and restrain that of China. However, Chinese leaders insist that China opposes all forms of aggrandizement and power politics, and that it will never seek hegemony or engage in ruthless expansion.

The USA is clearly neither a claimant to the Diaoyu/Senkaku Islands nor to the resources in the South China Sea, but for decades it has had a strategic national interest in the maintenance of peace and security in the region, and the pursuit of prosperity and well-being for the people there. In fact, since early 2009 the progressive Obama Administration has intensified its focus on Asia. Specifically, greater attention has been paid to East and South-East Asia given that both are economically vibrant regions that have sought deeper ties with the USA—mainly in reaction to China's rising powers and North Korea's increasing belligerence. Some argue that, as part of its strategic plans for the region, the USA is using Japan as a strategic tool in an effort to increase its presence in Asia, a policy that is said to be heightening tensions between China and Japan. This narrative is not without merit. As an Asian democracy, Japan has contributed to the peace and prosperity of the entire world, and it has counted on its alliance with the USA in order to do so. On the other hand, Japan continues to reiterate that China's peaceful, robust and stable development presents a tremendous opportunity for the global community, including Japan and abutting economies.[5]

A good example of geostrategic diplomacy on the part of the US Administration occurred in early September 2012, when the former US Secretary of State, Hillary Clinton, visited Chinese Communist Party (CCP) officials in Beijing to request that China should seek a peaceful resolution of its disputes with South-East Asian neighbours over claims (maritime and territorial) in the South China Sea. Clinton, as a preemptive measure, also asked representatives of South-East Asian countries also in attendance at the meeting to present a strong, cohesive front when dealing with China, and to work towards a steady dissipation of the increasing tensions in the South China Sea. The US Administration urged China and other involved parties to embrace a non-coercive dispute resolution mechanism and to abide by a fair code of conduct.[6] In more pluralistic forums held in late 2012 delegates at meetings of the Chinese Ministry of Foreign Affairs have insisted to senior government officials that ongoing discussions between China and Japan should examine ways in which to reduce the risk of clashes between Chinese and Japanese patrol vessels sailing perilously close to the islands. The overarching message has been that commerce, investments and trade are far more important than the ownership of the islands.

One of the countries attending these meetings was Indonesia. Indonesia, while not a claimant itself, together with China and Japan has been spearheading efforts in South-East Asia to draw up and implement a code of conduct for handling claims and disputes. Many countries in the region realize that a stable Sino–Japanese relationship produces stability and geopolitical certainty.

Chinese hard power: strength through force

In the international arena, the rapid rise of China as a key participant in foreign affairs is likely to emerge as a salient feature of the geopolitical

62 *Country case studies*

landscape of the early 21st century. As China steadily assumes the status of a superpower, it will start to take on an increasing number of roles and responsibilities. One of these responsibilities is the reinforcement of international codes, norms, rules and standards that enhance peace and security in the Asian region and around the globe.

The international community welcomes a prosperous, robust and vibrant China, but China has argued that in order to fulfil its roles and responsibilities it needs to undertake a comprehensive and sequential modernization of its military. Indeed, since 2004 the People's Liberation Army (PLA) has been mandated by the Chinese Government to carry out missions beyond the mainland's immediate territorial interests. This guidance has propelled the country's military to engage in surveillance, counter-piracy, disaster relief, humanitarian assistance, and international peace-keeping operations.[7] However, some regional actors have voiced concerns about China's accelerated military expansion.[8] They argue that a modern military could increase China's ability to achieve greater diplomatic leverage or favourable conditions in dispute resolutions.

The details speak for themselves: China's total military expenditure for 2010 amounted to more than $160,000m. (by comparison the Obama Administration sent to Congress a proposed defence budget of $663,800m. for the fiscal year 2010. The budget request for the US Department of Defense included $533,800m. in discretionary budget authority to fund base defence programmes and $130,000m. to support overseas contingency operations, in particular activities in Iraq and Afghanistan[9]). In 2011 China began developing its own aircraft carriers, and was already in sea trials with a refitted Soviet-era carrier from Ukraine. It has also developed anti-ship ballistic missiles, potentially capable of attacking US aircraft carriers. Finally, China has been working on a new generation stealth jet fighter, which it boldly tested in Beijing in January 2012 during a visit by former US Defense Secretary Robert Gates. China's PLA (with some 1.25m. ground troops it is the largest in the world) is on track to achieve its goal of building a modern, regionally focused force by 2020. The US Department of Defense's annual report to Congress entitled *Military and Security Developments Involving the People's Republic of China 2011* revealed that the speed and breadth of China's military expansion and modernization could augur a wave of destabilization in East Asia and the Pacific. The report provided details on China's latest acquisitions, such as aerial and combat vehicles, fast-attack submarines, ballistic missiles, jet aircrafts, military tactics, warships and weaponry.[10] The details suggest that China is serious about hard power.[11]

In addition to hardware, numerous intrusions into computer systems around the world (between 2010 and 2013) appeared to have originated in China. The development of capabilities for cyber warfare is in line with authoritative Chinese military doctrines: that information warfare is integral to achieving information superiority and is an effective means of countering a stronger foe.

Most importantly, as a source of economic prosperity and national security, China is increasingly looking to the maritime domain. CCP officials emphasize the growing relevance of maritime power to the country's strategic interests. In 2010 China's State Oceanic Administration released a report entitled *China Ocean's Development*, which stated that the most significant task for China in the 21st century is to build up its maritime power and that the stage for realizing this task is from 2010 to 2020.[12] Military build-ups, however, are highly scrutinized. US Department of Defense officials have expressed concern about China's military intentions in the Pacific. In the European Union (EU), questions have been raised given the overall trends and trajectory in the scope and the scale of China's military modernization efforts.

Despite criticism and scrutiny, senior Chinese government officials continued to push for a more powerful China in regional and international affairs. Former President Hu Jintao, in a report to the 18th National Congress of the Communist Party held in November 2012, explicitly outlined his country's policy to resolutely safeguard China's maritime rights and interests, and build China into a maritime power. These pronouncements have attracted recurrent denunciations in Japan. For example, Japanese Prime Minister Shinzo Abe asserted in early 2013 that Chinese power is increasingly transfiguring the South China Sea into 'Lake Beijing'. Japan frets that China will misuse its naval might and that it cannot be trusted to use its novel military power responsibly.[13]

The overarching rationale against the build-up of power is that China's drive towards military aggrandizement will push other countries into anti-China coalitions that reduce rather than enhance China's diplomatic influence. As China can effectively deter direct military actions in the region, nations seeking to counteract its rise will be bound to choose a blend of containment, deterrence and preemption strategies that slow, rather than speed up, the economic growth China requires in order to maintain internal stability, political legitimacy and regional leadership.

For many observers, the anger-laden actions witnessed in Chinese cities in recent years are cause for concern, given that they are rooted in nationalism encouraged by the government, radicals and provocateurs. Clearly, erratic economic growth in 2013 was poised to weaken the government's legitimacy, and it is possible that the Chinese Government may become increasingly dependent on nationalism and patriotism in order to entrench an intrinsic utilitarian validity with its citizenry. However, not all Chinese government officials are bent on belligerence, militancy and truculence. Key actors of the Chinese Government and state-run media outlets understand the risks to China of an increasingly bellicose stance on the world stage. From late 2012, as many observers expected, there was a spate of calls in state news media for rational patriotism, in an attempt to quickly curb pugnacious impulses.[14]

The Japanese reaction: we take it easy until we can't

In 2012, as China and South Korea entered into delicate territorial contestations with Japan, foreign commentators expressed trepidation over Japan's shift to the right of the political spectrum (i.e. conservative and reactionary).

64 *Country case studies*

This right-leaning positioning appeared to be reinforced by the rise to power of the 'traditionalist' Shinzo Abe, who was returned to the post of Prime Minister on 26 December 2012, after serving his country in that role from September 2006 to September 2007. In view of Abe's belligerent pronunciations prior to his election, some observers concluded that his return as premier signalled that Japan would rashly opt to alter its stance on pacifism (a position Japan settled on following the Second World War), becoming instead more robust and truculent, influenced heavily by nationalistic sentiments. News media outlets warned that Abe's right-leaning team of ministers was composed of belligerent nationalists and extreme conservatives, and that as such the cabinet could have negative consequences for East Asia. Given such sentiments, the public was expected to rationally conclude that Japan would be keen to contain China and North Korea, and assume a much firmer diplomatic position with regard to Russia and South Korea.

This rationale has no firm basis, so let's explore it to gain valuable insights into Japan's actions, behaviours and reactions. First, there is growing alarm that the current Government is reassessing Japan's analysis of its conflict-prone past, thus hinting at an agonistic, war-like stance. China and South Korea have expressed concern that Japanese officials will persist with visits to a memorial honouring Japan's war casualties: the Yasukuni Shrine.[15] To China and South Korea, the shrine is a pertinent reminder that Japan has not yet fully acknowledged its hegemonic past, especially its imperial expansion in the region. Additionally, China and South Korea continue to be uneasy that the Prime Minister will amend or annul the two official apologies (i.e. the Kōno and Murayana pronouncements made in August 1993 and August 1994, respectively[16]) that past Japanese leaders tactfully advanced to put the brash behaviour of the Imperial Army of Japan between 1938 and 1945 into a more acceptable perspective.

In addition, foreign observers expected that Japan would take a more firmer stance in response to the increasing tensions emanating from North-East Asia. Prior to his election, Shinzo Abe spoke of the need to establish a stronger position with China, South Korea and Russia regarding his country's territorial and maritime disputes. By early January 2013 the vigorous harangues gained momentum after Japan insisted that there could be no flexibility in any negotiations over the legality of contested islands because this matter had been settled long ago. As expected, the Japanese cabinet led and chosen by Abe was reluctant to give into China's persistence to amend the 'normal state of affairs' in the East China Sea via its customary patrolling of the waters and routine flights over ill-delimited airspace. Within the region, some pundits went so far as far as to state that the current Prime Minister and his political coterie were aiming to change Japan's peace-laden post-war architecture with the intention of moving towards rearmament, initiation of hostilities, and an escalation of intimidation, thus auguring a wave of destabilization in East Asia.

The inference that Japan is suddenly moving from pacifism to bellicosity is flawed. These are some of the narratives that clash with such a conclusion: in

Japan, strong opposition to China is not a 'new' foreign policy paradigm—Japan has always defended its sovereignty over its land and water. For instance, Yoshihiko Noda, Prime Minister from 2011–12 and leader of the Democratic Party of Japan, took a similar stance against China regarding territorial disputes. Importantly, it is worth mentioning that some of these blanket criticisms about the Japanese Government's policies with its neighbours tend to emphasize Japan's tempestuous rapprochement with China and South Korea, while ignoring the Japanese Government's sweeping foreign policy of seeking further integration and unity within the region. Regardless of misperceptions, it is clear that China, Japan and South Korea are likely to maintain their positions on territorial and maritime sovereignty, as well as other critical multilateral concerns, but what remains certain is that all three countries will work together to advance economic and regional growth, and social cohesion. The Japanese Government has repeatedly asserted that bilateral ties with China and South Korea are of great significance. For example, the Government has persisted in its efforts to launch a free trade accord with China and South Korea, a gargantuan plan that could result in the merger of two of world's biggest economies. However, it would be naïve to assume that such an accord would move ahead without difficulty or setbacks.

As can be expected in these situations, critics tend to be one-sided. They emphasize the narratives that best fit their arguments. This is the case with Shinzo Abe—his detractors have overlooked his 'very practical' push, which has been revived by the objective material circumstances of active statecraft. Prior to his election the Japanese Prime Minister did indeed make some unusual and worrying statements, but thereafter his opinions and views changed; that is, his comments appeared to be less feisty and more amicable. Since December 2012 Japan has been signalling to China and South Korea its desire to reach an improvement in bilateral ties with both countries, even if this means that some sensible concessions will have to be made on the territorial and maritime issues. Certainly, the shuttling of envoys between Japan and South Korea in early 2013 hinted that some progress was in sight. Also, some timely decisions were taken to avoid causing discontent. Japan rejected a proposal to upgrade Takeshima Day[17] to the unprecedented level of national holiday. This is relevant because Takeshima Day marks the Japanese claim to small territories currently under the control of South Korea. In summary, the Japanese Government has shown that it is adept at assessing reality on its own merits.

The next section will examine Japan's strategic ties with ASEAN and other powerful agents.

Counterbalancing China: ASEAN, Japan, and powerful 'others'

What is integral to this argument is that the maintenance of strategic relations goes beyond China and South Korea, as Japan has been seeking a rapprochement with Russia, and did so by launching a series of actions to find a

66   *Country case studies*

solution to the claims over the Northern Territories (known by Russia as the South Kuril Islands). Japan has hinted to Russia that it is willing to consider relinquishing the largest of the islands.

Abe's first period in office as Prime Minister was marked by expediency and practicality, so his business-like approach to governance in 2013 should not have been surprising. However, before being elected to the post of leader of the Liberal Democratic Party and of Chief Cabinet Secretary of the administration led by Junichiro Koizumi, Abe was lauded as a rising star in his country for his uniquely strong political stance and outspokenness against North Korea. However, later, as often occurs in local politics, his allegations and harsh rhetoric diminished, so much so that one of his first political acts in 2006 was to amend and revive Japan's relationship with China and South Korea—by conducting official visits and meeting with their leaders. In summary, the Japanese Government has not forgotten its ability to excel amid mediocrity.

If we step aside from the Japanese Government's pragmatic approach to a number of interstate issues, it is worth placing in context Japan's strategy vis-à-vis its Asian neighbours as a forward-looking foreign policy that considers all the countries in East and South-East Asia, rather than focusing telescopically on two individual states. Evidence of this broad approach to regional cohesion emerged as an official document entitled *Asia's Democratic Security Diamond*. This frank document offered guidance on Japan's intentions to bring collective actions to the fore and to call for robust multi-party work to advance complete freedom of naval passage in Indo-Pacific waters, enhanced water-based trade, and maritime security. The Japanese Government aims to achieve these targets by advocating a tactical collaboration between Japan and growth-oriented actors such as Australia, India, Indonesia and the USA. As expected, critics regarded this document as a tangible act of provocation towards China and South Korea, but what it offers instead is Japan's moderate version of collective security in Asia. While there is no doubt that Japan will continue to defend its territorial rights in the East China Sea and its maritime rights in the South China Sea and elsewhere against undermining actions by regional actors, it is true, however, that the Government is not a shrewd promoter of quick containment or military encirclement. It became readily evident to political observers that Japan's neighbourhood policy was to attract allies and like-minded partners in its immediate vicinity to pursue a situation where the balance of power in Asia is maintained by all countries and not tilted overwhelmingly to the right or left by any given state.

The Japanese Government's strategic objective to renew and strengthen critical ties in its neighbourhood were further confirmed through Shinzo Abe's official visits to several South-East Asia countries during his first foreign tour. This common-sense practicality and tendency towards regional cohesion revealed Japan's approach to 'outcome-based diplomacy' which developed a varied programme of financial and economic activities that buoyed the region generally: Japan's trade with China declined from approximately 18.5% of total exports in 2000 to about 11% in 2011, a steep decrease for a country with a traditional role as leader in regional exports. However, this decrease in trade with China was quickly counterbalanced by an increase in exports to Vietnam, Indonesia, Singapore, Thailand and the Philippines, which soared in 2012 from close to 9.5% to approximately 11%, according to the Japan Research Institute. These figures suggested that Japan's regional policy for growth, power-balancing, and security should not be analysed through an examination of the country's most recent discord or friction with China (and South Korea). Overall, the Japanese have learned to construct a dense network of regional ties that are expected to provide a compass for its foreign and regional policies in a pragmatic and matter-of-fact manner.[18]

The Sino–Japanese relationship: co-existence without defiance

Conflict and tension between China and its neighbours are not recurrent scheduled events, but it is not uncommon to hear of government spokespersons complaining publicly about China's actions in the region—including unfair trade sanctions, rapid military build-ups, territorial contestations, immigration issues, sanitary violations or maritime disputes. With this in mind, forceful debate between government officials in China and Japan over the uninhabited Diaoyu/Senkaku Islands could be interpreted as routine diplomatic posturing between two states that are redefining their positions under a new economic-political context; a dispute that is unlikely to end up in full-scale war but that it is not impossible to rule out as a catalyst for armed conflict.

In February 2013 reports indicated that an escalation in tensions demonstrated just how sensitive the stand-off was, so much so that a skirmish was narrowly avoided. The Japanese Government claimed that a Chinese battleship had engaged in a regrettable, provocative act when it beamed a 'locked-on' radar signal at a Japanese destroyer (part of group of ships from the Maritime Self-Defense Force that patrol the area). This unilateral action was perceived by Japan as an initial, premeditated step in preparation for launching an attack at a target. This event, which took place approximately 60 miles from the Diaoyu/Senkaku Islands, was understood as one of China's repeated attempts to 'test' its boundaries with nearby rivals. Earlier, in mid-January 2013, China had already beamed a similar radar signal at a Japanese helicopter from one of its warships. To some Japanese officials, these acts are not only understood as threats but also as challenges to Japan's control of and sovereignty claims over the uninhabited islands. These provocations, when properly assessed within the context of 'nationalistic' statecraft, could only be answered with counter-provocations, which meant that both states took on the responsibility to oversee and patrol what they 'believed' to be theirs and moved ahead with the deployment of air and naval power to respond to what they considered to be maritime and territorial incursions, all of which resulted in a list of internationally sensitive incidents that heightened regional risks.[19]

68 *Country case studies*

As these incidents occurred, they attracted the attention of neighbours and major international actors. One of these was the USA (see Chapter 6). While the USA has not taken sides over who should control the islands, US government officials wasted no time in asserting that the USA is tightly bound to Japan through the 1951 bilateral Security Treaty between the USA and Japan, China appeared indifferent to these assertions when they were made public, but paid close attention to the way in which strategic positions aligned in the international sphere. Chinese officials did not ignore the constant shuttling of US diplomats into East Asia calling for calmness, comity, co-operation and restraint. In fact, the new leaders of the CCP in Beijing recalled history very well and remembered that, during the tense years of the Cold War, Russia and the USA devised numerous strategies to avoid and prevent accidents, errors and misinterpretations that could have resulted in irreversible armed conflict. Similarly, today, when leaders on both sides bring the past to bear on the present, they also realize that China, with its young army and navy, has not developed reliable risk-reduction mechanisms to prevent conflicts.

The involvement of foreign actors in Asia's regional struggles is not new. Both the EU and the USA have intervened at different times and to varying degrees. However, international relations in 2013 have not changed since 1953. Nowadays, countries in general try proactively to work out their differences with or without international involvement. In East and South-East Asia, for instance, conferences, meetings and summits are used to resolve multilateral concerns and bilateral issues, and to mend relationships that have gone awry. If, however, the matter is critically urgent, it is not uncommon to hear of emergency gatherings in which heads of states meet in order to discuss, ponder and find short- or long-lasting solutions to problems.

Sometimes certain countries use clever tactics to oversee and protect their strategic interests without being perceived as openly militaristic. China, according to facts, fits a pattern of mendacious inveiglement. The Chinese Government is known to make use of pertinent civilian bodies instead of military units to patrol the Daioyu/Senkaku Islands. Boats and ships belonging to research agencies, universities and environment-oriented bodies have been used to conduct inspection rounds on strategic outposts. However, this tactic has attracted internal criticism. As the *Economist* reports, news outlets aligned with and influenced by the orthodox CCP have made cautionary calls, 'recalling China's history of being set back in its development by Japanese aggression—in the 1890s and again in the 1930s and 1940s'.[20]

It is noteworthy that not every politician in Japan is anti-China. Progressive and young actors in the political milieu of Japan's officialdom have advanced the possibility that the incident in February 2013 was not a top-down decision emanating from the highest echelons of Chinese power, but instead a foolish and immature act by a low-ranking naval officer on board the warship. Moreover, representatives of Japan's Liberal Democratic Party believed that had the provocation been found to have taken place on the instructions of senior CCP officials, this would have been a blow to the Chinese

Government's all-too-often quoted slogan of 'peaceful growth and non-interventionism'. More likely than not, it would have been interpreted within the region as an 'arrogant China' seeking to extend its economic and military influence. However, just because this incident could end up being catalogued as an unintentional mishap of sorts it does not detract from the possibility that the Government does has not firm control on its generals and military apparatus, which is what Japanese authorities fear the most. If China is unable to curb its military forces, then who is really in charge?

In speeches, senior Japanese officials reiterate long-held government positions, one of which is that the disputed islands form an inviolable part of Japanese territory and that no dispute exists with China regarding control or ownership. In fact, during a parliamentary meeting in February 2013 Prime Minister Abe quoted the former British Prime Minister, Margaret Thatcher, recalling her comments regarding the Falklands War between Great Britain and Argentina in 1982, when she mentioned that her attempts were, at all times, geared to uphold the principle of international law, which, above all existing principles must prevail against the use of force in order to avoid chaos and destruction.[21]

Observers inside and outside Japan are not so sure that this was a reckless miscalculation. Many have gone so far as to suggest that the decision to target the Japanese vessels was intentional and calcuated, and taken at the most senior level of the CCP. If they are right in this assessment, then China and Japan are surely heading towards a full confrontation. The Lowy Institute of Australia published a report on China's foreign policy and proposed the argument that the Chinese Government's actions and reactions in the East and South China Seas are calculated and assessed policy directives issued by Xi Jinping. In fact, the report purported that a new unit had been set up by the Chinese Government to deal with the continuing impasse regarding the islands, and that China's new leadership was fully aware of the drawbacks and consequences but that, regrettably, senior Chinese decision-making officials are exposed to inaccurate accounts, outright exaggerations, manipulations and faulty geopolitical assessments by advisors determined upon bullish approaches.[22]

With this situation in plain view, Japanese foreign policy pundits asserted that China is calibrating and gauging Japan's cheek-to-cheek alliance with the USA, and to find out quickly how much regional latitude China may be given on a crisis-by-crisis basis. Also, more hawkish voices in Japan wasted no time in claiming that the spate of clashes in the East China Sea is nothing more than a calculated approach to undermine senior Japanese officials, many of whom favoured the bullish statements and bellicose narrative of Shinzo Abe during his campaign.

Is there a way forward?

Inasmuch as the world would welcome the news of a meeting between China and Japan jointly to attempt to resolve all the issues regarding the islands, it is predictable that this is unlikely to happen. Both Xi and Abe are new figures in

70 *Country case studies*

high-stakes politics in East Asia, and both are leaders with big egos and grandiose plans for their countries, so it is improbable that either will take steps to publicly propose a way forward and show a willingness to adjust positions that the general population may perceive to be feeble concessions. This being the case, and in consideration of the full historical background that weighs down on the Sino–Japanese relationship, it seems only reasonable to suggest that both countries should acquiesce to potential win-win scenarios, such as shared exploration, navigation and fishing rights, and the oversight of territorial and maritime delimitations on alternate schedules. However, this reason-based suggestion hinges on the assumption that the word 'sharing' is not too insulting for any party to embrace. A resolution means that Japan would have to accept, publicly, that the tiny Senkaku Islands are in fact subject to a sovereignty dispute, and it would also mean that China is willing to maintain a calmer and a less intrusive approach to what the country now considers to be its vicinity. A reduction in tensions between China and Japan would also depend on how Japan plays its regional security card with the USA: as the US Administration tackles soaring debts, a sluggish economic recovery, and cutbacks in defence spending, it seems that the Japanese Government is counting on US backroom diplomacy and its pre-eminent status to deter the Chinese Government from acting rashly, and that statements backing Japan unconditionally (in case of a war) will make China reconsider.

The core of the issue: potential windfalls

At the core of the territorial and maritime dispute between China and Japan lie three separate but interconnected issues—Chinese projection of power in a region where it is emerging as its engine of growth; securing the natural gas and crude oil deposits that may (or may not) be found under the seabed in the East and South China Seas; and the potential economic windfalls derived from energy sales and from up- and downstream savings achieved through reduced dependence on foreign oil.[23]

If we view contemporary Sino–Japanese relations under this lens, it is not difficult to comprehend that the two leaders of the CCP, Xi Jinping and Li Keqiang, will continue to utilize the armed forces to cement their country's political authority and to present a tough stance by China in growing territorial disputes in the region. Indeed, during the opening ceremonies of the National People's Congress in 2013, both politicians exploited their airtime to spike nationalistic sentiments and embolden their bases to unite and support. This stance can help to explain why China accused Japan of harassing Chinese ships, and continues a succession of allegations that reflect increasing distrust between the two countries. In response, Japan asked the Chinese Government to explain why Chinese ships had strategically placed several buoys in the East China Sea near a group of the disputed islands. As expected, denial continued to be China's first response to claims and accusations. Ultimately, this has resulted in a situation whereby China accuses Japan, and

Japan accuses China, and both dispatch ships to the same location to keep each other under close observation. However, such antagonism only serves to weaken a regional momentum for cohesion, comity and co-operation.

Concluding remarks

China and Japan share strategic interests not only in terms of bilateral relations but in a variety of areas (i.e. cultural, financial and technological). Both are committed to building 'win-win' ties through co-operation and reciprocation. Despite these commitments and interests, it is some time since Chinese consumers staged a boycott of Japanese products in late 2012 over the uninhabited islands; sales of Japanese cars in China have yet to recover; Chinese factories continue to favour South Korean component suppliers, and the USA has displaced China as Japan's largest export market. It is evident that the commercial costs of failing to resolve this dispute keep rising fast.

Citizens and politicians of both countries would do well to remind themselves of the tremendous efforts made by former Chinese and Japanese leaders as they devoted themselves to normalizing interstate relations, and decided to establish a mutually beneficial relationship based on common strategic interests, thereby propelling the bilateral relationship to a higher level. Yet, it is interesting that immediate economic ties have been overshadowed by the fact that the Diaoyu/Senkaku Islands offer the prospect of rich fishing grounds, potential oil reserves, and a maritime strategic military outpost for both China and Japan. Clearly, these spats have changed the landscape of Sino–Japanese relations, especially since territorial and maritime disputes are prone to spirals of escalation and retaliation. Put into perspective, it is not difficult to foresee that both regional economies will, inevitably, lose more than they gain—Japan could potentially lose a giant market for its products, and China may prove to be unable to exploit Japan's technological know-how and capital investment necessary for further economic growth.

There is sincere hope in China that Xi Jinping will achieve the long-delayed economic, political and social reforms required to transform the country into a growth- and peace-seeking economy, but truly substantive changes in Chinese foreign policy are not likely to follow the selection of a new and younger government leadership team. Sooner or later China will enter a phased progression into an increasingly open situation, a two-way conversation—one where people with diverse backgrounds are able to make greater contributions. Furthermore, this evolution could very well include a system based on equitability, rule of law and greater accountability. Nowadays, it is politically customary to draw up plans under a penumbra of secrecy. For instance, it has been reported that the Chinese authorities are sensitive to media coverage of the wealth amassed by some of those occupying the highest echelons of power. Such reports are evidence of the 'increasingly corrupt system of interlocking ties between the Communist Party and state-owned banks, industries, and monopolies'. The vast internal assemblage of knots and ties allow high-ranking

72   *Country case studies*

CCP officials and their families to become affluent, and even facilitate the rapid shuttling of monies out of China.[24]

There are encouraging signs that change is near. Not everyone is tightlipped in China. It has been argued that the lack of political reform is the root cause of public discontent, including stalled economic restructuring, income disparity and pollution.[25] Also, China's lack of transparency and its trends in military prowess have been denounced. Chinese commentators have stated that 'being nationalist in China is politically correct, and the government has long relied on a muscular nationalism to bolster its legitimacy'.[26] Even staunch allies are progressively searching for options. In November 2012 Myanmar hosted a visit by US President Barack Obama, which marked a dramatic shift in policy for a strategically important neighbour that had long been considered to be aligned reliably with China. This means that the region is also listening.

In future, the world can only hope that students of foreign affairs, international law and political science will be expected to learn that China and Japan acted as responsible members of a peace-reinforcing international community, and that finally the two countries were prepared to stabilize official relations with each other after realizing how much was at stake.

Notes

1 Some of the paragraphs included in this chapter appeared in a peer-reviewed article published by the same author in the *Georgetown Journal of International Affairs*, online, 2013.

2 Kimie Hara, '50 Years from San Francisco: Re-Examining the Peace Treaty and Japan's Territorial Problems', *Pacific Affairs*, Vol. 74, No. 3, 2001, 361–82.

3 Zhongqi Pan, 'Sino-Japanese Dispute Over the Diaoyu/Senkaku Islands: The Pending Controversy from the Chinese Perspective', *Journal of Chinese Political Science*, Vol. 12, No. 1, 2007, 71–92.

4 Koichiro Genba, 'Japan-China Relations at a Crossroads', *New York Times*, 20 November 2012, available at: www.nytimes.com/2012/11/21/opinion/koichiro-genba -japan-china-relations-at-a-crossroads.html?_r=0.

5 Claude Meyer, *China or Japan: Which Will Lead Asia?* (New York: Oxford University Press, 2012).

6 'Clinton seeks Chinese accord on South China Sea', *CBS News*, 4 September 2012, available at: www.cbsnews.com/8301–501712_162–57505428/clinton-seeks-chinese- accord-on-south-china-sea/.

7 Andrew Scobell and Andrew J. Nathan, 'China's Overstretched Military', *The Washington Quarterly*, Vol. 35, No. 4, 2012, 135–48. For an expanded examination of China's goals, see: Sigfrido Burgos Cáceres and Sophal Ear, *The Hungry Dragon: How China's Resource Quest Is Reshaping the World* (New York: Routledge, 2013).

8 The Chinese military remains focused on Taiwan, which it claims as part of its sovereign territory, and reports allege that it has deployed as many as 1,200 short-range missiles aimed in its direction.

9 US Department of Defense, 'DoD Releases Fiscal 2010 Budget Proposal', News Release No. 304-09, 7 May 2009. Available at: www.defense.gov/releases/release. aspx?releaseid=12652.

10 Office of the Secretary of Defense, 'Military and Security Developments Involving the People's Republic of China 2011', Annual Report to Congress (Washington, DC:

Department of Defense, 2012), available at: www.defense.gov/pubs/pdfs/2011_cmpr_final.pdf.

11 See: Christopher Hughes, *Japan's Remilitarization* (New York: Routledge, 2009).

12 State Oceanic Administration of the People's Republic of China. See: www.soa.gov.cn/.

13 James Holmes, 'The South China Sea: Lake Beijing', *The Diplomat*, 7 January 2013, available at: http://thediplomat.com/the-naval-diplomat/2013/01/07/the-south-china-sea-lake-beijing/.

14 Richard Bush, *The Perils of Proximity: China-Japan Security Relations* (Washington, DC: Brookings Institution Press, 2010).

15 The Yasukuni Shrine is a Shinto shrine in central Tokyo that commemorates Japan's war dead. The shrine was founded in 1869 with the purpose of enshrining those who died in war for their country and sacrificed their lives to help build the foundation for a peaceful Japan. Since 1978, political controversy surrounds this Shrine because fourteen war criminals are among the 2.5 million people enshrined at Yasukuni.

16 Between 1993 and 1994 the Japanese Chief Cabinet Secretary Yōhei Kōno and the former Prime Minister, Tomiichi Murayama, expressed regret and remorse over acts of aggression and military rule that caused pain, hardship and suffering for many people in Asia, including China and South Korea. These statements are believed to be connected to a public relations exercise by Japan on the eve of the 50th anniversary of the ending of the Second World War.

17 Takeshima, or Dokdo in Korean, are a string of uninhabited volcanic outcroppings in the Sea of Japan. Both Japan and South Korea claim them, a dispute going back at least 60 years. The holiday, for its part, only goes back to 2007, when a local Japanese council signed it into law. Takeshima Day remains a reminder that Japan and South Korea haven't always been friendly. See: C. Dewey, 'Japanese Holiday 'Celebrating' Disputed Islands Sparks Backlash in South Korea', *Washington Post*, 23 February 2013.

18 J. Berkshire Miller and Takashi Yokota, 'Japan Keeps Its Cool: Why Tokyo's New Government Is More Pragmatic than Hawkish', *Foreign Affairs*, 21 January 2013. Available at: www.foreignaffairs.com/articles/138770/j-berkshire-miller-and-takashi-yokota/japan-keeps-its-cool.

19 Aaron Friedberg, *A Contest for Supremacy: China, America, and the Struggle for Mastery in Asia* (New York: W. W. Norton & Company, 2011).

20 'China and Japan: Locked On—The Dangerous Dance Around Disputed Islets Is Becoming Ever More Worrying', *The Economist*, 9 February 2013, available at: www.economist.com/news/asia/21571466-dangerous-dance-around-disputed-islets-b ecoming-ever-more-worrying-locked.

21 Shingo Ito, 'Japan PM Quotes UK's Thatcher on Island Dispute', *Agence France Presse*, 28 February 2013.

22 Linda Jakobson, 'How Involved Is Xi Jinping in the Diaoyu Crisis?' *The Diplomat*, 8 February 2013, available at: http://thediplomat.com/2013/02/08/how-involved-is-xi-jinping-in-the-diaoyu-crisis-3/?all=true.

23 Edward Luttwak, *The Rise of China vs. the Logic of Strategy* (Cambridge, MA: Belknap Press, 2012).

24 Thomas L. Friedman, 'The Talk of China', *New York Times*, 15 September 2012, available at: www.nytimes.com/2012/09/16/opinion/sunday/friedman-the-talk-of-china.html? src=me&ref=general.

25 *The Economist*, 'China's New Leadership: Vaunting the best, Fearing the worst', 27 October 2012.

26 Didi Kirsten Tatlow, 'The Meaning of the China-Japan Island Dispute', *International Herald Tribune*, 19 September 2012; Dai Tan, 'The Diaoyu/Senkaku Dispute: Bridging the Cold Divide', *Santa Clara Journal of International* Law, Vol. 5, No. 1, 2006, 134–68.

5 The Philippines

Introduction

Brunei, China, Malaysia, the Philippines, Taiwan and Vietnam lay claim to overlapping portions of the South China Sea.[1] This sea extends over 1.4m. square miles of the Pacific Ocean. It is dotted with over 250 small islands, atolls, cays, shoals, reefs and sandbars, most of which have no indigenous people (i.e. they are uninhabited), and are naturally under water at high tide, some of which are permanently submerged. The South China Sea is important to all these countries because one-third of the world's shipping transits through its waters, and in addition it is believed to hold significant oil and natural gas reserves beneath its seabed.[2]

Economists and historians tell us that a rapidly growing economy requires critical inputs, especially energy sources, natural resources and raw materials. Thus, the robust economic growth of East and South-East Asia has boosted demand for critical inputs in the region. In order to provide an indication of Asia's rising energy needs, we need to look at figures. A Western research entity 'projects total liquid fuels consumption in Asian countries outside the Organisation for Economic Co-operation and Development (OECD) to rise at an annual growth rate of 2.6 percent, growing from around 20 percent of world consumption in 2008 to over 30 percent of world consumption by 2035. Similarly, non-OECD Asian natural gas consumption grows by 3.9 percent annually, from 10 percent of world gas consumption in 2008 to 19 percent by 2035.'[3] These annual growth rates for oil and gas consumption suggest that a competition for energy sources is expected, and many commentators and observers believe that the ongoing disputes over maritime and territorial sovereignty in the South China Sea reflect this competition.

Analysts in Eastern and Western think tanks posit that China is trying to substantiate its claims of 'absolute and indisputable sovereignty' over most, if not all, of the South China Sea by conducting scheduled naval patrols in the area. As we learned in Chapter 4, the Chinese Government is using a similar approach (i.e. regular maritime surveillance) in its heated dispute with Japan regarding the Diaoyu/Senkaku Islands in the East China Sea.[4] Clearly, as Asia's energy demands continue to grow through development and prosperity, the international community expects a greater share of oil from producers in Africa, Central Asia and the Middle East to pass through the South China Sea. This increased transit of oil from foreign sources to China is regarded by government officials as a strategic vulnerability, a weak point that can be exploited by traditional hegemonic powers to stifle China's growth potential and as punishment for behaving rashly against its neighbours. In order to reduce this vulnerability (i.e. manage associated risks), high-ranking Chinese strategists have formulated a strategy that includes full control of the South China Sea.[5]

The USA considers the Philippines and Japan to be its partners, and is actively seeking measures to increase regional security following the various maritime and territorial tensions. China has never been comfortable about the US presence in the region. In the past China was not in a position to do much about it, but now that the country has accumulated significant economic, military and political power, it has demonstrated its strength by warning the USA to be careful with its actions and language. Such warnings are usually made following public opposition on the part of the US Department of State to any unilateral actions that might undermine Philippine or Japanese sovereignty over any disputed territories in the East and South China Sea.[6]

Sino–Philippine relations: not so smooth

China and the Philippines have been in dispute over reciprocal claims of sovereignty over large parts of the South China Sea (also known as the West Philippine Sea). To clarify, China's ongoing dispute with the Philippines is only one of several tense disagreements between the Chinese Government and its South-East Asian neighbours over waters in the region. The Philippine Department of Foreign Affairs has stated that the country has in effect exhausted almost all diplomatic and political avenues for a peaceful and long-lasting settlement of its maritime dispute with China.[7] In view of the mounting difficulties in dealing with China's recalcitrance, in 2013 the Philippine Government challenged China at the International Tribunal for the Law of the Sea, in Hamburg, Germany, over the many Chinese claims to the South China Sea, including the waters off the west coast of the Philippines. During the trial, the Philippine Government cited the United Nations Convention on the Law of the Sea (UNCLOS) to press for a final and binding resolution to the dispute. So acrimonious are the disagreements between China and its neighbours that the Association of Southeast Asian Nations (ASEAN) has compared the situation in the South China Sea to that of the ongoing tensions between Israel and Palestine.

Disagreements and tensions between China and the Philippines increased in 2012 (and were ongoing in 2013) owing to a naval stand-off over the remote and rocky but strategically located Mischief Reef[8] in the South China Sea. The reef is a sea-based territory located just 80 nautical miles from the province of Zambales, Philippines. As a result of the ensuing interstate crisis,

76 *Country case studies*

both countries called in each other's ambassadors to complain about reactive responses and reckless behaviours. The tensions escalated quickly to the point that ASEAN feared that an open Sino–Philippine conflict would ensue.

This development can be explained in part by China's priorities and viewpoints. The new Chinese leaders, Xi Jinping and Li Keqiang, have started to focus on domestic problems (e.g. income inequality, unemployment, inflation, popular unrest, pollution and corruption). This inward focus has thus precipitated a Chinese foreign policy that is bold and reactive. However, this handling of foreign affairs may have serious consequences and impacts on China owing to the potentially explosive nature of the country's most pressing foreign policy challenge—how to reduce tensions with the USA and with South-East Asian states over diverse territorial claims in the East and South China Seas. Indeed, US government officials have continued to reiterate that US policies for the region do not take a definitive position on the ultimate sovereignty of the Spratly Islands, but that the USA is resolute regarding its commitments to uphold defence and security treaties with its regional allies.

Despite US affirmations and assurances, China has not changed its behaviour. Reports from news agencies in the Philippines and Japan have revealed that Chinese surveillance vessels and naval patrols continued to carry out regular inspection missions in the South China Sea. Furthermore, the director of the State Oceanic Administration stated that China would continue its maritime patrols 'to secure the nation's maritime rights and interests' in areas it claimed as its territorial waters.[9] In response to these actions, Europe and the USA have urged ASEAN to enforce and strengthen an existing code of conduct in the South China Sea, even if China objects.

Lately, Sino–Philippine relations have not been constructive, nor have they improved. In June 2012 Philippine President Benigno Aquino hinted that he would order government ships to return to the Scarborough Shoal if China did not abide by its promise to remove its vessels from the area in dispute. However, the Sino–Philippine stand-off over the Shoal came to an abrupt end when an incoming typhoon forced fishing vessels and navy ships flying the Philippine flag to leave the disputed area. Unsurprisingly, following the passage of the typhoon, the Philippine military returned to the Shoal and discovered two Chinese law enforcement ships and six fishing vessels docked there. The Philippine Government expressed its dissatisfaction over this finding because China had agreed previously to withdraw all ships from the sheltered lagoon following allegations that Chinese fishermen were poaching corals, exotic species of fish, sharks and turtles from the Shoal.[10]

Chinese policy-making: continual tweaking

The Chinese Government defines the objectives of foreign policies through consultation with other ministries and members of the Central Committee of the Chinese Communist Party (CCP). These objectives follow somewhat predictable orientations, which annually align with the most pressing issues of

The Phillipines   77

the time. Since 2011 three objectives have emerged: (1) domestic political stability; (2) sovereign security, territorial integrity and national unification; and (3) China's sustainable economic and social development. It is noteworthy that China's primary objective is domestic stability; that is, pacification of its citizenry to ensure that the CCP stays in power, that the model of autocratic capitalism keeps on delivering results, and that the socialist system remains intact. In addition, high-ranking CCP officials acknowledge that a stable external environment (regionally and internationally) is conducive to achieving these three objectives. Regional stability is thought to be maintained by ensuring that neighbours do not resort to violence or start to work with pariah states (e.g. North Korea), and thus an environment that is calm enough to carry out unimpeded interstate commerce is fostered.

Some Chinese military officers have publicly challenged the legality of claims advanced by the Philippines, citing that China will protect its territorial sovereignty at all costs. However, senior Chinese officials and political leaders have repeatedly reaffirmed the country's abidance to guidelines for dealing with China's maritime and territorial conflicts. The argument is that China wishes to focus on sustained economic co-operation while delaying the final resolution of any underlying claims. Meanwhile, the presence of armed vessels patrolling contested islands and waters does not seem to harmonize with the 'pacifying rhetoric' emanating from the Government. Many East and South-East Asian countries continue to perceive China's behaviour as being provocative and pugnacious—a sign of the country's willingness to adopt a more unilateral and confrontational attitude in the region.[11]

High-ranking CCP officials have come to realize that richer, more actionable insights are identified from what is learned in the context of the real world, which explains why they are so keen to observe how regional actors react to Chinese tactical moves in the South China Sea. China tinkers with power projection and military provocation towards the Philippines with the intention of gauging the extent of attention and coverage it gets from the foreign press, news outlets and the international community. It can also be argued that China has concluded that it is worth souring relations with the Philippines as a way of discovering how its neighbours and the USA will respond to bullying. The Chinese Government understands that direct observation of actions, behaviours and reactions is preferable to logical deduction of outcomes simply because it has learned that foreign governments and their leaders are insincere.

History also provides lessons that have been heeded. Ian James Storey asserts that 'China's occupation of Mischief Reef in 1995 was part of a dual strategy of negotiation and occupation, influenced by domestic political factors'. This falls in line with current behaviours which suggest that the Chinese Government tinkers first with weaker states in the region to test opinion and regional reactions. Storey explains that 'the weakness of the Philippine armed forced provided the People's Republic of China with an opportunity to extend its claims in the South China Sea, avoiding the possibility of military

78 *Country case studies*

confrontation'. From China's perspective, gaining ground in disputes with the Philippines enables the country to adopt a more proactive approach to tougher rivals (i.e. Japan and Vietnam) and sets a bankable precedent for moving claims forward without the risk of armed conflict. According to Storey, in response to Chinese bullying, the Philippines chose to employ 'diplomacy to resolve the disputes, employing both bilateral and multilateral negotiations. Whilst these negotiations have met with some success, the primary issues remain unresolved.' ASEAN gave strong support to the Philippines throughout its maritime and territorial dispute with China, especially because its neighbours were concerned that China's actions would aggravate the possibility of regional instability. Interestingly, the USA remained silent.[12]

US indifference: not all friends are powerful allies

The USA provides very little assistance, encouragement and support to the Philippine Government in its disputes with China because it has calculated that critical US strategic interests are not significantly affected. Yes, the Philippines is a friend of the USA, but not a powerful ally that the US Administration could use should it come to deflecting China from further assertiveness and expansion in South-East Asia and the South China Sea. Furthermore, when US officials are asked to comment on disputes over contested islands and waters in the East and South China Sea, they resolutely affirm that the USA has no position on sovereignty issues but strongly opposes any use of coercion, force, intimidation or manipulation to seek resolution.

In true collaborative spirit, the USA asserts that the Obama Administration takes a position on the importance of dealing with maritime and territorial disputes through dialogue and diplomacy, and calling on parties to avoid the use of coercion and intimidation as viable options. The attitude of the US Administration towards the Philippines could be interpreted as well-intended neutrality or strategic indifference. In fact, it has been noted that the USA could, on occasion, serve as a good-faith mediator between the disputants. However, it would appear that the USA is less neutral than assumed. Indeed, the US involvement in the region is more geared towards violent conflict than debating issues through the usual diplomatic channels.[13]

Renowned US foreign policy experts claim that the Obama Administration has unleashed a pragmatic foreign policy, which tackles one issue at a time in a thoughtful way. Overall, the Administration's performance has been competent and solid, and in foreign affairs it has chosen reasonable policies (or the least worst options, at a minimum) with an approach typified by multidimensionality, thoroughness, reasonably good teamwork and flexibility when needed.[14]

If we are to take the above claim at face value, the USA will rejoin the Sino–Philippine conflict as it evolves, and it will assess the advantages and disadvantages of US involvement in light of the measurable and objective circumstances of the time. Both China and the Philippines should not expect partial or total defence and security commitments by US forces in the view of the low priority assigned by the USA to the conflict between the two countries. In April 2013 US Secretary of State John Kerry reiterated US commitment to a peaceful resolution to the South China Sea dispute even if such an outcome does not suit China. The USA will continue to work with the Philippines in resolving the conflicting claims in the South China Sea. Moreover, the US favours arbitration as the main instrument to reach a binding solution between the claimants, but the Chinese Government has taken its case to the UN to argue against plans to resolve the dispute in this way, insisting that areas claimed by the Philippines form parts of China's cultural and historical domain.

Concluding remarks

Scholars will eventually surmise that beyond the immediate economic benefits to be gained through controlling the islands and waters in the South China Sea, the Chinese Government believes that after recovering Taiwan, all of these outcomes will signal a final dismantling of the imperial yoke of Japan and of traditional Western hegemons. Meanwhile, the other five claimants assert that retaining control or ownership of the islands, their resources, and their surrounding waters are necessary acts of defiance in light of China's growing assertiveness and bullying behaviour in the region.

Notes

1 Six countries claim conflicting territorial rights in the South China Sea. This vast area is rich in oil, gas, fishing and mineral resources. For interactive maps, see: www.nytimes.com/interactive/2012/05/31/world/asia/Territorial-Claims-in-South-China-Sea.html?_r=0, 'Territorial Claims in South China Sea', *New York Times*, May 2012.

2 The US Energy Information Administration estimates that there are reserves amounting to approximately 11,000m. barrels of oil and 190,000,000m. cu ft of natural gas in the South China Sea. These numbers represent both proven and probable reserves, and thus a high-end estimate. However, it is difficult to determine the amount of oil and natural gas in the South China Sea because of under-exploration and territorial disputes. Most of the discovered fields are clustered in uncontested parts of the sea, close to the shorelines of the coastal countries. For more details, see: US Energy Information Administration, 'South China Sea', (Washington, DC: EIA, February 2013). Available at: www.eia.gov/countries/regions-topics.cfm?fips=SCS.

3 The US Energy Information Administration collects, analyses and disseminates independent and impartial energy information to promote sound policy-making, efficient markets, and public understanding of energy and its interaction with the economy and the environment. See: www.eia.gov/about/.

4 Linda Jakobson, 'China's Foreign Policy Dilemma', (Sydney: Lowy Institute for International Policy, 5 February 2013). Available at: www.lowyinstitute.org/publications/chinas-foreign-policy-dilemma.

5 Will Rogers, 'India's South China Sea Gambit Redux', Natural Security Blog (Washington, DC: Center for a New American Security, December 2012). Available at: www.cnas.org/.

6 Kenneth G. Lieberthal, 'The 2013 People's Congress: A New Government, A New Direction?' Audio interviews with a panel of experts (Washington, DC: Brookings

80   *Country case studies*

Institution, 28 March 2013). Available at: www.brookings.edu/blogs/up-front/posts/2013/03/28-china-congress-roundtable-lieberthal.

7 Roy C. Mabasa, 'Only Philippines, China Can Solve Territorial Row', *Manila Bulletin*, 3 April 2013.

8 Daojiong Zha and Mark J. Valencia, 'Mischief Reef: Geopolitics and Implications', *Journal of Contemporary Asia*, Vol. 31, No. 1, 2001, 86–103.

9 Jethro Mullen, 'Philippines takes Territorial Fight with China to International Tribunal', *CNN*, 22 January 2013.

10 Jane Perlez, 'Vietnam Law on Contested Islands Draws China's Ire', *New York Times*, 21 June 2012.

11 John W. Garver, 'China's Push through the South China Sea: The Interaction of Bureaucratic and National Interests', *China Quarterly*, Vol. 132, December 1992, 999–1028.

12 Ian James Storey, 'Creeping Assertiveness: China, the Philippines, and the South China Sea Dispute', *Contemporary Southeast Asia*, Vol. 21, No. 1, April 1999, 95–118.

13 Michael T. Klare, 'The United States Heads to the South China Sea: Why American Involvement Will Mean More Friction, Not Less', *Foreign Affairs*, Vol. 92, No. 1, January/February 2013. Available at: www.foreignaffairs.com/articles/139023/michael-t-klare/the-united-states-heads-to-the-south-china-sea.

14 Martin S. Indyk, Kenneth G. Lieberthal and Michael E. O'Hanlon, *Bending History: Barack Obama's Foreign Policy* (Washington, DC: Brookings Institution Press, March 2012).

6 The United States of America

Introduction

Long regarded as a major source of instability and tension, the South China Sea has posed significant challenges to regional relations in East Asia. Much of the political discourse revolves around managing the risk of possible conflict over disputed claims by a number of countries.[1] The prospects for prosperity and security in the South China Sea are matters for the attention and concern of regional countries (i.e. Brunei, China, Malaysia, the Philippines, Taiwan and Vietnam) and non-regional countries (i.e. India, Japan, Russia and the USA) owing to their economic and strategic interests in this location. As expected, tensions between claimants continued to escalate in 2012 with a series of events related to arrests, litigations, overexploitations and transgressions.[2]

Before moving forward, we first need to ask why the South China Sea merits the close attention of the international community of nation states. The answer is simple. The geostrategic importance of the South China Sea is huge, especially due to the exploitable resources that lie therein. Furthermore, its geographical position makes it the link between the Indian Ocean and the Western Pacific. The South China Sea is the location where international sea lanes come together, representing billions of dollars in annual trade. It is a water body where six nations have 'overlapping territorial claims over a seabed with proven oil reserves of seven billion barrels as well as an estimated 900 trillion cubic feet of natural gas'.[3]

It is now widely known that freedom of navigation and non-intrusive shipping transit in the South China Sea is a very contentious issue, especially between China and the USA over the right of US military ships to operate in China's 200-mile exclusive economic zone. Yet, while considering all of the above, these rationalizations do not fully explain why the South China Sea is so strategically critical to China and the USA. Some contend that it has to do with oil security; others posit that its relevance is due to trade protection and power projection.[4]

The growing consensus among many scholars is that China's rapid economic growth has led to a massive increase in its domestic energy requirements. As the Chinese Government deals with its growing need for oil imports, the country is shaping its international economic and diplomatic strategies, which are

82 *Country case studies*

subtly affecting global political relations and behaviours.[5] This accelerated growth has produced an unprecedented 'energy vulnerability' that could threaten the sustainability of its economic development—a linchpin to social stability and the legitimacy of the Chinese Communist Party (CCP), as well as the foundation for China's rising power aspirations.[6] Put simply, the South China Sea is the main transit area through which oil tankers pass en route to Chinese ports, as well the location of extensive reserves of oil and gas. Similarly, the USA has significant economic, political and security interests in the South China Sea, which explains the large number of military personnel stationed at bases throughout the region.[7]

In view of the common strategic interests at stake—coupled with the heterogeneous set of countries asserting historical, jurisdictional and territorial claims—China has undertaken a progressive and significant modernization of its military forces (i.e. air, army and, more importantly, naval) with the explicit intention of enforcing its sovereignty, jurisdiction and resource exploitation rights. The sustained development of China's military capabilities could rapidly put US military forces in the East Asian region at risk of conflicts and wars, thus potentially denying access to US naval forces in the Western Pacific.[8]

The following sections examine the complex dynamics between China and the USA more closely, especially how control of the South China Sea can be achieved and the measures needed to avoid this.

Literature review and study approach

This chapter seeks to understand the 21st-century security dynamics in the South China Sea in relation to China and the USA. The questions that arise are: (1) how and why is China dominating and claiming rights over the South China Sea? And (2) what are the responses that can be anticipated by the USA and its allies? These questions guide the discussion throughout the chapter, as well as making selected links to multidimensional issues. This research contributes to an increasing body of work on China, the USA and the South China Sea by authors such as Robert D. Kaplan, Patrick M. Cronin, Peter Dutton, Aaron Friedberg, Ian Storey and Timo Kivimäki, among many others.

This chapter begins by examining geography, security and warfare, the emerging power struggles in East Asia and the Pacific, and the geopolitical configurations at the South China Sea; followed by an overview of the evolving security dynamics that include naval build-ups, military strategies, the probability of conflicts or war, and the potential responses by old and new powers. The chapter concludes with a summary of these findings and a forward-looking analysis.

Wars, security and the role of geography

The Thirty Years' War (1618–48), followed by the Napoleonic Wars (1803–15), and much later, the two World Wars, were mainly fought on the European continent. The landscape upon which these armed conflicts took place was defined by mountains, plains, rivers and valleys. In East Asia conditions are somewhat different—the geographical features consist of numerous islands, long coastlines and many waterways; in short, a seascape. As one tries to understand conflicts and wars in the 20th and 21st centuries, there is a need to fully appreciate the differences in geography, as well as the principal motives that led to the dire outcome of war.

States have the inherent right to defend themselves against aggression, but history tells us that this is not the sole justification for going to war. In the case of Europe, a political assassination and German territorial expansion into Eastern Europe triggered the two World Wars. Some years earlier, however, countries in Europe allied together in order to tame France's hegemonic ambitions when Napoleon's armies were conquering European lands. During the past 100 years, territorial contests in Africa and Europe have produced evidence suggesting that regional security is rightly upheld by fighting over populated and unpopulated terrains, many of which allowed for the advance of troops on foot. However, with the spread of globalization, particularly during the first 13 years of the 21st century, the economic and population centres of the world have moved from West to East. In the case of East Asia the geography of the region means that the dynamic contacts between countries are both territorial and maritime.

Military interventions necessarily differ in how land and sea deployments are conducted. The tactics required to claim victory or avoid losses are in many ways linked to the nature of these engagements. Military interventions that take place over land involve people, animals and productive assets, thus always carrying with them legal dimensions related to codes, duties, norms, rights and discourses about social justice and fairness. On the other hand, interventions that occur in oceans and seas are connected to water, ships, aquatic resources and far fewer people, thus transforming these events into bureaucratic, technical issues that reduce conflicts and wars to algorithms and equations. The stakes are the same; what differs is the way in which the interventions are carried out.

Given that warfare, humanity and the geographical elements of sovereignty are so tightly enmeshed, it has always been difficult to justify the collateral damage caused by armed conflicts. Three examples illustrate this point. When the Second World War was perceived to be dishonest, dishonourable and wicked, some of the predominant ideologies of the time had to take into account the ethical implications raised by the deaths and injuries of innocent civilians. Later, the Cold War was considered by many to be immoral, indecent and sinful, with the arms race and proxy wars claiming lives and redirecting resources to non-productive purposes. Finally, it is likely that the post-Cold War era will be remembered as unethical, unrighteous and evil, with vitriolic admonishments aimed at tyrants and dictators in Africa, Central Asia and South-East Asia.

At the present time the justifications for US involvement in large-scale military interventions in Afghanistan, Iraq and Pakistan have met stern

84 *Country case studies*

opposition and demands for reconsideration, especially following the deaths of thousands of non-combatants in attacks, bombings and skirmishes. Thus, the discussion about conflict and law-making, and about peace and co-operation, had to leave the hallways of power and the executive offices in major world capitals—war became a forum for the collaborative exchanges of ideas, proposals, and solutions by academics, diplomats, generals, geo-graphers, lawyers, policy-makers, pundits and scholars. Whether on land or at sea, combat is no longer an isolated occurrence in distant lands. Our modern interconnections make the entire world vulnerable to warfare. With regard to conflict at sea, the general consensus is that it is less disruptive. It is not.

Political geography, broadly understood as the way in which political pro-cesses are affected by spatial structures, has been helping academics and policy-makers to make sense of priorities, strategies and tactics, as these relate to national and regional actions in response to territorial or maritime claims. With this in mind, when one considers the borders of East Asian countries and the contours of their lands, it is easier to surmise that in the 21st century there will a strong focus on fleets and navies. Of course, these include air, land and sea military forces given that they are all tightly interdependent (e.g. flights land near seaports in order to supply naval ships).

Clearly, naval power is built for a purpose. Regardless of the country and the region, this purpose can be either preventive or reactive. In relation to China in East Asia, and more to the point, with regard to the South China Sea, there is mounting evidence that the Chinese Government is expanding its navy, a move suggesting its readiness to be perceived as an equal power to the USA in terms of economic throughput and military might. It can be argued that Chinese territorial borders have become increasingly safe and secure due to the relative peace that the country has achieved with Mongolia and Russia to the north and India to the west. In fact, territorial security in China's main-land is at an all time high, especially when contrasted to the period of cohesion and tranquility that pervaded during the Qing dynasty during the latter part of eighteenth century. Such security, however, is not enjoyed on the maritime borders.

The CCP leadership has embraced economic success and military build-up as a hermetic lid that will, at long last, stifle debilitating memories of the period of repeated subjugation and humiliation suffered by China under Japanese and Western imperialism. The accumulation of land and sea power is making China's neighbours anxious about the future, and is prompting them to react ever more tactfully to Chinese overtures.

East Asia and the Western Pacific: power struggle epicentre

The countries and territories conventionally included in East Asia are China, Hong Kong, Japan, Macau, Mongolia, North Korea, South Korea and Taiwan. East Asia represents approximately 28% of the Asian land mass and about 40% of the population of Asia. The Pacific Ocean covers an area measuring 64m. sq miles, representing almost 46% of the Earth's water surface. The Western Pacific comprises only the western part of the Pacific Ocean, its waters washing the shorelines of East Asia.[9] The combination of a massive land mass, a vast ocean, and a number of large market economies experiencing growth makes East Asia and the Western Pacific a dynamic hub for commercial exchanges and maritime flows.

Indeed, the many ethical predicaments and moral quandaries that warfare generated in the 20th century are not likely to be reproduced in the 21st century, mainly because international organizations seem to provide some restraints and because economic ties serve as effective deterrents to conflicts and wars. Some commentators believe that security dynamics in East Asia and the Western Pacific will tend to be concentrated on naval domains, where intelligence and military officers, in consultation with experts in defence, will thrash out the minutiae without the intervention of civilians. The more disciplined and steadfast handling by military men is said to be much preferred given the political profile of some leaders in East Asian countries—China and North Korea appearing more assertive, authoritarian, defiant and determined than their peers.[10]

Should a country seek to impose its hegemony upon the region, it is unlikely that this will immediately lead to conflict or war. Naturally, misunderstandings or skirmishes are bound to occur, but a progressive accumulation of power will be achieved through a combination of inveiglement and diplomatic manoeuvering. When looking at the behaviours of nation states over an extended period of time, it is quite safe to conclude that alliances, ententes and partnerships between actors in a specific region take place at variable speeds and under revisionist modes: a careful, tactical and utilitarian affiliation to a dominant economic, military and political power. Even if there is a race for supremacy in a region in which two actors are moving towards a confrontation, the rational expected outcome need not be conflict or war. It will be recalled that the Cold War taught the world that a contest between superpowers does not necessarily result in the annihilation of both.

Since history provides evidence of peaceful co-existence between countries, and a growing body of evidence suggests that strong trade links override belligerent behaviour, it is not difficult to imagine that the Asian continent, and indeed the whole world, will be able to achieve shared prosperity, power and security if China and the USA handle their *most striking* differences and disparities amicably, tactfully and intelligently. While it is clear that cultural and social homogeneity is not the desired result of co-operation, it is agreed by all that the objective of minimizing conflicts is a collective goal.[11]

Now, let's consider the following question: are East Asia and the Western Pacific more prone to conflicts and wars in the 21st century than in the previous century? I believe that they are not, because the specific contextual conditions of the time and place do not make it so. A geographical sketch of East Asia reveals vast, sometimes unpopulated coastlines and dispersed island groupings; the huge and treacherous Pacific Ocean serves as a natural obstacle to the successful initiation of military interventions; large attack craft—even

86 *Country case studies*

the most modern ships—are slow to progress across the waters, thus providing conflicting parties with the opportunity to re-evaluate decisions or to negotiate stand-offs; and naval forces differ from armies in that they are not considered to be occupiers of land (i.e. transgressions can be resolved by repositioning ships a few miles away); and productive assets are rarely disrupted. One could say that the presence of a large ocean and seas, and the resulting water-based trade that enables countries to build their economies, are, in fact, factors that reduce the likelihood of conflicts.

However, this has not always been the case, especially if one looks at the 20th century. Then, the ocean and its surrounding seas did not prevent the wars in Cambodia, Korea, Laos and Vietnam; combat during the Second World War in the Pacific; the adventurism of the Japanese during the era of imperialism; and the war between Japan and Russia. These historic events are now perceived as having been national struggles to break apart or to come together. Today, the media continually remind us that military forces in East Asia are technologically advanced, politically driven and striving to project power.[12]

Context, forces and players in North-East and South-East Asia

In order to facilitate an understanding of the security dynamics in the region as a whole, it is suitable to partition the eastern part of Asia in two sub-regions: North-East and South-East Asia.

North-East Asia is characterized by the importance of the Korean Peninsula. Much of the security discourse revolves around the political and military outcomes in Pyongyang, North Korea, which is now internationally known as an authoritarian and totalitarian country which has been ruled for decades by a succession of leaders from a single family line. Viewed through the global context of capitalism, democracy, free and open trade, and liberal ideals, it is highly probable that North Korea will remain marginalized and not involved with the major decisions effected by world leaders. It is not just these factors, but also the economic stagnation, hunger and poverty that afflict the country, which are likely eventually to cause North Korea to disintegrate. Should this happen, China, Japan, South Korea and the USA will be expected to provide civilian and military forces in order to deploy humanitarian and rescue operations, as well as aid, unwelcome state-building, and institutional support. Powerful actors and their allies will use these intiatives to argue in favour of their respective positions and domains of influence. Given that China and South Korea are territorially connected to North Korea, the immediate business of resolving land affairs will take priority; however, a reunified Korea means that maritime affairs will gain importance. In the meantime, the focus will remain on military exercises on land and sea.

South-East Asia is characterized by the importance of the South China Sea—the body of water that serves as the central hub for the naval outposts of a number of countries. As a sub-region, it is defined by its entrepreneurship and vibrancy, as well as its focus on regional co-operation and the importance of intergovernmental associations (e.g. the Association of Southeast Asian Nations—ASEAN), which tackle challenges and obstacles facing the region. For example, Cambodia has demonstrated that an export-led approach and open tourism can sustain economic growth and foster political stability. China, while embracing authoritarian capitalism, has shown the world that an alternative growth model can co-exist with democratic and liberal ideologies, and that being an active, decisive and semi-responsible member of the international community is optional, not mandatory. Indonesia, a predominately Muslim state that survived a period of strict military control, has emerged as a progressive democracy that is using its macroeconomic success and institutional membership to ensure equality in the distribution of money, power and security. Malaysia, nestled between Thailand and Singapore, has for decades been enjoying the spillover benefits of burgeoning trade, regional consultation and financial concord. Singapore, the city-state known as the London or New York of South-East Asia, has for years sought to align itself with China and the USA, while simultaneously striving to attract assets, investments and trade. Thailand, despite the political turmoil and ensuing popular revolts that have afflicted the country, continues to serve as a centre for commerce and tourism, attracting investors and hosting numerous meetings and summits. Finally, Vietnam is a capitalist country that is still ruled under communist principles, which enjoys access to the western part of the South China Sea and has in the past allied itself with the West to foil the interest of its northern neighbour, China. To some degree all of these states have experienced colonization, democratization, disasters, financial crises, genocides, transitions, trafficking and wars—and all are staking their claims of rights to land to water, and beyond.

From a security perspective, it is impossible to overstate the importance of the South China Sea to most countries in North-East and Southeast Asia. Conveniently, many are standing shoulder to shoulder with China as the locomotive of regional growth, while others are warily observant of the ongoing naval build-ups and the handling of mini-crises resulting from exploitative and jurisdictional claims.

China, the USA and the South China Sea

Via its many routes the South China Sea connects and brings together countries in South-East Asia and grants them access to the Western Pacific. In short, the South China Sea is the vital link to the world's oceans. Its pivotal role as trade conduit and provider of natural resources is accentuated by the strategic usage of four straits: Lombok, Makassar, Malacca and Sunda. Some of the countries that border these straits have experienced strong lobbying from powerful states to protect their waterways, given that approximately 30% of all shipping traffic and more than 50% of global maritime tonnage transits through them. Indeed, the USA has consistently sought in Asia, generally, and in South-East Asia, specifically, to prevent any single country from dominating the region; and since the US Administration perceives that this is precisely

88   *Country case studies*

what China intends to do, it has been predicted that the strategic interests of China and the USA will eventually collide.[13]

Of the four straits, Malacca has received the most attention internationally. The Strait of Malacca is a narrow, 500-mile stretch of water between the Malay Peninsula and the island of Sumatra, Indonesia. Oil shipments coming from the Indian Ocean all the way to East Asia have to pass through the Strait of Malacca and the South China Sea. The volume of maritime traffic passing through this strait is reported to be greater than that sailing through the Panama Canal and Suez Canal. In terms of trade, this is of significance given that exports to and imports from Europe and Central, South and West Asia have to pass through these tight waterways, where there is always the risk of interdiction. Given that during the past 20 years China has evolved into the world's low-cost manufacturing hub, and now heavily depends on oil imports to sustain economic growth, it is easy to understand why China might be interested in controlling or securing this global sea route. Owing to the complex nature of potential threats to vital sea lanes, there is the temptation for China to address this 'evolving situation' unilaterally as the Government moves to modernize its military forces.[14]

More generally, ASEAN and the international community have raised concerns over the likelihood of blockages or closures in the Strait of Malacca, which would result in the immediate increase in sea freight rates. Such an increase could put some low-cost producers at risk of losing clients and market share because their prices are no longer competitive. However, if one takes a much larger perspective and includes the potential for conflict in the South China Sea, one sees that claimants will be particularly affected—close to 70% of South Korea's energy imports, approximately three-fifths of Japan's and Taiwan's oil shipments, and nearly four-fifths of China's energy supplies are brought from the Indian Ocean into the Straits of Malacca and pass directly to the South China Sea.

It would be logical to assume that the key geostrategic relevance of the South China Sea hinges on its geographical positioning, its function as a maritime conduit, and its deposits of oil and gas, but this would be short-sighted. For decades, this body of water has witnessed internecine strife over disputed boundaries and territories. The large majority of territorial claims revolve around ownership of and sovereignty over the Paracel and Spratly Islands. The Paracel and Spratly archipelagos are undeniably two of the world's most strategically important inter-ocean basins and they also serve as China's southern maritime frontier.[15] Brunei, China, the Philippines, Taiwan and Vietnam all have laid full or partial claims to the South China Sea and, of course, the islands lying in the Paracel and Spratly archipelago. The Chinese Government has been bold in asserting its claim, based on various historical records dating back up to 2,000 years, to the central parts of the South China Sea, a bulb-like shaped loop that runs from Hainan Island in Southern China all the way down to the waters that wash up on the island of Borneo, Malaysia, Western Philippines and Singapore.

As a direct consequence of the Chinese Government's numerous claims over such an extensive area, all of the regional countries that surround the South China Sea have rallied themselves in one way or another against the Chinese Government. As China has emerged as the region's locomotive of growth, many fear that it will use its economic, military and political power to take these territories by force, if necessary. This said, regional countries have come to rely more and more on the USA for advice, protection and support. In 2012, as tensions rose, CCP officials in Beijing released several strongly worded statements, including warnings to their rivals to cease mineral explorations in the area.[16]

The number of claims and counterclaims are expected to escalate as the energy needs of North-East and South-East Asian countries continue to increase.[17] In time, the South China Sea will gradually evolve into the region's pivotal feature that will guarantee the cohesion, prosperity and well-being of the countries in question. Countries surrounding the South China Sea continue to become militarized—media reports have been published claiming that countries that have been arguing over maritime rights and possession of islands have been strengthening their naval forces, and that their coastguards have been training in preparation for conflicts or emergencies. Tellingly, considerable diplomatic effort has been exerted during the past decade in establishing a co-operative management regime[18] for the South China Sea that is intended to defuse the potential for conflict. Ironically, while it is well known that the situation in the South China Sea is the most problematic of the maritime jurisdictional challenges confronting East Asia, equally it is here that most progress is being made to achieve effective regional co-operation.[19]

Let's examine China in more detail. The geographical contours and orientation of China enable it to assume a key position in the race to command assets in the South China Sea. The Sea lies to the south of the Chinese mainland and is a natural forum for the projection of power and influence. For example, in mid-2012 the Chinese State Council granted approval for the establishment of a new national prefecture, which is headquartered on Woody Island in the Paracel archipelago. Interestingly, Woody Island has no indigenous population and there are no natural water supplies, but it boasts a runway capable of handling military aircraft, a bank, a post office, a convenience store and a clinic. According to Xinhua, a Chinese official news agency, the new prefecture administers over 200 islets and 2m. sq km of water. These initiatives, motivated by strategic and political forces, have been matched by economic and military expansion. China's Central Military Commission has publicized the deployment of a garrison of soldiers to guard the islands in the area. The countries surrounding the South China Sea, many of which are weak and politically divided, can do little to contest China's actions, especially since China is known to to be quick to exert its power and influence.

Senior CCP officials frequently appear to display the same behaviour and enact the same policies as those put in place by leading US decision-makers

90 *Country case studies*

during the 19th and early 20th centuries with respect to the forceful projection of power in the Caribbean and, to a larger extent, in Central America. China has taken note of US history and its foreign policy travails, and the Government has been swift to emulate its practices since China wishes to model itself on the USA when it was the ambitious, vibrant and young country of the western hemisphere. At the time, the USA recognized the claims and exploitation rights of European countries over Caribbean islands; however, as the de facto hegemonic power government legislators persisted with moves to dominate the region. Historians posit that the emergence of the USA as a global power to be reckoned with was the consequence of its engagement in the US–Mexican War (1846–48), the US–Spanish War of 1898, and later through the excavation, construction and management of the 51-mile-long Panama Canal (1904–14).

Logically, Chinese military historians and political scholars have drawn parallels between the situation regarding the Caribbean islands and that of the South China Sea (i.e. with respect to the Paracel and Spratly islands). From a historical standpoint, it is undeniable that domination over the Caribbean islands and their surrounding waters gave the USA control and influence over some, if not all, of the western hemisphere. This overarching regional dominance facilitated the tilting of the balance of power in other regions, such as the eastern hemisphere. Today, notwithstanding the irony of history repeating itself in the East, China is in a very similar position in relation to the South China Sea and competing claims over its islands and resources by others. China craves domination of or influence over the Indian Ocean, not only to protect its oil shipments from the Middle East but also to consolidate its control over the region.

China therefore sees no problem in mimicking the actions and initiatives of the USA. And as if this were not enough, the recurrent vacillations stemming from consensus-seeking US administrations have emboldened China for years. US policy regarding sovereignty issues in East Asia and the Western Pacific has been ambiguously centrist; that is, the USA has adopted a neutral and nonagressive stance. Practically, Washington has declared that such affairs must be resolved peacefully among the parties involved. However, weaker countries repeatedly call for greater international involvement: if not the USA or a European major power, then which country will offer assistance?

Aware of these facts, former US Ambassador James Dobbins, now director of the International Security and Defense Policy Center at the RAND Corporation, asserts that 'since the disappearance of the Soviet Union, China has become America's default adversary' and that in years to come 'China could become the most powerful adversary the United States has ever faced'.[20] Yet, it must be recalled that the Chinese Government's 'security interests and military capabilities will remain focused on its immediate periphery'—China does not appear to be interested in achieving a similar global reach to that of the USA, and is not 'in a position to assume defense commitments beyond its immediate sphere' of influence.[21] All in all, the unpalatable question remains whether a modern China wishes to resolve the key issues regarding the South China Sea through acceptable international standards, and whether the US President has the capacity and will to insist that this is the only means to achieving regional stability.

Ulterior motives: China wants the West out of mind and out of sight

Initially, it might be supposed that control and domination of the South China Sea are the overarching motives for China's actions and rhetoric, but underlying this is a sort of historical hatred—a desire to settle scores arising from extended humiliations. For thousands of years, China was an enviable power and progressive civilization, but in 1949, at the tail end of Chinese Civil War, the West helped to bring about the division of one great China into two Chinas.[22] However, there are other factors to take into consideration. During the 19th century, as the Qing dynasty in East Asia was on the verge of disintegration, China lost territories to Britain, France, Japan and Russia. Later, Japan returned to capture Manchuria and the Shandong Peninsula. From 1839 to 1949, the so-called century of humiliation, China experienced losses of sovereignty at the hands of Western powers, many of which enforced extra-territorial arrangements to facilitate trade and avoid legal prosecution, in the form of treaty ports.[23] During this period, China's sufferings at the hands of foreigners were such that by the late 1930s there was a fearful expectation that 'China was about to be dismembered, that it would cease to exist as a nation, and that the four thousand years of its recorded history would come to a jolting end'.[24] Some commentators have suggested that this traumatic period in China's history will not reach closure until Taiwan is reunified with the Chinese mainland.[25] China's power in the South China Sea is tantamount to a signal that it will no longer abide by the rules of others.

Regional dramas, Chinese nationalism and foreign comebacks

In the future the boundaries between national borders and the South China Sea may be redrawn as the new military front lines of the 21st century. As an increasingly ambitious and militant China proceeds with its naval expansion, there is a real risk that its Asian neighbours will be forced to build up their own navies in an attempt to defend their sovereignties, especially since Chinese claims over assets or islands in the South China Sea conflict with existing claims made by other countries. It is also possible that, in an attempt to bulwark China, that some claimants will request US naval support, even though this is already finely stretched by its peace-keeping duties in North Africa, the Middle East and Central Asia. Commonly, there are multiple forces acting in any region, but in the South China Sea there is a clash of the interests of two forces.

With regard to power projection on the oceans and seas, the presence of naval fleets and powerful warships act as deterrents; few casualties result from conflicts unless bombs are exploded from nearby shores. In this particular theatre of war neither genocide, tribal warfare nor ethnic cleansing can occur. China, still referred to as communist or red, does not seem to attract the widespread hatred against ideological clashing that the Soviets once attracted. The world now sees what China is all about: a modern rendition of authoritarianism, embracing capitalism on its own terms, and dealing with dissidents with an iron fist, for fear that it might incentivize others to rebel. Additionally, it is expected that in the future China will become a more open society. Greater exposure to the Western world may act as a catalyst for younger generations to reject conflagrations and violence, while accepting collaboration and co-operation as a route to progress. It is likely that China will be characterized by nationalism instead of militarism—and further still, harmonious unity instead of irreconcilable divisions.

Nationalism, a sense of state-wide consciousness that exalts one country above all others and places fundamental emphasis on the promotion of its culture and interests as opposed to those of other countries, is frequently thought to hark back to 19th-century politics. This notion should not be disregarded. It is important to emphasize that in Asia political discourse is mainly driven by nationalistic sentiments. As populations continue to be threatened by the perception of an exploitative regional power, so are they likely to promote their interests over those of neighbours. Today, it is this influential nationalism that is fuelling the growth of naval, army and air forces in the region, with the explicit mandate to defend citizens, protect sovereignty and forcefully protest over natural resources that are critical to national interests. In a real sense, an intemperate struggle over the balance of power conducted nevertheless with cool and realistic calculation is developing across the South China Sea.

Regardless of the breadth and depth of any evolving crisis in East Asia and the Western Pacific, power politics and forceful responses are likely to be moderate instead of provocative. The smaller, weaker countries in the region will subsume much of the vituperations out of the Chinese Government's pulpit, but the sheltered rationale of South-East Asian nations will very likely become a tactical alliance with the USA without loosening the economic ties that bind them to China's ambitions. James Webb, a US senator for Virginia, stated that 'since World War II, despite the costly flare-ups in Korea and Vietnam, the United States has proved to be the essential guarantor of stability in the Asian-Pacific region, even as the power cycle shifted from Japan to the Soviet Union and most recently to China'.[26] The validity of the role of the USA has yet to be tested in Asia.

The security dynamics that are emerging in the South China Sea are altogether different from the ones that most countries and people are accustomed to. As conflict and contestation are deeply embedded in human nature, it is unlikely that they will cease to occur altogether. However, as peace and stability are experienced alongside war and instability, a future outcome may comprise a combination of both, with humanity going forward with progress and momentum as states work out all remaining issues between them. Now, as then, the prospect of war ignites the creativity and inventiveness of citizenries.[27]

From a security perspective, it is important to ask if clashes and schisms in the South China Sea can be adequately managed. An argument can be made that large-scale wars will not ensue in the region, under the premise that extensive economic ties tend to diffuse belligerent temptations,[28] and that South-East Asian countries can find it even more practical to strategically position vessels in the South China Sea while haggling for a balanced allocation of assets and resources under contestation. However, this argument, while simplistic, neglects China's claims on Taiwan, and its resentment towards Vietnam resulting from the two countries' historical disharmony and setbacks. Both Taiwan and Vietnam could be belittled and insulted by China. It is worth mentioning, however, that China is not the only country in the region to seek to build up its arsenals and military forces. Neighbouring countries have inflated their defence budgets over the past decades, even as other regions have seen their defence budgets dwindle. Imports of light and heavy weapons have risen in some countries in the region. For example, since 2000 Indonesia has increased imports by 84%, Singapore by 146%, and Malaysia by more than 700%. Much of this expenditure has gone on air and water-related artifacts and weaponry, such as fighter jets, guided missile systems, submarines and warships.[29]

Following the Asian financial crisis in 1997–98, defence spending was reduced significantly, despite the fact that weaponry and military transportation were clearly becoming outdated. During 2012 the Asian economy made a swift recovery and state budgets improved, as a result of which many South-East Asian countries now appear to be taking advantage of their economic and financial windfalls to build up and upgrade their military assets. Observers note that this does not imply the beginning of an arms race, but instead that countries are seeking to modernize their military capabilities during periods of prosperity. In fact, smaller countries look to their potential adversaries for guidance: the Chinese Government has been doubling its defence budget during five-year periods and in 2012 the Indian Government announced a 17% increase in defence expenditure, to about $40,000m.[30]

It is clear that earlier commitments made by the USA are guaranteeing the delicate balance and stability of the South China Sea. The USA's ubiquitous military presence acts as a deterrent to China's aggressive impulses and functions to restrain the Chinese Government and military officials, many of which are keen to demonstrate the recently acquired capabilities of the country. The continued presence of the USA is perceived primarily by South-East Asian countries as a substantial force that will react decisively if provoked, but it is much less regarded for its backing of democracy, freedom and the promotion of human rights. As long as the USA is able to keep China in check, regional neighbours are content to remain vigilant. Fortunately, as long as China keeps the USA's activities in its sights and vice versa, some space appears that is sufficiently clear of political issues to allow regional collaboration and interstate co-operation to develop. This is partly the reason why ASEAN has been so keen to bring China closer to the region, especially

94 *Country case studies*

since a number of free trade agreements have yielded tremendous benefits to all parties involved. This, of course, hinges on the restraint China can exercise over its ambitions in the South China Sea: the conflicts in the South China Sea between some ASEAN members and China may derail the Association's attempt to consolidate its economic, political and military ties with China's elite. There is an opportunity for South-East Asia as a closely knit region to take on diplomatic challenges whereby smaller countries can effectively perform a role in peace-making between major rivals.[31]

Capitalism as catalyst for contention: searching for truths beyond the obvious

This chapter is about security, but security inevitably takes place within an economic and geopolitical context, and one cannot comprehend the world without considering the fundamental geopolitical facts of the 20th century: the crumbling of socialism[32] and the collapse of the Soviet Union.

Initially, the dismantling of this ideology took place in China. In 1978 Deng Xiaoping, as leader of the CCP, steered his country towards a market economy and capitalism. This initiative occurred two years after the disintegration of radical political movements and the defeat of Maoist extremists who sought to restart the Great Proletarian Cultural Revolution, which took place from 1966 through 1976. It is noteworthy that Deng moved ahead only three years after Vietnam was pronounced a victory under a Communist banner. Slowly but surely, in the years that followed, millions of Chinese people abandoned Marxism as their intellectual focal point, but the rest of the globe did not immediately grasp the far-reaching consequences of this move. By the early 1990s it was clear that world leaders and scholars alike had failed to grasp the full extent of China's transformation from regional backwater into influential global powerhouse. Writings of the period reflected a common theme: the global economy would thenceforth encompass Europe, Japan and the USA.

At the time, China was considered to be a secondary actor, if that, and part of an emerging bloc dependent on Japanese growth. As it turned out, and as the world now knows, the rise of China as the locomotive of growth in Asia, coupled with the sustained vibrancy of Asia's market economies, 'subtly but deeply demoralized the Soviet regime, by making its claim to have history on its side ever less plausible'.[33] Following the humiliating failure of the Soviet Union and the demise of the socialist dream, capitalism had gained supremacy. This meant that cheaper air and sea transport, improved telecommunications, minimal impediments for investments, and lower barriers to trade helped to minimize the challenges and disadvantages encountered by developing countries.

As capitalism spread around the world, the benefits of export-led economic growth to vast numbers of people in transitioning economies signified the advent of an economic system that delivered remarkable prosperity and ever-rising opportunities for upward mobility. To many governments, this approach to economic and social progress represented a renewed opportunity to compete in world markets for manufactured and industrial goods, many of which are traded via the oceans of the world. In a matter of three decades, maritime trade regained its traditional primacy. The long-standing liberal hypothesis is that commerce and trade ties facilitate interstate peace, but Western scholars also claim that extreme interdependence, whether symmetrical or asymmetrical, has the greatest potential for increasing the likelihood of conflict and contention.[34]

If this is the prevailing situation between these countries, and given that a third of the world's maritime trade—including vital energy supplies for China and Japan—transits through the South China Sea, these waters open up the probability for countries to enact overzealous military interventions to protect and secure these critical global trade and energy sea routes.

Security dynamics

An affordable, safe, secure and sustainable energy supply is vital to the economic and strategic interests of any global player. Today, conventional energy sources such as oil are becoming scarcer and as a result of shortages increasing energy prices could have the potential to diminish global prosperity and quality of life. Looking ahead, the growing global competition for energy is likely to cause conflict or war in certain parts of the world, especially in resource-rich regions. One of these regions is the South China Sea, with its vast deposits of crude oil, gas and minerals.

World-wide, media outlets have reported on, and frequently expressed concern over, the growth of Chinese naval power.[35] Government officials in the West are also anxious about the pace and scope of China's military build-up.[36] Specifically, there is fear that this rapid build-up could eventually prove to be a potentially destabilizing phenomenon in the Pacific.[37] In addition to a growing surface fleet, the Chinese military has developed a series of anti-access capabilities designed to exclude US carrier battle groups from any conflict near China's shores.[38] These details are relevant to the US Administration's national security interests and strategic regional alliances because the Chinese military remains focused on Taiwan, and it has deployed as many as 1,000 short-range missiles aimed in its direction.

It is important that US civilian and military leaders understand the current Chinese mentality—one of the biggest fears confronting CCP officials concerning the presence of the USA is that China does not wish to re-experience manipulative hegemonic power such as it did when the Soviet Union held sway.[39] Western commentators have noted that the Chinese Government believes that the ongoing stand-off between China and the USA will ultimately tilt in favour of China, chiefly owing to its growing role as the engine of regional economic growth and its geographical importance.[40] In practice, China's military preparations are based on two factors: to distance external

96   *Country case studies*

actors from the country's regional affairs; and to maintain a firm grasp on the region's national dynamics, which it perceives as a collection of unco-ordinated and weak states. In view of this and amid concerns about China's growing military power and its claims to disputed territories, Thailand, the Philippines and Vietnam have cautiously rekindled their friendship with the USA. However, even with new military hardware, Thailand, the Philippines and Vietnam still would be no match for Asia's new superpower, should it come to war. Nevertheless, the presence of local and foreign rivals might make China pause before engaging in conflict, and buy time before the USA—presumably—came to the rescue.

Australian scholars have noted that from their strategic viewpoint, Australia wishes the situation in Asia to remain largely the same (with the exception of North Korea's radicalization and accumulation of weapons). They hope that the Chinese economic behemoth will advance as the global economy recovers from the protracted financial slump so that Australia can continue to export its products and services, backed by the USA's powerful presence in the region—thus serving as a guarantor of freedom and security for Australia. However, the challenge is that this relatively stable state of affairs is not likely to persist for long; economic transformations in Asia will undoubtedly attract a number of diplomatic changes and political reforms, and this will reinforce Chinese antipathy to the presence of the USA in the region or to it making offers of allegiance in exchange for protection. However, during visits to Washington, DC, Chinese military officials have stated that China has no interest in challenging the US military. There seems to be a lack of comprehension on China's part regarding the reasons for which concerns have been raised about its military build-up.[41]

That China has the right to build up, modernize and upgrade its military during prosperous times has found support in many quarters, especially other countries seeking to do the same (e.g. Iran and North Korea) without provoking the ire of the USA. The Chinese Government is swift to reiterate its position as a non-threatening, non-controlling power, one that does not interfere in the national affairs and policies of other countries. However, the US Congress and Administration have failed to find this convincing. In the logical thinking of technocrats, the US presence in East and South-East Asia is formulated on the premise that as China is an authoritarian and repressive country, then it is only likely that it will act brashly and irresponsibly beyond its borders. Not everyone is this pessimistic, however. John Garver argues that if China keeps its commitment to rise economically without any regional hegemonic intentions, the USA will welcome the emergence of peaceful and prosperous China, one that co-operates with the USA to address common challenges and mutual interests.[42] This notion is far-fetched but worth bearing in mind.

It stands to reason that audiences around the world may be paying too much attention to the specific features of China's regime, such as authoritarianism, direct control, acute power consolidation, popular repressions, iron-fisted enforcement of laws, the one-child policy, aggressive state-owned enterprises, and one-party rule, while at the same time attempting to criticize and limit the Chinese Government's actions and initiatives overseas simply because its national policies are deemed to be archaic or simply different. However, it appears that the international community of independent states seems to be overlooking the fact that regional prosperity and stability is likely to be achieved through balance, not coercion or manipulation. It is also noteworthy that the fundamental principles of international relations, including hard power, continue to be relevant today in East Asia, and that the world needs to give China some breathing space and the benefit of doubt with regard to its policies.

Indeed, the USA cannot afford significantly to decrease its military presence in Asia; as its stay has been for some duration, it is now considered a fixture of the geopolitical scenery. Even if a naval redeployment to the Strait of Hormuz were to occur or if the USA were to lose an aircraft carrier strike team in the Western Pacific due to budgetary reallocations, it is likely that any movement in the military domain would incite debate in the region about the possibility of US decline in power and the subsequent attempts to make amends with the Chinese Government and side with Chinese interests. Despite all this, it is acknowledged that a US military presence is desirable for the region, should China decide to secretly unveil a hidden agenda. The fact that US military personnel are stationed at bases and on vessels all over the Asian region indicates that the US Administration is watching and waiting while the Chinese Government upgrades its army and navy to the level of modernity that is expected from a superpower.[43] Even though China's total military expenditure for 2010 amounted to approximately $160,000m., this still lags far behind US expenditure.

As concord and normality in the South China Sea are of considerable importance to most ASEAN member countries—which are both ambitious and friendly—they must do more to preserve an open political and economic order in East Asia. This being so, US security in the region will improve if the USA adapts to changing circumstances by exercising restraint and placing greater responsibility on allies and on the diplomatic efforts of intergovernmental organizations.[44] The equilibrium of power offers a reliable guarantee of freedom and peace in East Asia, even if democratic ideals have to assume a lower profile. In the search for shared prosperity and regional stability, ethical, moral and virtuous imperatives will have to co-exist with the not-so-righteous behaviour of China and its military. If there is a lesson to be learned from the South China Sea, it is that flexible positions are necessary when engaging with China.[45]

Concluding remarks

Although the possibility of a major military conflict in the South China Sea is low, the potential for clashes and contestations in the near future is high, especially when one considers the past behaviour of countries in the region, the suspicions concerning rising powers, and the growing stakes. At the heart of the problem lies the question of the USA and its allies allowing China to emerge as the dominant Asian power in the 21st century. The USA has been cautious about denying (or at least not confirming) that its interest in increasing its military presence in East Asia and the Pacific has been designed to contain China, which has alarmed many ASEAN members by making expansive territorial claims to the resource-rich South China Sea.

In 2013 the USA was under the impression that China, as member of the six-party talks, had not acted in its relationship with North Korea as the US would have expected it to do. As anticipated, Japan joined in the condemnation. Indeed, Japan is apprehensive about the real prospect of being replaced by China as the manufacturing hub of Asia, and of losing its dominance in the South-East Asian economic sphere in the wake of preferential Chinese trade agreements.[46] Sheila Smith contends that greater predictability and transparency in Sino–Japanese maritime activities will go a long way in developing confidence in what has to date been a very uneasy and publicly sensitive aspect of the bilateral relationship.[47] Now, the military build-up in South-East Asia, together with the wars in Afghanistan, Iraq and Pakistan, indicate that economic and military power has been moving swiftly from West to East. However, care must be taken when making these linear assumptions given that in countries where military officers have become involved in politics, civilian politicians have used larger defence budgets to obtain political compliance from the military intelligentsia—a case in point is politics in Thailand.

Diplomatically, ASEAN and various think tanks have repeatedly warned against bold actions by countries to stake their numerous claims over resources in the South China Sea given that misinterpretations and miscalculations may pose a threat to security, stability and prosperity in the region, and may invite the presence of external powers all too eager to capitalize on chaos. In September 2012 former US Secretary of State Hillary Clinton urged South-East Asian nations to present a unified front when dealing with China in an attempt to ease rising tensions in the South China Sea.[48] The overarching argument offered by the USA is that China must resolve its maritime disputes without coercion, and that its dealings need to be passed through ASEAN as a bloc, not individually with each member country. This suggestion clashes with China's principles of non-interference, and puts the USA at odds with China, which recently has become more aggressive in pressing its territorial claims with its smaller neighbours and wants the disputes to be resolved with each country, giving it greater leverage. Also, let's not forget that the Chinese people regard themselves as the rightful citizens of the Middle Kingdom, and that the country's justification for regional control is grounded in its historical centrality to world affairs, rather than in an economic-political system it wishes to enforce on its neighbours.

Finally, I argue that increasing individual freedoms, an evolving leadership transition in the CCP, market-oriented economic reforms, and greater openness to the global community all point towards a more balanced approach to the handling of Japan, Taiwan and the South China Sea. Moreover, claimants to resources and territories in the South China Sea need to emphasize the relationship between social equity, economic productivity, environmental quality, and unity.

Reflections

China depends on foreign imports for over 50% of the oil it consumes, with one-half of its oil imports coming from the volatile Middle East. The European Union and the USA face similar challenges with regard to energy security. Both are net energy importers, and both depend on oil to an unhealthy extent.[49] However, the USA has been slow to comprehend that a competitive, low-carbon economy is already the most cost-effective approach to move into the future sustainably. The EU, for instance, has chosen to confront these challenges through a strategy to substantially reduce greenhouse gas emissions, increase the contribution of renewable energy, and improve energy efficiency in numerous sectors by 2020. For China, the challenge facing the Government is to better manage its dependence on oil and to define a sustainable energy security path, rather than simply to seek resources beneath the South China Sea.

One wonders, what does China want? The CCP may crave the extensive hegemonic power that the USA wielded over the western hemisphere after securing control of the Caribbean Basin. The calculus is that if the USA did it, then China can do it as well—via the assets and islands in the South China Sea. Under this panorama, China envisages a situation in which Asian neighbours are free to act as they like when it comes to the running of their governments, but with the clear understanding that Chinese ideas and views need to be given complete consideration, over and above any proposals by foreign actors. The only difficulty with this wish is that Japan will not tolerate Chinese hegemony, even to a modest degree. What is left for East Asia and the Western Pacific is the traditional Concert of Powers, that is, a situation in which ASEAN, China, India, Japan and the USA discuss the concerns and issues as equal members. It remains to be seen if the USA will settle for this arrangement, especially since it has for some time linked East Asia's well-being with its own prosperity.

Still, the handling of affairs in the South China Sea provide an indication of China's determination to promote its national interests, and the general ambition of the Chinese leadership to integrate with the international system on its own terms and at its own speed. As for the region, countries with active naval forces in the South China Sea—including China, Philippines, Vietnam, and the United States—might be better served if they adopt and apply the safety measures and standard operating procedures outlined in the Code for Unalerted Encounters at Sea (CUES) to reduce uncertainty and improve communications in the event of a maritime incident. More precisely, senior CCP officials should stand by their pledges of support for risk reduction actions and confidence-building initiatives among claimants in the South

100   *Country case studies*

China Sea. Moreover, existing collaborations should be expanded, while new co-operation ideas should be developed. More frequent visits by ships should become the norm, along with bilateral and multilateral military exercises, and improved operations to combat piracy, radicalism and terrorism. In addition, co-operation on energy, ecological stewardship, fisheries, and the training of relevant experts should be promoted further.[50]

Fitting the pieces together

At the time of writing, in January 2013, Hillary Clinton had left her post as US Secretary of State and Senator John Kerry had taken over her role as the USA's most senior diplomat. This is relevant because in early April 2013 the new US Secretary of State visited China and met senior CCP officials in order to elicit the Chinese Government's assistance in dealing with an increasingly truculent nuclear-armed North Korea. The international community looked at this Sino–US collaboration with interest because it was a genuine attempt to try to reduce tensions and mitigate hazards on the Korean Peninsula that threatened to spiral out of control. However, China has been careful in acquiescing fully to US requests. In the past, the Chinese Government has feared that instability in North Korea after Western provocations would lead to a collapse of the CCP and would deliver the entire Korean peninsula and parts of the East and South China Seas to the USA's sphere of influence, and this could open up the possibility of causing US troops in Japan and South Korea to move even closer to Chinese borders. The USA regards China's co-operation as essential to maintain peace and promote trade.

Notes

1 Timo Kivimäki, *War or Peace in the South China Sea?* (Copenhagen: Nordic Institute of Asian Studies, 2002); David Shambaugh, *China Goes Global: The Partial Power* (New York: Oxford University Press, 2013).

2 For a unique legal angle, see: Nong Hong, *UNCLOS and Ocean Dispute Settlement: Law and Politics in the South China Sea* (New York and Oxford: Routledge, 2012), www.routledge.com/books/details/9780415505277/.

3 Patrick Cronin, Peter Dutton, Robert Kaplan, Will Rogers, M. Taylor Fravel, James Holmes and Ian Storey, *Cooperation from Strength: The United States, China, and the South China Sea* (Washington, DC: Center for a New American Security, 2012). It is worth stressing that nation states that master the reciprocal inter-relationships among economic wealth, technological innovation and the capacity to efficiently access their resources for prolonged military preparedness, military modernization and war-making procedures are the ones with the relatively greater ability to maintain a balance of military and economic power that ultimately results in a clear hegemonic lead.

4 Sigfrido Burgos Cáceres and Sophal Ear, *The Hungry Dragon: How China's Resource Quest Is Reshaping the World* (New York: Routledge, 2013), www.routledge.com/books/details/9781857436860/.

5 For an expanded examination of the relationship between China, non-renewable energy resources and the world, read the scholarly works of Philip Andrews-Speed

and Roland Dannreuther, *China, Oil, and Global Politics* (New York and Oxford: Routledge, 2011) and Sigfrido Burgos Cáceres, 'Understanding China's Global Search for Energy and Resources', *Central Europe Journal of International and Security Studies*, Vol. 7, No. 1, March 2013.

6 See: Suisheng Zhao, *China's Search for Energy Security: Domestic Sources and International Implications* (Oxford: Routledge, 2012), www.routledge.com/books/details/9780415627931/.

7 To connect law, politics and the high seas, see: Yann-Huei Song, *United States and Territorial Disputes in the South China Sea: A Study of Ocean Law and Politics* (Baltimore, MD: University of Maryland School of Law, 2002).

8 Bonnie S. Glaser, 'Armed Clash in the South China Sea', Contingency Planning Memorandum No. 14 (New York and Washington, DC: Council on Foreign Relations, 2012); www.cfr.org/east-asia/armed-clash-south-china-sea/p27883.

9 Steven A. Leibo, *East Asia and the Western Pacific* (Washington, DC: Stryker-Post Publications, June 2000).

10 Robert D. Kaplan, 'The South China Sea is the Future of Conflict', *Foreign Policy*, Vol. 188, September/October 2011, 78–85. The author charts a path that links the past and present, and makes predictions for the future.

11 The growing significance of global interdependence is well understood, as is the inherent difficulty of managing global problems through the voluntary and ad hoc co-operation of nation states. Maintaining peace and prosperity in the South China Sea between China and the USA will be a breakthrough in global governance arrangements.

12 Owing to the geographical endowments of East Asia, China is likely to emerge as a naval superpower with competent air force capabilities—this explains why much of the discourse revolves around China's naval build-up.

13 Richard Bernstein and Ross H. Munro, *The Coming Conflict with China* (New York: Alfred A. Knopf, 1997).

14 Marc Lanteigne, 'China's Maritime Security and the Malacca Dilemma', *Asian Security*, Vol. 4, No. 2, 2008, 143–61; Susan Shirk, *China: Fragile Superpower* (New York: Oxford University Press, 2008).

15 The economic, geostrategic and political significance of these islands is invaluable. Economically, their surrounding waters host marine resources (e.g. fisheries) and seabed deposits of oil and gas. Geostrategically, they are habitable islands in which naval outposts and research centres can be built, as well as refuelling stations in case of extended conflict on the high seas. In the bigger islands landing strips can be built, and these could grant a significant military advantage. Politically, securing control over these islands satisfies a long-held ambition of the CCP, and it bolsters credibility and legitimacy, particularly with nationalistic agents in China. See also Marwyn Samuels, *Contest for the South China Sea* (New York: Routledge, 2005).

16 'The most serious trouble in recent decades has flared between Vietnam and China. The Chinese seized the Paracels from Vietnam in 1974, killing more than 70 Vietnamese troops. In 1988 the two sides clashed in the Spratlys, when Vietnam again came off worse, losing about 60 sailors.' For more information: 'Q&A: South China Sea dispute', *BBC News* (London), 27 June 2012, www.bbc.co.uk/news/world-asia-pacific-13748349.

17 So far, China has gained control of 12 geographical items, Malaysia five, the Philippines eight, Taiwan one, and Vietnam 25.

18 Through iterative consultations between members of ASEAN and China.

19 For a review on politics and regional security, see: Sam Bateman and Ralf Emmers, *Security and International Politics in the South China Sea: Towards a Cooperative Management Regime* (New York: Routledge, 2009).

20 See: James Dobbins, 'War with China', *Survival: Global Politics and Strategy*, Vol. 54, No. 4, 2012, 7–24.

102 *Country case studies*

21 For an entry on the debate over the extent to which national wealth should be used for military purposes, see: 'What's the Potential for Conflict with China, and How Can It Be Avoided?' Research Brief No. RB-9657-A (Santa Monica, CA: RAND Corporation, 2012). Also, for an assessment of the interaction between economics and strategy over the past five centuries, see the academic work by Yale historian Paul Kennedy, *The Rise and Fall of the Great Powers* (New York: Vintage Books, 1989). Kennedy's book might explain why China is expected to rise.

22 To whom Taiwan actually belongs is a convoluted and legally complex issue that is currently unresolved. This arose in large part due to the USA and the Allies of the Second World War handling of the surrender of Taiwan from Japan in 1945, which led to a temporary custodianship by the Republic of China troops under General Order Nr. 1. There followed the 1951 Treaty of Peace with Japan, to which neither the Republic of China nor the People's Republic of China was invited to contribute, and left Taiwan's sovereignty legally undefined in international law and therefore in dispute.

23 Britain established the first treaty ports in China by the end of the First Opium War. This occurred in 1842, under the Treaty of Nanking. In addition to ceding Hong Kong to the British in perpetuity, the Treaty also established five treaty ports at Shanghai, Canton, Ningpo, Fuchow and Amoy. Concessions to France and the USA soon followed.

24 See, also: Jonathan D. Spence, *The Search for Modern China* (New York: W.W. Norton & Company, 1991).

25 For more information, see: Muthiah Alagappa, *Taiwan's Presidential Politics* (New York: M. E. Sharpe, 2001).

26 James Webb, 'The South China Sea's Gathering Storms', *The Wall Street Journal*, 20 August 2012.

27 Karl F. Helleiner, 'War and Human Progress', *The Canadian Journal of Economics and Political Science*, Vol. 18, No. 2, May 1952, 205–08. True enough, wars are known as destructive and debilitating, but from the view of sociologist and ethnographers wars are events that bring out the essence of what modern societies are made of.

28 G. John Ikenberry notes that 'status quo states are most likely to cooperate and balance against a rising power if they have strong economic ties with each other but not with the adversary. When economic ties with the adversary are extensive, however, a balancing strategy is difficult to sustain.' For more information, see: Paul A. Papayoanou, *Power Ties: Economic Interdependence, Balancing, and War* (Ann Arbor: University of Michigan Press, 1999).

29 According to a report from SIPRI (Stockholm International Peace Research Institute), Singapore accounts for 4% of the world's total expenditure on arms imports. Its per caput defence expenditure beats every country except for Israel, Kuwait and the USA. Singapore is now the fifth largest arms importer in the world after some obvious behemoths like China, India, Pakistan and South Korea. For more information, see: 'Military Spending in South-East Asia: Shopping Spree', *The Economist*, 24 March 2012, www.economist.com/node/21551056.

30 Craig Whitlock, 'U.S. Eyes Return to some Southeast Asia Military Bases', *Washington Post,* 22 June 2012.

31 'Will ASEAN Step Up to Try to Bridge Japan-China Rift?' *The Japan Times Online*, 7 September 2012.

32 To clarify, socialism is to be understood as a stage of society in Marxist theory that is in transition between capitalism and communism, and is distinguished by the unequal distribution of goods and pay according to work done.

33 Paul Krugman, *The Return of Depression Economics and the Crisis of 2008* (New York: W.W. Norton, 2009).

34 For more information on this subject, see: Katherine Barbieri, 'Economic Interdependence: A Path to Peace or a Source of Interstate Conflict?', *Journal of Peace Research*, Vol. 33, No. 1, February 1996, 29–49.

35 It is important to note that Indonesia, Malaysia and Singapore have also undertaken onerous naval expansions.

36 It is important to note that the Chinese People's Liberation Army—with some 1.3m. ground troops it is the largest army in the world—is on track to achieve its goal of building a modern, regionally focused force by 2020.

37 Elisabeth Bumiller, 'U.S. Official Warns about China's Military Buildup', *New York Times*, 24 August 2012.

38 Robert Farley, 'The Future of U.S. Naval Power', in: *The Future of Maritime Security*, ed. Zachary Hosford, Abraham Denmark, Robert Farley and Mark J. Valencia (*World Politics Review*, 14 September 2010).

39 For more information, See: Amy Click, 'Book Review: The Coming Conflict with China by Richard Bernstein and Ross H. Munro', *Tulsa Journal of Comparative and International Law*, Vol. 5, 1997–98, 413–17.

40 Two excellent sources of analysis, comments and data are: Elizabeth Economy, 'China's Rise in Southeast Asia: Implications for the United States', *Journal of Contemporary China*, Vol. 14, No. 44, 2005, 409–25; Suisheng Zhao, *China–US Relations Transformed: Perspectives and Strategic Interactions* (New York: Routledge, 2008).

41 Hugh White, 'Power Shift: Australia's Future between Washington and Beijing', *Quarterly Essay*, No. 39, 2010, www.quarterlyessay.com/issue/power-shift-australia %E2%80%99s-future-between-washington-and-beijing.

42 John W. Garver, 'The Diplomacy of a Rising China in South Asia', *Orbis*, Vol. 56, No. 3, summer 2012, 391–411. For a broader coverage of China, see: Henry Kissinger, *On China* (New York: Penguin Books, 2012).

43 A US viewpoint dotted with progressive outlook can be found: 'South China Sea: Cooperation, Conflict, and U.S. Interests', webpage introduction, Center for a New American Security, www.cnas.org/node/5641.

44 See: Doug Bandow, 'Strategic Restraint in the Near Seas', *Orbis*, Vol. 56, No. 3, summer 2012, 486–502.

45 For a viewpoint on the intersection of law and security, this scholarly work is illustrative: Peter Burgess, 'The Politics of the South China Sea: Territoriality and International Law', *Security Dialogue*, Vol. 34, No. 1, March 2003, 7–10.

46 Takashi Teradaa, 'Forming an East Asian Community: A Site for Japan–China Power Struggles', *Japanese Studies*, Vol. 26, No. 1, 2006, 5–17. This author claims that ASEAN has more power than it thinks to tame China.

47 For more information on this and other relevant topics, see: Sheila A. Smith, 'Japan and the East China Sea Dispute', *Orbis*, Vol. 56, No. 3, summer 2012, 370–90; John Milligan-Whyte and Dai Min, *US–China Relations in the Obama Administration: Facing Shared Challenges* (New York: New School Press Limited, 2011).

48 Matthew Lee, 'Clinton Seeks Chinese Accord on South China Sea', *Washington Times*, 4 September 2012.

49 See: Burgos and Ear, *The Hungry Dragon: How China's Resource Quest Is Reshaping the World*. For further information, see: Andrew J. Nathan, *China's Search for Security* (New York: Columbia University Press, 2012).

50 For an extensive discussion on interstate co-operation in conflict situations, see: Zhiguo Gaoa, 'The South China Sea: From Conflict to Cooperation?' *Ocean Development and International Law*, Vol. 25, No. 3, 1994, 345–59.

7 Vietnam

Introduction

Most South-East Asian nations have witnessed the rapid rise of China with admiration and fear. China's neighbours have been impressed by the successful reconfiguration and re-launch of a country that was in decline for 500 years. This turnaround will be remembered as one of the most significant economic-political events of the 20th century. Commentators such as Nicholas Kristof have stated that 'the rise of China, if it continues, may be the most important trend in the world'.[1] This growth curve has proved accurate, as China continues to perform well. In the 1990s the Chinese economy grew at an impressively rapid pace, at about 10% per annum. However, from 2011–12, growth rates were affected by the financial crises experienced by the European Union and the USA, and the global economic slowdown. In 2012 China's gross domestic product eased to 7.8%, down from 9.2% in 2011, the lowest since 1999.[2]

Accelerated economic growth propelled by rising exports, higher internal investments, and increased domestic consumption levels has made China the preferred destination of overseas investors. For instance, during the first six months of 2012, China overtook the USA to become the world's largest recipient of foreign direct investment[3] (FDI), according to a report released by the United Nations Conference on Trade and Development (UNCTAD).[4] Moreover, from January–September 2012 China attracted the largest share of global FDI flows with \$170,000m., followed by the USA (\$104,000m.), Brazil (\$48,000m.), the United Kingdom (\$47,000m.), and France (\$46,000m.).[5] These investment inflows, when added to the US dollar denominated payments of exports, have accumulated \$3,300,000m. in foreign reserves.[6]

These trillions of dollars in Central Bank reserves have long been used to support Chinese companies expanding their operations overseas and by the Government in order to facilitate a number of strategic acquisitions. The Chinese State Administration of Foreign Exchange helps the Chinese Government to seek 'innovative uses of the reserves and supporting financial institutions in serving China's economic growth and going-out strategy'.[7] In addition, the Chinese Communist Party (CCP) has also decided to allocate a portion of these funds to undertake a significant build-up and modernization of the People's Liberation Army (PLA) and other security-related bodies. Among these upgrades, special attention has been given to air and naval power because China's combat landscape is characterized by bays, islands, seas and seashores.

As noted in previous chapters, the combination of one-party rule, increasing military strength, rising nationalism, strong economic growth and solid foreign exchange reserves has caused many observers in East and South-East Asia wondering what the Chinese Government intends to do with the seductive mix of economic, military and political power. Since the 1990s Western commentators and observers have warned that 'China has increasing weight to throw about. But its neighbors still question whether this weight will be thrown behind efforts to build a more secure and stable Asia'.[8]

One of the chief causes of concern is the maritime and territorial disputes in the East and South China Sea. More specifically, members of the Association of Southeastern Asian Nations (ASEAN) continue to witness with increasing frequency the use of military power to coerce and intimidate neighbours into giving up their claims over the same islands and waters that China claims. Following the end of the Cold War, these overlapping claims and disputes emerged as the chief source of tension in East and South-East Asia. The driving strategic rationale among civilian and military members of the CCP is that 'in a world of shrinking natural resources, the mainland Chinese have clearly stated what flag they think should fly over the potentially oil-rich island group'.[9] China is in dispute with Vietnam over maritime boundaries, reefs and the Paracel and Spratly islands.[10]

Historical background: China versus Vietnam is nothing new

The origins, contexts and consequences of the long-standing disputes between China, Taiwan, Vietnam and the Philippines over the Paracel and Spratly archipelagos in the South China Sea are wide-ranging and not fully understood. The incomplete understanding of these disputes stems from the growing number of factors at play and the convoluted way in which issues and problems have been connected by these nations to their respective priorities: for some actors the disputes have economic ramifications and for others they have sociopolitical consequences.

It is understood that inter-state rapprochement can be affected by multiple factors and that it changes according to leaders' interests and viewpoints, and in this context we will examine the periods of conflict and collaboration between China and Vietnam. These two countries have been been in conflict over islands and resources in the South China Sea for almost 40 years.[11] However, the situation was different during the 1940s, not only with regard to changing contexts but also in terms of shifting priorities: Mao Zedong considered the Vietnamese national liberation movement to be a powerful geopolitical catalyst, one that deserved support because it fitted into his strategy of creating an anti-imperialist world order and China's interest in balancing

106 *Country case studies*

the Soviet Union and the USA against one other. During the 25-year period following the founding of the People's Republic of China in 1949, China helped Vietnam diplomatically and economically in its struggle against France and the USA. Furthermore, during the 1960s China gave substantial assistance to the Vietnamese President, Ho Chi Minh, when 320,000 Chinese volunteers were permitted into North Vietnam to help to build infrastructure for the country, thereby freeing a similar number of People's Army of Vietnam personnel to go south and engage in fighting against the USA.[12] As the Vietnam War drew to a close during the early 1970s, and as the Chinese Government amended its strategic calculation by making overtures to the United States to offset rising threats from the Soviet Union, China's relations with Vietnam started to become increasingly complicated and vitriolic, resulting in a direct clash in 1979.[13]

By the late 1970s China began to construct the elaborate framework of what would be known as the most significant shift to the right in its economic and social stance since 1949. Both China and Vietnam, at that time, were looking beyond their borders in search of fresh capital, know-how, technology and trade by courting the industrial, neo-liberal democracies of Australia, Europe and North America. During this time ASEAN also enjoyed a boost in attention and confidence given that two major regional economies were focused on growth and development, and there was renewed hope for the emergence of a region in which freedom, prosperity, peace and security were perpetuated, along similar lines to that which was originally proposed by Malaysia in the Zone of Peace, Freedom and Neutrality Declaration signed in Kuala Lumpur in 1971.[14] It could be argued that Chinese and Vietnamese interests converged at about the same time, and that their relationship could easily have switched from collaboration to conflict as both would then perceive the other as a regional rival competitor. Indeed, following the fall of the South Vietnamese capital, Saigon, to North Vietnam in April 1975, China had to attempt to resolve border and territorial disputes against its ally, Vietnam, which also happened to be an ally of China's adversary, the Soviet Union. This was a difficult political-diplomatic situation for the Chinese Government, especially when it came to balancing benefits and costs (or the balancing of advantages and disadvantages).

Chinese conceptualization of power and its uses

As the Chinese Government struggled to find its place on the economic-political spectrum, it may have set out goals and objectives that clashed with the objective circumstances of the time. Tellingly, Charles McGregor examined the Chinese Government's efforts to reconcile its conflicting aims of putting pressure on Vietnam to become more pro-China while simultaneously projecting itself as a force for growth, peace and stability in the region.[15] The overarching theme is that China had only a limited number of diplomatic measures available to it through which to pressure neighbours to acquiesce to its aims. Vietnam, for its part, had plans of its own, and was flirting with suspicion-attracting supporters (i.e. the Soviets) and with a governance model widely lambasted for its inequities and iniquities (i.e. communism). Yet, both countries knew that they needed regional support in order to launch their planned reforms and to achieve international perception as constructive members and not as destabilizing forces. However, insofar as the South China Sea is concerned, Vietnam and other members of ASEAN have long believed in the Chinese Government's prestidigitation: a cleverly executed deceptive plan starting with a pacifying rhetoric (i.e. peaceful and non-intrusive rise) to avoid detection and ending with a powerful neighbour forcing its way through its unilateral plans (i.e. reunification with Taiwan and buffering the USA in Asia).

Regarding this issue of power projection and regional perception, Zhiguo Gao studied the national policies behind the evolution of events related to the Spratly Islands disputes in the South China Sea and examined in particular some of their implications on regional relations and the future of the South China Sea, with special emphasis on China's policy towards the issue.[16] It is often argued that the Chinese Government is rethinking the regional concept of Eurasia, not only in terms of the analysis and interpretation of 'influencing power' by members of the international community but also as a geographical area. Chinese strategists have examined the dynamic geopolitical links that are reconfiguring Eurasian spaces from the western edge of Europe (and shaky model of a Union) through to the eastern edge of Asia, including the Korean peninsula and Japan. While current scholarly debates presume that Eurasia is merely a catch-all term for ambition and geostrategic wrangling at the hands of old and new power players, it is true that the world perceives the Eurasian region from the perspective of 'power competitions' between China, Europe, India, Japan, Russia and the USA. According to ASEAN, China's rethinking of Eurasia is merely a useful conceptual framework that hammers down a broad vision of blurred borders—from the eastern edges of the Sino–Vietnamese zone through the Himalayan corridor and the abutting Central Asian countries—that will be used in the future by China to distinguish those peripheral players who 'align closely and favorably' instead of those who are especially antagonistic.[17] Michael Leifer posited in 1995 that a strong connection exists between China's economic reform and its security policy. Leifer argued that this 'positive link' was demonstrated in China's increased capability to project power in the South China Sea while pursuing maritime and territorial claims. In short, the rationale is that economic success leads to increased revenues, and that prosperity has allowed the CCP to allocate economic resources in support of defence, security and power projection roles 'by the armed forces in general and the navy in particular'. This support to the military can be politically justified 'on the grounds that it will lead to future economic advantage' and that leaders can pitch popular proposals advocating for greater expenditure on defence and security when social reforms and economic well-being are at a high point. Also, there is the desire to carefully 'accommodate a disaffected domestic constituency', that is, diasporas and

108   *Country case studies*

groups within Chinese cities that for long have been critical of the Government for not taking a strong stance on issues that are critical to China, especially against troublesome neighbours.[18]

At stake: energy and national security, surveillance of sea routes and buffering hegemons

Among the numerous maritime and territorial disputes between China and its regional neighbours, the Paracel and Spratly Islands dispute is increasingly attracting the attention of ASEAN and the international and regional news and media outlets. Primarily, the dispute concerns the control and absolute ownership of some 200 mid-ocean islets in the South China Sea, most of which are shark-infested, coral-surrounded outcroppings which at first glance are without much value in themselves. However, the dispute, and the issues associated with it, is complicated by the reasonable expectation that whoever eventually owns the islands will be entitled to all of the natural resources[19] (fisheries, oil and gas) and economic windfalls that may be developed from the islands' offshore waters.

Since mid-January 1974, following a tense two-day skirmish between China and South Vietnam (this military engagement is known as the Battle of the Paracel Islands and was considered a victory for the PLA's navy), the Paracel Islands[20] have remained firmly under Chinese control and are currently under the administration of Hainan Province, while the Philippines, Taiwan and Vietnam share control of some of the Spratly Islands. The Paracel archipelago is situated approximately equidistant from the coastlines of China and Vietnam; that is, 330 km, or 210 miles, south-east of China's Hainan Island, and one-third of the distance from central Vietnam to the northern Philippines.

As a trade-critical sea lane between the two archipelagoes is the only major route to link East Asia with Africa and Europe, strong strategic interests in the South China Sea have been advanced and sought by major powers in East and South-East Asia. It is believed that, unless direct provocation occurs, none of the parties involved in the dispute are likely to use armed forces to gain control of the Paracel and Spratly Islands, nor is it widely expected that they would seek international adjudication or other forms of third-party involvement to settle the dispute under international law. As long as control and ownership of the islets is argued by actors in the region, delimitation of maritime boundaries among the disputing parties will be conveniently delayed, and this in turn will necessarily impede the development of the sea resources that exist in immediate proximity to the islands. For economic and geopolitical reasons, the actions, attitudes and reactions of China and Vietnam towards the issue will play a decisive role in finding a solution to this and other territorial disputes.[21]

With regards to national security, Stein Tønnesson argues that 'Vietnam's interests in the South China Sea may be divided into traditional national security interests and interests linked to the broader category of human security ... connected with a trend toward a greater regional, less nationalist approach, which may give Vietnam a key role in resolving the multiple disputes in the South China Sea'.[22] This argument assumes that Vietnam is chiefly interested in protecting its population against the depletion of fisheries, floods, pollution, piracy, typhoons and wars, all with the aim of improving the living conditions of Vietnamese citizens. However, this rationalization does not seem to incorporate the broader forces of sovereignty and instead permits the setting of a precedent in which China bullies Vietnam, again, into relinquishing its claims over territories through sheer force. Also, while Tønnesson claims that 'muted nationalism' is the path to resolving these issues, it seems counterintuitive given that China marshals support for its actions in nearby foreign lands by fuelling the same nationalistic sentiments that neighbours seem to be curbing. China, on the other hand, is not shy to assert that control of the South China Sea fits exactly with it policies for energy and national security sinced it relates, first, to state survival, and second, to showcasing its governance model. All in all, the Chinese Government is trying to secure energy resources in order to continue its stellar economic growth and to legitimize further its political approach to statecraft. To do so, the South China Sea is the theatre in which China buffers the long-standing influence of the USA in Asia.[23]

A source of fire in the middle of the sea: the scramble for oil and gas deposits

On 14 March 1988 Chinese and Vietnamese troops and warships exchanged fire on and near Sinh Ton Island. This violent exchange occurred as a result of disputes over ownership of the Spratly Islands and the natural resources lying within the 200-nautical mile exclusive economic zone (EEZ). As for the existence of resources, it is no secret that public and private sector reports have surfaced indicating that potential oil deposits are at issue. However, the existence of such resources does not provide a full explanation for China to launch territorial disputes against its neighbours. At stake, also, is the acquisition of the capacity to project power through military might (air and sea). The Spratly Islands are considered by claimants as strategic outposts where naval bases can be built for the defence of sea lanes, interdiction, surveillance of vessels and for the mounting of land attacks. This being the case, the national security interests of major powers (Japan and the USA) are also at stake. This is explained by the inevitable passing of ships and tankers through the South China Sea close to the Spratly Islands and to the positioning of the port of Hong Kong and the port of Singapore, which are key access points for ships carrying valuable merchandise to East and South-East Asian economies. Moreover, the sea routes adjacent to and within the Spratly Islands transit area are important trajectories for oil and gas tankers, many of which are en route to China or Japan. It is noteworthy that countries in the region have good memories for history: politicians are quick to remind civilian and

110   *Country case studies*

military officials that during the Second World War the Japanese Navy used Taiping Dao, the largest of the Spratly Islands, as a submarine base from which it launched invasions on the Philippines, the then Dutch East Indies and Malaya. It just so happens that, at one point, the Imperial Navy did in fact succeed in cutting off the Allied forces' shipping routes in the critical South China Sea.[24]

When Chinese resource security and Vietnamese sovereignty claims intersect, one can start making connections in terms of interests, motivations and rationales. The Chinese Government has a vested interest in maintaining a balanced supply of oil and gas to the mainland, and has for some time sought to develop its offshore exploration, drilling and extraction of crude oil and natural gas in the South China Sea; however, to attain its long-term goals, the Chinese will have to find binding and lasting solutions to geopolitical and strategic problems that have been further complicated by overlapping territorial claims which analysts and observers believe could lead to tensions or conflicts between China and abutting countries (including ASEAN members), and with Vietnam in particular.[25]

Considerable debate exists over the extent of the recoverable oil and gas deposits in the vicinity of the Spratly Islands. The Chinese Government has kept the islands under close observation since 1989 when the *China Geology Newspaper* published findings arguing that ongoing surveys by the then Ministry of Natural Resources and Geology estimated that about 18,000m. tons of oil and natural deposits might lie in that region.[26] A 2013 US Energy Information Administration (USEIA) report estimated that the extended seabed around the Spratly Islands holds energy sources of approximately 11,000m. barrels of oil reserves and 190,000,000m. cu ft of natural gas reserves.[27] Meanwhile, in November 2012 the Chinese National Offshore Oil Company (CNOOC) estimated the area holds around 125,000m. barrels of oil and 500,000,000m. cu ft of natural gas in undiscovered resources, although independent studies have not confirmed this figure. Finally, the US Geological Survey (USGS) estimated that the South China Sea 'may contain anywhere between 5 and 22 billion barrels of oil and between 70 and 290 trillion cubic feet of gas in as-yet-to-discover resources'.[28]

If any these figures are correct, then these maritime reserves would become indisputably some of the largest in the world. However, at present it is impossible to reach many of the reservoirs but experts predict that the technology required for their extraction will become available in the near future.

Tug of war: diplomacy, soft power and the struggle for supremacy

Now let's turn our attention to the actions, behaviours and reactions of China and Vietnam in the South China Sea to exercise control and protection of the areas surrounding the Spratly Islands. As noted above, the controversy over the Spratly Islands and its waters remained relatively dormant until 1988, when China and Vietnam fought over Sinh Ton Island, resulting in a number of fatalities. Since then, clashes and hostilities have erupted regularly in the area, with both sides offering diplomatic options, promises, false concessions and short-term assurances.

By mid-2012 China and Vietnam had exchanged verbal hostilities in order to demonstrate to each other their intention to remain steadfast on claims over the South China Sea. For example, in June 2012 China criticized Vietnam for enacting a law that assumed Vietnamese control over the Paracel and Spratly Islands. The Chinese Government has continued to insist that the islands and its resources belong indisputably to China. Nguyen Van Tho, the Vietnamese ambassador to China, was summoned to a meeting at the Chinese Ministry of Foreign Affairs where officials protested against the law, and expressed their opposition to what they perceived to be a direct and serious violation of China's territorial sovereignty. Officials insisted that Vietnam's declaration of jurisdiction and sovereignty over the islands was an act of provocation, and a hinderance to the building of cohesion and peace in the region. The summoning of the Vietnamese ambassador was one of the many instances during which the Chinese Government exhibited its determination to reiterate other South-East Asian countries its exclusive ownership of the South China Sea, its islands and its resources. Interestingly, these acrimonious exchanges and legal protests took place two weeks prior to an ASEAN meeting of ministers of foreign affairs in Phnom Penh, the capital of Cambodia. China aimed to put the issues surrounding the South China Sea at the top of the meeting agenda.[29]

In November 2012 Chinese officials informed reporters that China had elevated the level of governance on three island groups in the South China Sea, the Nansha, Xisha and Zhongsha Islands—in other words, the Spratly and Paracel Islands, and the Macclesfield Bank (an underwater atoll of reefs and shoals). A government statement released by the Chinese State Council noted that the islands and their surrounding waters had been placed under the administration of the city of Sansha, that is, a management which ranks at the level of prefecture rather than the level of county, which is considered a lower rank. The underlying argument for this move was that this new arrangement would strengthen the Chinese Government's administration of these islands and that Asian neighbours should assume that this action reinforced China's desire to unambiguously assert its strategic interests in the South China Sea.[30]

China and Vietnam are determined to advance their claims to gain control of resources. In 2007 Vietnam reiterated that the British Petroleum-led US $2,000m. natural gasfield and pipeline project in the South China Sea was within the bounds of its sovereignty. Vietnam argued that division of the South China Sea islands and territorial waters into blocks for the purposes of oil and gas exploration conformed to international law and should not be contested by China given that they lay within the confines of Vietnam's EEZ and continental shelf. The gasfields in question were not part of an ongoing joint seismic exploration project being undertaken in the Spratly Islands by the national oil entities of China, the Philippines and Vietnam. In response,

112   *Country case studies*

China counterposed that Vietnams's actions infringed upon Chinese sovereignty, sovereign power and consensus-based administrative rights in the Spratly Islands.[31] In the end, the interstate struggle for control of the islands and its resources hinges on the willingness of either country to abandon its ambitions and plans, which are tightly linked to national identity, cultural legacy, economic growth and international status.

Dashed lines, intergovernmental organizations and expected outcomes

Most maritime and territorial disputes are concerned with disagreements and misunderstandings related to borders, delineations, distance, frontiers, identifiable marks, reference points and lines.

This is the case with China and its neighbours in the South China Sea. At the core of the sovereignty disputes between all claimants to the South China Sea lies the so-called nine-dash line, depicted on Chinese maps as nine long dashes across the sea. In reality, the U-shaped line designates China's claim to over 80% of the South China Sea. However, this was not always the case. The original line, which was denoted by eleven dots, was first ordered and drawn by the Kuomintang Government in 1947. This map included regions as far as the Gulf of Tonkin, off Vietnam's northern coast. The change from eleven dots to nine dashes came about after China decided to alter the maps. It achieved this by removing two dots on the Gulf of Tonkin.

From the early 1950s to the early 2000s there were some minor disturbances in the South China Sea but nothing that merited much attention from the Asian states or the international community. During this period of increased trade, buoyant commerce and accelerated economic growth the South China Sea served its essential purpose: as a conduit for sea-based transportation of people and goods. However, in May 2009 the Chinese Government issued an official note concerning emerging security issues within the nine-dash line, and this action formally brought the controversy behind the map with a nine-dash line to the attention of regional institutions, neighbours and the rest of the world.

The issuance of the official note in early 2009 was interpreted as a declaration of the Chinese Government's view that this relatively old map held serious international and regional significance. In fact, this and subsequent statements were a direct response to Malaysia and Vietnam's joint submission to the UN expressing and validating their own claims in the South China Sea. When examined in this context it is easier to see that China was merely reacting to a legal-political move by Malaysia and Vietnam, who sought to raise awareness in the international community that China had in effect arbitrarily claimed a large portion of the South China Sea, and the basis for such a claim rested upon historic understandings.

In early 2010 Chinese government officials considered elevating China's maritime and territorial claims in the South China Sea to that of a core national interest; that is, allowing it to be understood that the South China Sea now ranked at the same level with outright control of Tibet and reunification with Taiwan. The Chinese Government, of course, has never publicly confirmed this, and very likely never will. Interestingly, the CCP leadership has not issued a formal denial despite the apprehension aroused by its actions in the surrounding area. This acceptance–denial game is another tactic used by China: it claims to be developing peacefully but is building up its military; it claims to be a non-intrusive state but manipulates decisions and interventions through the UN Security Council; and it complains that the USA and Japan seek to stifle their growth but that they are using their power to influence Cambodia, Myanmar and North Korea.

By April 2011 the Philippines had filed a formal protest at the UN over China's nine-dash line across the South China Sea. According to the contested map, the Chinese-claimed waters include several oil- gasfields 'belonging' to Indonesia (Natuna Islands), Malaysia (fields lying offshore from Sarawak), the Philippines (Malampaya and Camago), and Vietnam (several blocks off the Vietnamese coast). The problem is really very simple: all these claimants disagree and misunderstand the distribution of the Spratly Islands. In summary, the Chinese Government continues to insist that China owns sovereignty and jurisdiction over the islands and adjacent waters, and other nations involved in the dispute contradict this claim, while basing their assertations on historical and legal arguments.

Law of the sea: history meets pragmatism

The tranquillity of the South China Sea has historically been disturbed by the occupation of the Paracel and Spratly Islands. This process of maritime and territorial dispute and subsequent occupation began in the 1970s and has continued up to the present day. Most of the islands and their respective surrounding waters within the South China Sea have been controlled by one littoral country or another, mainly as a tactical move to gain sovereignty over them. The reason that countries place such importance on controlling islands in the vast South China Sea stems from the belief that undiscovered resources exist under its seabed and because the area serves as a major trade route for Asian countries and the international community.[32]

In this process of claiming islands in the South China Sea one can find the interaction of history, law, politics and practicality, mainly connected with defining the extent of the continental shelf. As countries formulate what they believe is theirs to exploit, manage or control, the United Nations Convention on the Law of the Sea (UNCLOS) emerges as the mechanism through which to express differences and find solutions. In fact, it is under Article 76(8) of UNCLOS that countries around the globe submit the boundaries and limits of their national claims to the continental shelf up to 200 nautical miles from their coastal shores. This submission is sent to the Commission on the Limits of the Continental Shelf. In May 2009 the joint submission by Malaysia and Vietnam was contested by China. This 'arranged submission' by two South-East Asian countries brought about the exchange of unsigned diplomatic

114   *Country case studies*

communications prepared in the third person among the littoral countries making claims to islands in the South China Sea. In these written exchanges, the focus moved away from the claimed limits to the continental shelf and into a heated discussion about the role of the nine-dash line drawn by the Chinese Government. The controversy emerged as the countries in question started to respond to the maps provided by China to Malaysia and Vietnam.

A number of important questions were posed. These included logical questions, such as: what is the basis for the nine-dash line? Does the unilateral drawing of this line imply de facto sovereignty even if not recognized by others? What is the main function of this line to the Chinese Government? Does it have legitimacy in international law simply because a country has it on its maps? Is the nine-dash line gaining validity in the body of customary law simply because it has not been contested by other countries in the region?

The answers to these questions can only be found through repeated dialogues, iterations and reason-based interpretations. The outcomes need to explore and weigh the historical, legal, political and economic implications for all countries involved, as well as elaborating on the true nature of legal arguments, the future status in recognized maps, and the implications on security and sovereignty to China and Vietnam, as well as the other states that bring claims regarding the South China Sea.

Academics also play a role in framing questions and finding answers to difficult issues, and in this case two Chinese authors assert that 'the nine-dash line has always had a foundation in international law, including customary law of discovery, occupation, and historic title, as well as UNCLOS itself'.[33] Of course, there is a plethora of views on this subject. Two European authors claim that the ambiguity and vagueness of the term historic rights by the Chinese Government 'raises the issue of whether that very vagueness is being used as an element of political strategy'. They note that these so-called historic rights have been 'imbued with a certain degree of confusion and controversy in international law [and] play an important part in the arguments brought by states claiming sovereignty in this region and in particular by China'.[34] It is fair to say that China and Vientnam will have to find common ground.

Concluding remarks

Six South-East Asian countries have made overlapping claims to territorial sovereignty over all or part of the Paracel and Spratly Islands, the grounds for which are complex, misunderstood and have little commonality.[35] Lee Cordner argues that the real prospects for the Law of the Sea to provide the key to resolving the disputes are limited, even though each of the disputing parties variously refers to the 1982 United Nations Convention on the Law of the Sea to support its claims.[36]

Indeed, the South China Sea is an area where geopolitics, militarism and globalization are finding it difficult to converge. This is a direct outcome of power politics in the international arena. There are four clear factors that have contributed to this situation: its geostrategic location; disputes over the Paracel and Spratly Islands; competition for the control of the resources (e.g. fisheries, oil, gas and minerals); and updates to UNCLOS.[37] The 2009 joint submission made by Malaysia and Vietnam resulted in the resurfacing of complications and interstate tensions. The claims by these countries drew criticism and protests to UNCLOS from China, which restated its 'indisputable sovereignty' over the islands in the South China Sea and the adjacent waters.[38] The disputes in the South China Sea between China and Vietnam have the potential to become internecine power struggles. It seems that hard power and high politics are competing for primacy in South-East Asia. With regard to high politics, China, Taiwan and Vietnam have resorted to a balancing strategy; and in international relations, the smaller claimant countries, such as Vietnam, seemingly have adopted balancing strategies involving the USA.[39]

China and Vietnam will continue to clash in the South China Sea because neither wants to set the precedent of accepting debilitating terms or making advantageous concessions. The leaders of both countries know how to play the game of tit-for-tat; that is, they have learned that every action calls for a reaction, a measure calls for a countermeasure, and a provocation calls for a protest. Not doing so signals permissiveness and weakness. China wants Vietnam to know that it is playing this game for the long term, and Vietnam wants China to know that it feels the same way. In some ways, the Chinese Government expects neighbours to show signs of 'learned helplessness' because it will never relinquish its claims and want others to feel confused and tired. In other words, China is aware that at some point claimants will experience 'contestation fatigue' and at that point it will finally press its claims and resolve disputes with resolute force, but without going to war.

In summary, the South China Sea and its territories are poised to become one of the most dangerous international flashpoints in South-East Asia because its territorial waters and numerous small uninhabited islands and reefs are the subject of competing claims by a number of littoral countries. These anachronistic disputes have led to conflicts, and the ensuing tensions have from time to time led to clashes between vessels that have resulted in bloodshed and loss of life. It is worth stressing that the South China Sea is host to important shipping routes (i.e. sea lanes) for the international community; it is crucial for the economies of China, Indonesia, Japan and South Korea; and hosts very large fisheries, upon which many people depend for their livelihood and food.

This chapter has sought to present a comprehensive overview of the latent conflicts in the South China Sea and the legal and political measures being taken by ASEAN and regional countries to resolve them. It highlights the importance of the South China Sea and considers the interests of the different littoral countries. It also considers the strategic interests of external powers, notably the USA. It discussed the legal issues that have emerged and covered possible future developments.

The following two chapters cover numerous issues on power projection and resource security.

Notes

1 Nicholas D. Kristof, 'China's Rise', *Foreign Affairs*, Vol. 72, No. 5, November/December 1993, 59–74.
2 See: 'China's GDP Growth Eases to 7.8% in 2012', *China Daily* (Beijing), 18 January 2013.
3 Foreign direct investment is a category of investment that reflects the objective of establishing a lasting interest by a resident enterprise in one economy (direct investor) in an enterprise (direct investment enterprise) that is resident in an economy other than that of the direct investor. The lasting interest implies the existence of a long-term relationship between the direct investor and the direct investment enterprise and a significant degree of influence (not necessarily control) on the management of the enterprise. The direct or indirect ownership of 10% or more of the voting power of an enterprise resident in one economy by an investor resident in another economy is the statistical evidence of such a relationship. For more information on financial definitions and other matters, see: OECD, *Benchmark Definition of Foreign Direct Investment*. 4th Edition (Paris: OECD, 2008).
4 See: 'China the Largest FDI Recipient in First Half of 2012', *China Daily* (Beijing), 24 October 2012.
5 These five host economies received 45% of global inflows during first nine months of 2012, as opposed to 37% in the first three-quarters of 2011. For more information and updated tables, see: OECD, 'FDI in Figures', (Paris: OECD, January 2013). Available at: www.oecd.org/daf/inv/FDI%20in%20figures.pdf.
6 'Central Bank of China to Retain Dollar Reserves'. Available at: www.china.org.cn/english/BAT/210401.htm.
7 See: 'China to Use Forex Reserves to Finance Overseas Investment Deals', *Bloomberg News*, 14 January 2013.
8 For an excellent essay on this topic, see: 'A Job for China', *The Economist*, 20 November 1993, 18.
9 Michael Gallagher, 'China's Illusory Threat to the South China Sea', Vol. 19, No. 1, summer 1994, 169–94.
10 For information on China's search for energy and resources, see: Sigfrido Burgos Cáceres and Sophal Ear, *The Hungry Dragon: How China's Resource Quest Is Reshaping the World* (New York: Routledge, 2013).
11 China and South Vietnam fought over the Paracel and the Spratly Islands in 1974, and unified Vietnam (North and South) fought briefly with China in 1988 over the same islands. According to the International Crisis Group, after the conflicts were settled, China controlled the Paracel Islands, as well as the surrounding reefs and shoals.
12 Chen Jian, 'China's Involvement in the Vietnam Conflict, 1964–69', *China Quarterly*, No. 142, 1995, 366–69.
13 Qiang Zhai, *China and the Vietnam Wars, 1950–1975* (Chapel Hill, NC: University of North Carolina Press, 2000).
14 Sheldon W. Simon, 'China, Vietnam, and ASEAN: The Politics of Polarization', *Asian Survey*, Vol. 19, No. 12, 1979, 1171–88.
15 Charles McGregor, 'China, Vietnam, and the Cambodian Conflict: Beijing's End Game Strategy', *Asian Survey*, Vol. 30, No. 3, 1990, 266–83.
16 Zhiguo Gao, 'The South China Sea: From Conflict to Cooperation?' *Ocean Development and International Law*, Vol. 25, No. 3, 1994, 345–59.
17 For more information, see: Randall L. Schweller, 'Bandwagoning for Profit: Bringing the Revisionist State Back In', *International Security*, Vol. 19, No. 1, 1994, 72–107; Stephen M. Walt, 'Testing Theories of Alliance Formation: The Case of Southwest Asia', *International Organization*, Vol. 42, No. 2, Spring 1988, 275–316.
18 Michael Leifer, 'Chinese Economic Reform and Security Policy: The South China Sea Connection', *Survival*, Vol. 37, No. 2, 1995, 44–59.

19 This is a wide area believed to be rich in hydrocarbon deposits.
20 The Paracel Islands are also called the Xisha Islands in Chinese and the Hoàng Sa Islands in Vietnamese.
21 Choon-ho Park, 'The South China Sea Disputes: Who Owns the Islands and the Natural Resources?', *Ocean Development and International Law*, Vol. 5, No. 1, 1978, 27–59.
22 Stein Tønnesson, 'Vietnam's Objective in the South China Sea: National or Regional Security?', *Contemporary Southeast Asia*, Vol. 22, No. 1, April 2000, 199–220.
23 For an extensive review on China's aims in South-East Asia, see: Sigfrido Burgos and Sophal Ear, 'China's Strategic Interests in Cambodia: Influence and Resources', *Asian Survey*, Vol. 50, No. 3, May/June 2010, 615–39.
24 Mark J. Valencia, 'The Spratly Islands: Dangerous Ground in the South China Sea', *Pacific Review*, Vol. 1, No. 4, 1988, 438–43.
25 Mamdouh G. Salameh, 'China, Oil, and the Risk of Regional Conflict', *Survival*, Vol. 37, No. 4, 1995, 133–46.
26 Jorn Dosch, 'The Spratly Islands Dispute: Order-Building on China's Terms?', *Harvard International Review*, 18 August 2011. Available at: http://hir.harvard.edu/the-spratly-islands-dispute-order-building-on-china-s-terms.
27 US Energy Information Administration, 'South China Sea: Analysis Brief,' Institutional Website. Available at: www.eia.gov/countries/regions-topics.cfm?fips=SCS.
28 More specifically, USGS estimates for the Spratly Islands stand at between 800 and 5,400 (mean 2,500) million barrels of oil and between 7,600 and 55,100 (mean 25,500) of natural gas in undiscovered resources.
29 Jane Perlez, 'Vietnam Law on Contested Islands Draws China's Ire', *New York Times*, 21 June 2012.
30 Ibid.
31 For more information, see: 'Vietnam Defends Spratly Gas Project', *New York Times*, 12 April 2007.
32 Leszek Buszynski, 'The South China Sea: Oil, Maritime Claims, and U.S.–China Strategic Rivalry', *Washington Quarterly*, Vol. 35, No. 2, 2012, 139–56.
33 For further details, see: Zhiguo Gao and Bing Bing Jia, 'The Nine-Dash Line in the South China Sea: History, Status, and Implications', *American Journal of International Law*, Vol. 107, No. 1, January 2013, 98–124.
34 Florian Dupuy and Pierre-Marie Dupuy, 'A Legal Analysis of China's Historic Rights Claim in the South China Sea', *American Journal of International Law*, Vol. 107, No. 1, January 2013, 124–41.
35 Marko Milivojevic, 'The Spratly and Paracel Islands Conflict', *Survival*, Vol. 31, No. 1, 1989, 70–78.
36 Lee Cordner, 'The Spratly Islands Dispute and the Law of the Sea', *Ocean Development and International Law*, Vol. 25, No. 1, 1994, 61–74.
37 Nguyen Hong Thao and Ramses Amer, 'A New Legal Arrangement for the South China Sea?' *Ocean Development and International Law*, Vol. 40, No. 4, 2009, 333–49.
38 Nien-Tsu Alfred Hu, 'South China Sea: Troubled Waters or a Sea of Opportunity?', *Ocean Development and International Law*, Vol. 41, No. 3, 2010, 203–13.
39 Mohd Aminul Karim, 'The South China Sea Disputes: Is High Politics Overtaking?' *Pacific Focus*, Vol. 28, No. 1, April 2013, 99–119.

Part III
Conclusion

8 Power projection

Introduction

The power transition theory, which contends that the danger of full-scale war is greatest when a rising dissatisfied challenger threatens resolutely to overtake a declining satisfied hegemon, has been quoted in the literature and brought to the attention of scholars in order to analyse the economic rise of China, its subsequent military build-up and the likelihood of confrontations with Japan or the USA. While this theory is informed by the experiences of other major world powers and pertinent theories regarding international politics and foreign relations—such as those concerning extended deterrence, preventive war and democratic peace—it is frequently used as a tool to compare and contrast scenarios, and to orient policy-makers on perspectives that draw from contemporary power challenges.[1] In applying this and other relevant theories to the ongoing situation in the South China Sea between China and its neighbours, and the alliance of some actors with the USA, it is believed that China, when all factors are taken into consideration, is unlikely to instigate a confrontation with the USA, and that while military conflict over the South China Sea is possible, this is more likely to be due to China's inability to prevent US involvement than its willingness to provoke the USA.

Theories are useful analytical tools that help us understand the complex world we live in and its infinitely interrelated connections and ties. However, theories are not reality, and in using these tools and other mechanisms for the purposes of decision-making, the world has witnessed its fair share of dismal outcomes based on faulty facts, improper advice, unclear objectives and wrong assumptions. In fact, there is evidence to suggest that governments draw poor analogies from their past experiences. Political leaders get into difficulties when they start with 'a solution seeking a problem'. In typical analogical thinking, they search their repertoire of past experiences for analogies to current crises, conflicts or situations that they are trying to address. In some cases, however, political leaders begin with a solution which they advocate or prefer (e.g. threats, containment, etc.); perhaps a policy instrument or initiative that has been successful for them. That is to say, some leaders search for new crises/problems to which they can apply that solution. The

122   *Conclusion*

drawback is that, sometimes, this type of problem-finding or solution-fitting can be misleading and highly problematic when confronted with rapidly changing contexts and when dealing with unpredictable countries that are prone to misinterpretation. This being the case, it might be wise to consider that not only is China interested in fisheries, oil, gas and minerals, and in diminishing US and Japanese influence in Asia, but also the Government has been waiting for decades to settle old scores with old foes, and that China is using the disputes in the East and South China Seas to make the USA come to the East and not China go to the West. It may just be that analogies, formulations and theories are not at all good at revealing hidden agendas, bitter resentments and envy.

Analysts and scholars have stated that despite trepidation about Chinese belligerence in the South China Sea, the Chinese Government's absolute control of the Spratly Islands would not offset its poor power projection capability.[2] It is maintained in certain academic-military circles that the Spratly Islands are not strategically significant, especially given that they are located so far south from the main sea routes used by freight ships and megatankers. A military engagement in the high seas to defend them would drain, not enhance, China's power projection capability. It could, in effect, expose the weaknesses of the Chinese Navy, its inexperience and its inability to harmoniously orchestrate multiple military units to achieve a single purpose.[3]

Contain or engage China? And what outcomes can we expect?

The debate over containment versus engagement lies at the heart of narratives analysing relations between China and the USA. These narratives have centred on the development and deployment of the US Administration's policy for handling a rising power and a potential rival in Asia. Those who support containment believe that China will rise to become a truculent power and thus will create considerable instability in Asia that could, in turn, affect long-standing US interests in the region. The argument is that as China accumulates economic, military and political power it will gain the capacity and intent to bring to fruition a number of maritime, territorial and political plans. In order to curb these plans, the idea is for the USA to respond to Chinese advancements by reinforcing partnerships in East and South-East Asia, building alliances with peripheral actors and networks (e.g. ASEAN, Australia and Singapore), and strengthening US military presence in Asian sub-regions, particularly at its bases in Guam, Japan, South Korea and within the South China Sea. On the other hand, those who pursue engagement posit that while it is true that the Chinese apparatus is becoming stronger and more assertive, China's ambitions continue to evolve as the country accommodates itself to changing contexts. Engagers turn to psychology and warn that the adoption of pre-emptive and defensive policies runs the risk of instilling anger, doubt, fear, suspicion and nationalism, which combined could eventually create a self-realizing prediction: if the USA labels China as the enemy, soon people will assume that it is so and it will become one. The engagers differ from those advocating containment in that they call for increased collaboration and co-operation, more interconnected economic ties, and a number of ententes ranging from climate change to regional security, from democratization to human rights, and the maximization of power, whatever the source, to do the most good in the world and in East and South-East Asia.[4]

East Asia and South-East Asia are characterized by a number of contemporary changes, reconfigurations and shifts that make them more prone to dangers, threats and instability. These modulations include widespread maritime and territorial disputes that mix energy security and non-renewable natural resource issues; the search for post-colonial identity and fervent nationalism; weak institutionalization of security frameworks; increasing but still relatively low levels of real economic interdependence between subregions in the Asian continent; cultural, political and social heterogeneity; tangibly uneven distributions of economic, military and political power between and within countries; and significant rebalancing of power among core and peripheral actors in the international arena. With the above in mind, and believing that this is indeed the case, analysts, observers and scholars in the East and West agree that international instability is more likely to occur in East Asia and South-East Asia that in Central Asia or Western Europe.[5]

The modern security dilemma theory states that doubt, compunction, mistrust and suspicion between two or more potential adversaries can easily develop into aggression, threats and reciprocal tensions when few or no disadvantages or disincentives really exist to avoid these outcomes, especially within an anarchic and uncertain international system. If we apply this theory to the dynamics provoked by China's actions in the East and South China Seas, and combine it with the presence of Japan and the USA in the region, it is easy to deduce that this situation increases the likelihood that tension and retaliation will rapidly follow. These waves of instability are likely to be magnified by the absence of an overwhelming military power; one strong enough to ensure the maintenance of peace in the region.[6]

The next section will examine the projection of power by countries, China's use of power to achieve its goals, the Chinese Government's approach to the Korean Peninsula and the intricacies of Chinese politics.

On the uses of power: as a tool or weapon?

Countries use power to achieve goals and outcomes. Power, with respect to international relations, relates to capabilities, control, influence and is a goal in itself. In many instances, one can match 'powers' with a country's goals or outcomes. For instance, I can match economic power with prosperity; military power with security; and political power with sovereignty. Of course, sources of power can be matched differently, and often are. Throughout the ages power has been used for many purposes. There is some truth in the saying: *power in the hands of a wise person is a tool, but power in the hands of*

124   *Conclusion*

a foolish person is a weapon. Let's now turn our attention to the projection of force or power by countries.

In diplomacy, military studies and political science, the term 'power projection' is used to refer to the capacity of a country to undertake expeditionary warfare. Put simply, it is a real option exercised by countries (some, but not all) to bully, coerce, compel, intimidate or pressure other countries into doing something they would otherwise not do. In modern times, power projection is used to support an initiative or to implement a policy by means of force, or the threat of the use of force, in geographical areas distant from the territory where it originates. This ability to project power in a landscape where the world is shared with other countries is a crucial feature of a country's power in international relations. To be exact, any country able to instruct its military forces to venture outside of the internationally recognized bounds of its territory, might be said to have some degree of power projection capability. However, it is worth clarifying that 'power projection' is mainly used with reference to a country able to deploy a full military force possessing a world-wide capability.[7]

In applying power projection to China it is clear that one can safely make strong linkages between economic, military and political power to the search for peace, prosperity, security and sovereignty.[8] In this regard, China is no different from the United Kingdom, France, Israel, Japan, and the USA. All these countries are accumulating and exercising powers to attain goals and achieve outcomes. As noted in previous chapters, China has been using its sustained economic growth to accumulate foreign exchange reserves (mainly US dollars but other currencies too) and is strategically investing these revenues or profits in several areas, countries, industries, sectors and segments. These investment decisions are not only aligned with country goals and desires, but are also informed by economic, energy, foreign, military and social policies formulated by the current Central Committee of the Central Communist Party (CCP). More precisely, the Chinese Government is fully aware that free-flowing inputs are necessary to keep producing outputs for export and domestic consumption, and that energy sources, natural resources and raw materials are critical and vital inputs that are prerequisites for economic and financial success. These inputs come by air, land, and water, but some can only come by water owing to the cost of transportation, safety and volume. The ships and vessels that move the bulk of this cargo must pass through the Strait of Malacca and the Singapore Strait in order to reach the South China Sea on its way to Chinese ports. Recognizing this, CCP officials support and validate the use of hard-earned reserves to build up and modernize the military, and to deploy military forces to more forcefully assert control of the South China Sea as a critical passageway for inputs into the Chinese economy.[9]

Tellingly, Chinese officials have said that the CCP is fully aware that the People's Liberation Army will not reach a point of excellence and international recognition if economic growth diminishes, and this is an assessment that seems to inform the Government's strategic patience with Taiwan (i.e.

indefinitely waiting for reunification) and with the settlement of numerous disputes in the South China Sea.[10]

China and the Korean Peninsula: learning to live side by side

The East Asian region is undergoing a period of political transition. Two new leaders have taken office in the Korean peninsula: Kim Jong Un was declared the Supreme Leader of North Korea in December 2011, and Chung Hong-Won was installed as Prime Minister of South Korea in December 2012. They are two different leaders for two vastly different countries that once were united. The Chinese Government is aware that it must contend with powerful personalities and with policy-makers who are informed by unique personal experiences and backgrounds. As things stand today, the leaders in North and South Korea will use 'hard' and 'soft' power not only to gain political currency internally and externally, but also to differentiate their leadership styles from those exercised by their predecessors. Kim Jong Un bears the burden of having to meet the high expectations of North Koreans, as well as following his celebrated father and grandfather. The young North Korean leader has not wasted time in trying to leave a legacy worth remembering by the citizenry used to decades of belligerence, condemnation, marginalization, sanctions and totalitarianism. Both leaders in the Korean peninsula are finding the world-wide attention and the exercising of power irresistably seductive; and the expectation in China is that the delicate entente that reigned between the North and South is close to collapse.[11]

In March 2013 it was reported that the North Korean leader had cut off the last remaining military telephone hotline to South Korea. The North Korean Government even accused President Park Geun-Hye of South Korea of 'pursuing the same hardline policy of her predecessor that the North blamed for a prolonged chill in inter-Korean relations'. North Korea's decision to cut off military hotlines with the Government in Seoul was taken seriously by South Korean officials because the two Koreas have used these few telephone connections 'to control daily cross-border traffic of workers and cargo traveling to the North Korean border town of Kaesong'.[12] Kim Jong Un has adopted a more agressive tone in response to UN sanctions (which were imposed after North Korea carried out a series of nuclear tests) and has expressed anger over joint military exercises effected between the USA and South Korea close to its border.[13] In response to heightened tensions, the US Administration and its military announced that it was increasing its missile defences on the US West Coast and Alaska, citing the threat of North Korea's KN-08 missiles. The Chinese Government, for its part, kept open communication lines with North and South Korea, and the international community expected China to act as an honest broker—a fair, neutral and unbiased arbitrator that is 'soft' with people and 'hard' on issues.

A potential crisis with the two Koreas would be bad for China: regional instability, vulnerability to critical sea routes, impediments to develop

126 *Conclusion*

strategic oil and gas deposits in the South China Sea, disrupted commerce and trade, potential immigration issues, and having to act as an arbitrator while risking an upset in the status quo. Senior CCP officials have stated that the acrimonious exchanges between North and South Korea are interpreted as a signalling mechanism to express grievances and to find unwritten diplomatic understandings without having to show weakness in public. However, scholars have warned that a continuation of meaningless chatter may lead to the exhaustion of diplomatic options, and that strategic ties among participating actors could erode faster than expected. Moreover, beneath the surface of relations between China and North Korea, the two countries share few common interests. It is said that 'the two countries can hardly agree to any matters between them, be it historical ties, ideological stances, political and economic programs, or diplomatic interactions ... heralding an uncertain future for the bilateral relation, and thus may further complicate the security situation in the Korean Peninsula'.[14]

The next section will examine Chinese internal politics and the complex sociocultural dynamics that inform some of the decisions taken with regard to foreign and military policies.

Ruminations on Chinese politics and how they tie with projection of power

During his first year in office, the new Chinese President, Xi Jinping, was expected to focus on domestic issues, including eliminating corruption,[15] addressing the growing income divide and rebalancing the Chinese economy. These are daunting tasks in a region experiencing dynamism. It is by no means certain that the Chinese people will accept the outcome of such experiments, and whether the populace will be be given an input on the direction being taken by the country. However, in China, a country without freedom of speech, asking citizens objectively to evaluate their leaders' performance is akin to giving voters no choice at all. Interestingly, surveys conducted in 2003, and that were cited in *How East Asians View Democracy*, revealed that 67% of the Chinese public polled said that democracy is 'suitable for our country now' and 72.3% said that they believed that a democratic government is 'desirable for our country'.[16] It remains to be seen if democracy takes hold in China.

While China's President will be very busy dealing with complex and difficult internal affairs,[17] he will also be forced to keep foreign policy constantly in mind. The former President, Hu Jintao, took office at a time when China was triumphant: hosting the Forum on Asia-Pacific Economic Cooperation and the 2008 Olympics for the first time, and winning approval for membership of the World Trade Organization. However, Xi Jinping's transition to power has been rife with uncertainties and a challenging foreign policy environment. It is noteworthy that there have been loud calls for democracy in China, with demands for reform and progressivism within the CCP gaining strength, and aided, for the most part, by recurrent calls from millions of Chinese citizens, who now have internet access, for accountability, honesty, transparency and competent leadership.

The most pressing challenge for the CCP in 2013 was to quell anti-China sentiments among the population. The Chinese President has taken steps to achieve this. He has revived active diplomacy and conciliation in order to emphasize his desire for 'win-win' outcomes and to remind neighbours that China is the engine of growth for the region. Yet, even as political bickering with neighbours continues, China has advanced its plans for a regional free trade agreement with South Korea and Japan. This pursuit of commercialism and entrepreneurship is ironic, since China presents rather dissonant stances: it functions under autocratic capitalism yet its political system has permitted a few entrepreneurial politicians to experiment with federalism, policy innovations[18] and subsidiarity, which are some of the foundational features of a modern, functioning democracy.

However, such public announcements heralding comity and peace do not augur a return to a gentler, kinder China. The new CCP leadership urges the need for a great rejuvenation of the Chinese nation. The Government remains steadfast in safeguarding the country's security, sovereignty and territorial integrity. Since 2011 Chinese regional policies have been increasingly assertive, and this reflects the intention of a country that is bent on control and independence, which in turn suggests that some CCP members may be yet more authoritarian and conservative. In fact, there is no evidence that Chinese officials with good economic and foreign policy track records are more likely to be promoted to the top than those who perform poorly. It seems that patronage is still prevalent.

If some CCP members are determined upon armed conflict and hegemony, Xi Jinping will be forced to check these actors and work on integrating disparate narratives that undermine a coherent and goal-driven foreign policy. For instance, provincial governments and the Public Security Bureau have been accused of undertaking some of China's most provocative moves in the South China Sea. Also, international perceptions of Chinese foreign policy are often shaped by incorrect information and misleading comments made in irresponsible online entries, by cyber hackers, intellectual property criminals, and marginalized, low-ranking employees of state-owned enterprises.

Few commentators focus on China's future identity; that is, how does China perceive itself—as a force for conflict or peace? Thus, one of the biggest questions confronting Chinese leaders is what type of power they would like China to become. For example, with regard to trade and investments, will leaders seek to align China with accepted international norms or will they attempt to reform current practices? Or, in terms of cyber security, where norms are still evolving, how interested will leaders be in engaging or even assuming a commanding role in developing acceptable standards? The international community wants to believe that China is fully committed to non-intrusiveness, a peaceful and safe development and 'win-win' foreign policies. The new leadership

128 *Conclusion*

needs to make substantive assertions that help the nation to thrive, instead of harming it with threats and bluster. This could be difficult since the CCP's Central Committee is composed of fiefdoms in which members compete for credit, power and recognition, often in concealed skirmishes that make their own performance appear superior and those of their rivals inferior.[19]

The way forward: less corruption, more democracy

Globally, there is little doubt that autocracies, taken as a whole, are far more corrupt than democracies. In fact, a 2004 report by Berlin-based Transparency International[20] revealed that the leaders who most extensively looted their countries' resources during the preceding two decades were President Suharto of Indonesia, President Ferdinand Marcos of the Philippines, and Mobutu Sese Seko, the former President of the Democratic Republic of the Congo.

China, just to be clear, is not lenient on corruption. In fact, the CCP routinely orders the execution of corrupt officials. The problem lies on the absence of checks and balances on the power of government officials, and on the well-known lack of transparency and a free press. Meanwhile, a 2007 report by the Asian Development Bank[21] estimated that 300m. Chinese suffer from food-borne diseases annually. It is believed that many of these woes are connected to poor management and corruption, which in themselves sometimes lead to collapsed buildings and bridge failures, as well as chemical factory spills that contaminate and poison China's environment.

Western commentators have observed that China's leaders are missing the opportunity to mix economic well-being and popularity among citizens to pursue a proactive reform plan to achieve a gradual, ordered and peaceful transition to democracy, while avoiding the disruptions and upheavals experienced in North Africa and the Middle East. Nancy Qian, a Yale University economist, supports this line of argument, and found evidence to suggest that the introduction of village elections in China has improved accountability and expenditure on public services. Certainly, in the past few decades China has made tremendous commercial, economic and social gains, but it has also proved ineffective at culling graft, minimizing environmental damage, reducing income inequality and stimulating inclusive growth. It is indeed interesting that the CCP has not adopted any genuine political reforms since 1989. It has mainly relied on high growth rates and widespread employment to perpetuate its rule. However, stability is not achieved through oppression and repression but through greater economic and political openness.

China has already crossed what some social scientists believe to be the per caput income threshold beyond which most societies inevitably begin to democratize, that is, between $4,000 and $6,000. Moreover, of the 25 countries with a higher gross domestic product than China's that are not free or partially free, 21 of them are sustained by exploitation of their natural resources.[22] China needs to open up to stronger non-governmental organizations, which would help the Chinese Government to deliver better services; a more independent media, which would keep corruption allegations in check; and intraparty democratic elections, which would help air the party's unethical acts and unbecoming demeanor. Surely, it would be far better for the political system to change gradually and in a controlled manner, rather than through popular uprisings or a violent revolution.

Concluding remarks

The South China Sea is traversed by critical sea routes that connect Africa, Central Asia, Europe and India with East and South-East Asia. As these vital sea routes facilitate the transport of critical energy sources, natural resources and raw materials, the Chinese Government has taken intense interest in controlling and protecting sea lanes in areas it deems to be its own. The Government's projection of power in East and South-East Asia, and in the East and South China Seas, needs to be understood as China's attempt to promote prosperity, enhance security and uphold sovereignty as the CCP contends with a more important role in regional and international affairs. Additionally, Chinese officials stress that the increase in China's maritime capabilities is intended to build capacity for disaster relief, humanitarian assistance and overseas peace-keeping operations.

The CCP leadership must learn that interstate reciprocity is based largely on faith and goodwill rather than on hard evidence, and therefore it is wise to present one's foreign policy with modesty. For a group of states to interact constructively, an unspoken compact dictates that ambition is acceptable, but if a state plays harshly, other states will unite against it.

The establishment of effective and reliable interstate communication networks between civilian and military agencies is absolutely critical because without them policy formulation and implementation aimed at maintaining strategic interests would be lost in a plethora of details.

Senior CCP leaders must seek counsel and perspective to conclude whether the USA and its allies are either containing or engaging, and this conclusion may give us some indication of what lies ahead. China's ascent should be peaceful and constructive, which is why the overarching rhetoric concerning the disputes in the South China Sea calls for co-operation. Also, it is worth remembering that leaders of countries succumb to the temptation to deceive in order to advance personal and national interests. They lie, cheat and give false impressions when it is to their advantage. However, this deception tends to harm society at large and generates suspicion, which in turn undermines trust and leads to the breakdown of social co-operation. In view of this, the international community of nation states must demand that its leaders cultivate a disposition for honesty and truthfulness, and society must praise and value those leaders who have the right attitudes and right desires to enable their countries to contribute positively to the world.

130   *Conclusion*

Notes

1 Steve Chan, *China, the US, and the Power-Transition Theory: A Critique* (New York: Routledge, 2007).
2 Chinese military analysts have concluded that tech-enabled logistics and sustained power projection are potential vulnerabilities in modern warfare given the need for the co-ordination of transportation and communication networks.
3 Aaron L. Friedberg, 'The Future of US-China Relations: Is Conflict Inevitable?' *International Security*, Vol. 30, No. 2, 2005, 7–45; Michael O'Hanlon, 'Why China Cannot Conquer Taiwan', *International Security*, Vol. 25, No. 2, 2000, 51–86.
4 Robert S. Ross, 'Beijing as a Conservative Power', *Foreign Affairs*, Vol. 76, No. 2, 1997, 33–44.
5 For more information, see the following essays: Aaron L. Friedberg, 'Ripe for Rivalry: Prospects for Peace in a Multipolar Asia', *International Security*, Vol. 18, No. 3, 1993–94, 5–33; Richard K. Betts, 'Wealth, Power, and Instability', *International Security*, Vol. 18, No. 3, 1993–94, 34–77; Stephen Van Evera, 'Primed for Peace: Europe After the Cold War', *International Security*, Vol. 15, No. 3, 1990–91, 7–57; and James Goldgeier and Michael McFaul, 'A Tale of Two Worlds', *International Organization*, Vol. 46, No. 2, spring 1992, 467–92.
6 Thomas J. Christensen, 'China, the U.S.–Japan Alliance, and the Security Dilemma in East Asia', *International Security*, Vol. 23, No. 4, spring 1999, 49–80; Also, see: Thomas J. Christensen, *Useful Adversaries: Grand Strategy, Domestic Mobilization, and Sino-American Conflict, 1947–1958* (Princeton, NJ: Princeton University Press, 1996).
7 David Slater and Peter J. Taylor, *The American Century: Consensus and Coercion in the Projection of American Power* (Malden, MA: Blackwell, 1999); John J. Mearsheimer, *The Tragedy of Great Power Politics* (New York: W. W. Norton & Company, 2001); Robert Gilpin, *War and Change in World Politics* (New York: Cambridge University Press, 1981).
8 Robert S. Ross and Zhu Feng, *China's Ascent: Power, Security, and the Future of International Politics* (New York: Cornell University Press, 2008).
9 Alastair Johnston, 'Is China a Status Quo Power?' *International Security*, Vol. 27, No. 4, 2003, 5–56.
10 For example, see: Major General Yang Chengyu, 'Logistics Support for Regional Warfare', in *Chinese Views of Future Warfare*, ed. Michael Pillsbury (Washington, DC: National Defense University, 1997).
11 David Shambaugh, 'China and the Korean Peninsula: Playing for the Long Term', *The Washington Quarterly*, Vol. 26, No. 2, 2003, 43–56. The author argues that 'halting North Korea's nuclear program is not the ultimate end that China hopes to achieve. China's calculations, interests, and goals are more long term and complicated.'
12 Choe Sang-Hun, 'North Korea Cuts Off the Remaining Military Hot Lines With South Korea', *New York Times*, 27 March 2013. Available at: www.nytimes.com/2013/03/28/world/asia/north-korea-shuts-last-remaining-hotline-to-south.html.
13 The United States has expressed its commitment to uphold the 1953 and 1954 mutual defence treaties with South Korea and Japan, respectively.
14 You Ji, 'China and North Korea: A Fragile Relationship of Strategic Convenience', *Journal of Contemporary China*, Vol. 10, No. 28, 2001, 387–98.
15 Unchecked corruption, cronyism, nepotism and abuse of power undermine the popular legitimacy of the CCP. In fact, senior Chinese officials have issued dire warnings that corruption and cronyism could lead to the collapse of the party and the state. However, uncovering corruption, cronyism and nepotism require free-flowing information and freedom of the press. That leaves only a sobering conclusion: truth, in a single-party political system, is scarce.

16 Yun-han Chu, Larry Diamond, Andrew Nathan and Doh Chull Shin, *How East Asians View Democracy* (New York: Columbia University Press, 2008).

17 Most recently, mighty China is exhibiting problems: widespread corruption, slowing economic growth, inadequate provision of social services and a growing divide between rich and poor.

18 Without political reform, historical tragedies such as land collectivization, the Great Leap Forward, and the Cultural Revolution may happen again, but on a much grander scale.

19 The Central Committee of the CCP appoints candidates to many of the most powerful positions in China, including the General Secretary and the members of the Politburo, Standing Committee and Central Military Commission.

20 'Global Corruption Report 2004: Political Corruption', (Berlin: Transparency International, March 2004). Available at: www.transparency.org/whatwedo/pub/global_corruption_report_2004_political_corruption.

21 'Dignity, Disease and Dollars: Asia's Urgent Sanitation Challenge', (Manila: Asian Development Bank, August 2007); *Key Indicators for Asia and the Pacific 2007* (Manila: Asian Development Bank, 2007).

22 Yasheng Huang, 'Democratize or Die: Why China's Communists Face Reform or Revolution', *Foreign Affairs*, January/February 2013. Available at: www.foreignaffairs.com/articles/138477/yasheng-huang/democratize-or-die.

9 Resource security

Introduction

When Chinese government and military officials refer to 'resource security' they are talking beyond oil. This is because China's resource needs include natural gas, crude oil, petroleum, diesel, kerosene, jet fuel, rare earths, aluminum, textiles, iron ore, copper, zinc, bauxite, gold, silver, platinum, rubber, timber, coal, nickel, cardboard, soybeans, fertilizers, logs, paper pulp, and plastics, etc. However, in this chapter the word 'resources' refers to raw materials, renewable and non-renewable energy sources, and artificial and natural resources.

China's hunger for energy and resources is creating many problems—nationally, regionally and internationally.[1] Owing to the country's large population, size and commercial weight in terms of imports and exports, China is a major consumer of resources, many of which are in steady decline, or limited, nearly exhausted and non-renewable. This means that as China grows demographically and economically it is also growing its share of resources demanded and used, which translates into other countries struggling to find new deposits or reserves to maintain their economies. US, Brazilian, Chinese, European, Indian and Russian companies are all involved in this search for current and potential resources, with China a key player. China perceives Africa, Canada, Central Asia and Latin America[2] as resource-rich areas (i.e. inputs to be imported)[3] and as highly significant markets for Chinese products (i.e. outputs to be exported),[4] which explains why China is unyielding in its desire to control and protect trade-critical sea transit routes along the contested South China Sea.

This global hunt for vital resources has attracted the attention of Eastern and Western commentators. For example, David Zweig and Bi Jianhai tell us that 'a booming domestic economy, rapid urbanization, increased export processing, and the Chinese people's voracious appetite for cars are increasing the country's demand for oil and natural gas, industrial and construction materials, foreign capital and technology'.[5] This acute need to secure inputs and shipping outputs is in part driving China's economic, foreign and military policies.[6] Resource security is critical to China owing to the uneven distribution of resources and fossil fuels around the globe, which inevitably results in

China being dependent on a few African, South American, South-East Asian and Middle Eastern states to supply the country's most basic inputs. Also under consideration by central planners is that the supply of resources may become more vulnerable over the near term due to the growing needs of other emerging economies, such as Brazil, Chile, India, Indonesia, Mexico, Russia, South Africa, South Korea, Thailand and Turkey.[7] Given this tense situation, Chinese government officials at different agencies and ministries have to work together to harmonize the initiatives and policies that support key Chinese goals: economic growth, political party continuation, internal stability, rising living standards, increased trade, regional cohesion and peace, and national security. This harmonization explains why resource security is so intimately linked to defence, economic, energy and foreign policies, while simultaneously reinforcing the numerous ties that China has with external actors—intergovernmental organization, nation states and private companies.[8]

However, it is one thing to need resources and another to secure them. To secure resources China has to locate them, negotiate the terms of trade, sweeten deals, finance purchases, and ship them where they are needed in mainland China. China's unique physical features and the quantities of resources required merit transportation by ships, and these ships have to pass through the South China Sea.

Oil: a scarce input that countries crave

The orthodox neoclassical economic growth model treats essential energy inputs as secondary whereas capital, labour and land are treated as primary factors. This treatment assumes that the role of energy in production is intermediate, neutral and peripheral. On the other hand, from the biophysical and ecological viewpoint, during the process of economic growth, energy plays a central and primary role in determining national incomes. With this in mind, countries that are heavily dependent on energy use will be affected economically by shifts in energy consumption.

China is today the world's second largest energy consumer and a significant emitter of carbon dioxide into the atmosphere. This fact may help us to understand the relationship between oil and gas consumption and economic growth, especially to scholars, the international community, and Chinese society. A national economy and oil supplies go hand in hand in a self-reinforcing cycle: the more the economy grows the more oil it needs. With China still reaching annual gross domestic product (GDP) growth rates of between 7% and 9% this cycle becomes accentuated by Chinese Communist Party (CCP) long-term plans for full employment, low inflation, rising exports, increased domestic consumption and political legitimacy as a result of planned prosperity. For 2013 China set a GDP growth target of 7.5%, and this is a level that economic strategists believe will create sufficient jobs while facilitating the delivery of the structural reforms required to put growth on a more sustainable trajectory.

134   *Conclusion*

As traditional Western hegemons continued to expand and to consolidate economic, military and political power, emerging economies paid attention and learned from the good, bad and advantageous actions, decisions and policies of their peers. China understood early on that European states and the USA achieved success because they leveraged power to attain specific goals: they forged alliances with resource-rich countries and even coerced, manipulated or invaded others to plunder their precious natural resources and energy sources in order to keep the economies running at full speed. The US military presence in the Middle East and Central Asia can be understood as means to more closely oversee energy transport to the oil-addicted West. The guiding rationale that China has learned from highly developed countries is that resource security is an essential component for superpower status and a primary factor for prosperity.[9]

The concept of energy security is tied to resource security in general because cars, trains, trucks, ships and planes needed to transport inputs run on hydrocarbons. In short, energy security can also refer to coal, oil and gas security, and all three are directly linked not only to the well-known relationship between supply and demand, but also to an open, global trading system—the main feature of globalization. Owing to globalized trade, energy security for any given country is more than an economic problem; it is also a diplomatic, military and political issue. China's energy insecurity concerns are related to its dependence on foreign oil, which is traded in international markets as a commodity and its price is influenced by supply and demand dynamics, but also by geopolitics and wars. Given that most oil shipments come to China by sea transport, government officials believe that the control and protection of sea lanes is a state priority, particularly bottlenecks that could be interdicted. The risks of having essential inputs cut off from the Chinese economic engine is deemed a strategic vulnerability,which therefore influences CCP officials in their decisions regarding regional and international relations. Currently, Chinese supply and demand for key energy sources is threatened by imbalances and uncertainties as China engages in conflicts with neighbours over maritime and territorial disputes in the South China Sea, and puts greater pressure on industries to search for alternative sources.[10]

Growth, oil and militarization: the connection with the South China Sea

Resource security is also motivated by internal factors, mainly linked to electricity generation, industrial and manufacturing raw materials, minimizing popular unrest, managing pollution, and strengthening domestic consumption levels. Bankers, financiers, investors and senior officials at the European Union headquarters in Brussels, Belgium, and in the USA remain positive about the future of the Chinese economy, and are also very optimistic about the balanced decisions that will need to be made by CCP leaders, in view of the accelerated rise of a new consumer class in China that demands goods and services as it

Resource security 135

experiences affluence at a level enjoyed in the West. However, Chinese policy-makers will have to rebalance the drivers of growth away from exports and capital investments which could present problems in the future.

By late April 2013 domestic consumption by the large Chinese middle class exercising its purchasing power emerged as the biggest driver of growth. If one were to split the 7.5% GDP growth target it would probably be made up from consumption (4.3%), capital formation (2.2%) and from exports (1.0%). However, the resource-intensive construction sector, which is a major component of domestic consumption, is likely to present problems as commentators have warned of a growing housing bubble in Chinese cities, mainly fuelled by the expectation that economic growth will continue to draw people from rural areas into urban settings en masse. It is worth highlighting that anxiety is creeping up as a result of this centrally planned boom in apartment and office buildings because this economic activity is still largely dependent on investment spending, which is currently worth around 50% of GDP.

As one considers the influence of internal dynamics such as rising domestic consumption, essential inputs for factories and industries, and the need to import the goods that the Chinese are consuming, it is much easier to understand that resource security is more than securing deliveries of oil and gas, and much more than the development and financing of alternative energy sources. According to the CCP, resource security is tantamout to national security; it can be equated with state survival and political legitimacy. As members of the Central Committee of the CCP are selected and tasked to attain state goals and objectives—China needs to secure resources nationally, regionally and internationally, and protect them during transport until they reach Chinese seaports, to ensure that the basic elements of state survival are in place, and that no foreign power determined upon crushing China will ever think about targeting resources as a way to maintain a unipolar world order. To protect the country, its shores and the safe passage of vessels through trade-critical sea routes, the Chinese Government has been strengthening and modernizing its military, and this pursuit of militarization is causing anxiety.

World audiences have learned that China has utilized its expanded fleet of civilian and military vessels (i.e. maritime law enforcement units) to dissuade its South-East Asian neighbours from trying fully to exploit resources in the South China Sea. This they have done even when the United Nations Convention on the Law of the Sea gives nations the right to exploit resources within their 200-mile exclusive economic zones. All claimants to territories and surrounding waters in the South China Sea perceive China's actions as coercive and provocative, and as countering the collective interest of the region in promoting prosperity, maintaining peace and stability, and the free flow of maritime trade that has been pivotal to South-East Asia's success. The Association of Southeast Asian Nations (ASEAN) and the USA have noticed that the Chinese Government has been ordering the commanders of maritime surveillance vessels to supervise traffic in and around the East and South China Seas. Some of these missions stretch beyond their traditional role of

136   *Conclusion*

patrolling territorial waters, and these actions worry disputants because the more boats are in the water on patrol, the higher the risk of an accident that might escalate into a full regional crisis.[11]

Launching a sea consensus: China, neighbours and the search for resource security

China views the disputes in the South China Sea from different angles. One of these angles is the running of a proxy blockade by the USA without having to be present. China believes that US efforts to establish more naval bases in South-East Asia and to build the military capacity of the Philippines and Vietnam are the US Administration's method of strengthening its ability to confront China's maritime agencies and the navy of the People's Liberation Army. Without doubt, the escalating competition between China and the USA has been noticed by other regional leaders and diplomats as both countries try to assert their influence on a region that is already burgeoning with growth and entrepreneurship. While the US Administration itself is not directly engaged in the exploration and extraction of oil, gas and mineral deposits in the South China Sea, a number of private US multinational companies are. In addition, the USA remains steadfast in its support of regional allies, and it wishes to see a South-East Asia that is not dominated by a single country, but more like an open trading block in which countries co-operate to achieve common goals. China does not see this situation as one that aligns with its regional ambitions, which is why the Chinese Government is reluctant to abide by any Code of Conduct or dispute resolution framework. As long as the disputes remain unresolved, the spate of accusations and recriminations will continue to drive littoral countries to acquire greater military capabilities (e.g. long-distance missiles and warships), to foster increased tensions in diplomatic, political and military circles, and to initiate regional instability.[12]

With this in mind, resource security takes on a more pragmatic approach, one that hinges on the deployment of Chinese state-owned enterprises and government agencies in search of inputs that can be secured, processed and transported where they are needed. This approach is also convenient because it depends on the successful exploitation of resources that exist nearby. It is known that China is using the Mekong River to produce hydroelectricity, and that it 'rejects the concept of a water-sharing arrangements or joint, rules-based management of common resources'.[13] China has acquired land outright in Cambodia and has also secured exploitation rights to its forests and jungles.[14] Meanwhile, the Chinese Government has supported the military junta in Myanmar for some time in exchange for access to the Andaman Sea and for permission to build deep-sea ports that would in effect eliminate the passage of ships through the Strait of Malacca and the South China Sea.[15]

However, the Chinese Government is also looking further afield. In many African countries Chinese aid is linked to preferential agreements, oil shipments, mineral concessions and resource exploitation rights.[16]

If the Chinese Government has been able to enforce resource-securing accords, deals and pacts with neighbours either by friendly means or coercion, who is to say that it will not accomplish the same in its surrounding waters? Over the past two decades the steady expansion of Chinese power in the South China Sea has been a highly significant development in the region, especially after China gained control of the Paracel Islands.[17] The Chinese Government is forming strategic alliances, tactical partnerships and military relationships along trade-critical sea routes from the Middle East to the South China Sea in ways that suggest offensive and defensive positioning to oversee and protect China's resource interests, but also to serve broad security objectives (e.g. defending land, borders and frontiers). Denny Roy explains that 'despite Japan's present economic strength, a future Chinese hegemony in East Asia is a strong possibility',[18] and other scholars include South-East Asia in those plans. This augurs a situation in which ASEAN members resist coercion and control, while China presses yet more aggressively to have a region defined very much to its own advantage.

In summary, the South China Sea is the location for some of the most relevant trends in Asia-Pacific: the rising power of China in the region; the USA's rebalancing towards Asia; and ASEAN's increasing desire to shape the regional security milieu in favour of collective well-being.

Chinese resource security policies and manoeuvres

The Chinese Government's selfish acts in the South China Sea occur because it regards this body of water merely as a source of raw materials and energy sources, and because the country's leaders lack an ethical framework that encourages them to view it otherwise. The argument of Chinese officials is that historical rights bestow China with sovereignty over this vast area, yet they fail to understand that the South China Sea is to be shared fully with others, especially since collective prosperity, peace and security depend upon it.

However, this selfishness is not limited to resources in the South China Sea. Australian scholars note that the resource security policies enacted by the Chinese Government since 2005 have sought to address current record high iron ore prices through the use of foreign investment to sponsor new market entrants and the formation of an import cartel amongst the Chinese steel firms and that while these capital investments and cartel-like manoeuvres 'have catalyzed significant changes to the ownership and pricing structures of the Asia-Pacific iron ore market, they have carried only mixed benefits for the Chinese steel industry's resource security'.[19] This behaviour is illustrative of China's intention to shape trading environments on its own terms.

The pattern of accelerated economic growth and intensity of resource utilization in China are thought to be the principal factors behind increased energy and metal prices since 2003. There were immediate cyclical determinants that forced energy and metal prices to rise even more, and this happened because traders did not take into consideration the strong supply and

138   *Conclusion*

demand dynamics that arose as China took to the markets. It is believed that as China continues to grow, it will put further pressure on resource usage. In fact, the heightened intensity of resource utilization by all economic sectors (especially those experiencing rapid growth) is supported by increasing capital investments, increasing production of goods for domestic consumption and exports, and the increasing percentages of people moving to urban settings. It was hoped that growth and resource usage would dwindle in 2013 as GDP targets were modulated to accommodate external and internal economic conditions, and thus the expectation was that global commodity pricing would plateau and even descend as adjustments took place. The connection between national growth rates and global environmental damages at the hands of resource extractions is of concern to economists and conservationists since China and other rapidly growing emerging economies are narrowing the few options left to manage collective goods.[20]

J. D. Wilson, a lecturer at Murdoch University in Perth, Australia, argues that since 2005 China and other import-dependent resource consumers have been signing free trade agreements (FTAs) to handle resource security concerns. The rationale behind this strategic move suggests that resource-linked FTAs could significantly improve a given country's availability of resources internationally via targeted negotiations with large suppliers, extension of guarantees and protection of overseas capital investments, and trade liberalization with the aim of buying large amounts at lower prices. However, there are problems with this approach. Large suppliers of critical resources and inputs are not always willing to sign binding agreements with buyers that are located in resource-intensive sectors or regions. Suppliers naturally are anxious that buyers will use their contracts and buying power to lower prices further and to exact better terms and conditions on trade transactions. This indicates that FTAs are limited in their ability to enhance resource security, especially given that large suppliers are subjected to political pressures in their own countries. The drive for FTAs in the Asian region is unlikely to improve resource security.[21]

With this in mind, civilian and military CCP officials have been compelled to devise multipronged strategies in order to secure resources, in addition to strengthening China's ability to protect resources from origin to destination. Therefore, China's militarization and new-found assertiveness in the region must be understood as policies intended to serve multiple objectives.

ABC: assertiveness, balancing and control

Let's now turn our attention to this so-called Chinese assertiveness that has been regarded as the conventional wisdom in academic and scholarly circles since 2010. A. I. Johnston at Harvard University, USA, undertook a study of seven cases in Chinese diplomacy that lie at the centre of this assertiveness narrative and found that 'in some instances China's policy has not changed; in others, it is actually more moderate; and in still others, it is a predictable reaction to changed external conditions. In only one case—maritime disputes—does one see more assertive Chinese rhetoric and behavior'.[22] China's boldness in the South China Sea seems to be an accurate depiction of its behaviour because senior CCP officials and strategists are informed by reports that since 2008 the USA has been transformed from a commanding, mighty entity to a frugal, weak superpower.[23] In fact, F. G. Hoffman suggests that 'the slope of American decline is so steep that some analysts fail to accord *primus inter alles* status to a country that will retain the world's largest economy for at least a decade and whose military power roughly outspends the rest of the world and still bestrides the globe'.[24] These narratives, emanating from reputable Western entities, are the ones that empower China to behave vigorously in its immediate sphere of influence. Furthermore, the Chinese Government believes that the USA's continued military presence in East and South-East Asia is a waste of resources given that the probability of a full-scale war is low, especially when both China and the USA consider the economic and financial impacts that would arise from such an event.

China may as well opt for a balancing strategy, which many believe is taking place in the South China Sea with the USA's allies. Balancing is a soft strategic approach that embraces ambiguity, instability, regional competition and multipolarity as geopolitical facts of life. The Chinese Government seeks to build strong relationships and partnerships with ASEAN members to achieve this, especially since the approach avoids the use of military power to reconfigure the politics of the region; instead it relies on allies and partners to contain threats and to advance selected interests.[25]

When it comes to control, obfuscation and the exertion of outright influence, Chinese officialdom has shown signs of mastery. The ongoing maritime and territorial disputes initiated by China have created tensions among countries bordering the South China Sea. These conflicts are perceived as being driven by the CCP's scheme to gain access to hydrocarbon resources lying beneath the seabed. However, because these disputes have been accompanied by estimates of significant oil and gas deposits, they have encouraged disputants to be inflexible in their claims, which in turn have negatively impacted bilateral relations and have fomented mistrust in the region. An analysis by N. Owen and C. Schofield revealed that 'constraints on production mean that disputed South China Sea oil and gas may only constitute a small part of the solution to Southeast Asia's growing energy security challenges, and does not have the capacity to reverse the trend of growing reliance on imports to the region. Escalating demand for imported hydrocarbons would instead reinforce the importance of sea-lane security to regional energy security'.[26] This said, China's motives are multifactorial: resource security, potential income from resource sales, deflecting US and Japanese influence in Asia, being perceived as the core (and not as peripheral) point of contact to address regional challenges, and protecting the lifeline of China's economic success: free and open trade with the world. As for disputants, those with claims in the South China Sea are focused primarily on the associated benefits of any hydrocarbon

140 *Conclusion*

deposits for their potential to improve energy security, along with the opportunity to generate revenues from exports. It would therefore seem reasonable to expect that China would move swiftly to conduct assessments of oil and gas deposits to determine if those potential sources meet national resource security objectives, and if they are worth fighting for.[27]

Concluding remarks

The realms we call political, monetary, economic, sociocultural, military, and legal interlock to form what we call the fundamental basis of state sovereignty—that when packed together they constitute the domain from which all national discourses and narratives emerge to define state behaviours and positions. China's unified domain is different from that of Japan and Vietnam, which is why there is a need to understand the motives that influence the Chinese Government.

From a practical standpoint, if East and South-East Asian countries have a genuine desire to address critical challenges to resource security, they may act decisively to secure small to medium-sized resource deposits and reserves in nearby, strategically relevant areas such as the East and South China Sea. China's actions in its immediate neighbourhood are not unusual or unpredictable—given that the European Union and the USA acted unilaterally in the past to gain advantage in their spheres of influence and thus become wealthy, why would not China do the same? China calculates that if it does not pursue resources now, then any other country vying for the same resources will naturally pursue them through peaceful or non-peaceful means. The CCP currently enjoys popular support, trillions of dollars in foreign exchange reserves, relatively high employment levels, rising incomes, managed inflation, growing nationalist sentiment, political will and a committed, motivated and modern military eager to show off its capacity to put up a solid front against any rival. And it is with this internal recognition of advantages, assets, power, strengths and opportunities that China progresses with its ambitions in the South China Sea.

The crude oil and natural gas reserves that may exist beneath the seabed (not the oceanic crust) of the South China Sea that are subject to overlapping maritime claims form merely one of the central issues related to the South China Sea sovereignty disputes. The latent value (in terms of profits) of potential oil and gas reserves should not be ignored because economic factors are always a reliable incentive for a country to act brashly. The other resource-related issues have more to do with fisheries, minerals, the free flow of input-carrying vessels, sea route security and sovereignty concerns that together with associated nationalistic sentiment, historical resentments and strong ambitions are likely to remain among the more significant issues in the South China Sea maritime disputes.

To sum up, China's strategic interests in the South China Sea can be simplified as power projection and resource security. More precisely, the Chinese

Government aims to project military power in its sphere of influence in order to minimize US leverage in the region, to promote regional commerce with a sufficient inclusion of Chinese conditions, preferences and terms, and to gauge the reactions of neighbours and old powers to China's initiatives in the immediate neighbourhood. There is a need to secure resources in the South China Sea not only for internal use but also to derive revenues from exports, and in connection with the above, China seeks to control and protect trade-critical sea lanes that are essential to the transportation of its imports and exports.

Notes

1 Sigfrido Burgos Cáceres and Sophal Ear, 'The Geopolitics of China's Global Resources Quest', *Geopolitics*, Vol. 17, No. 1, 2012, 47–79.
2 Sigfrido Burgos Cáceres and Sophal Ear, 'China's Natural Resource Appetite in Brazil', *Asian Journal of Latin American Studies*, Vol. 24, No. 2, 2011, 69–89.
3 China's four main import partners are Japan (14%), South Korea (10%), the USA (7%) and Germany (5%).
4 China's five main export partners are the USA (18%), Hong Kong (13%), Japan (8%), South Korea (5%) and Germany (4%).
5 D. Zweig and B. Jianhai, 'China's Global Hunt for Energy', *Foreign Affairs*, Vol. 84, No. 5, 2005, 25–38.
6 Sigfrido Burgos Cáceres, 'Understanding China's Global Search for Energy and Resources', *Central European Journal of International and Security Studies*, Vol. 7, No. 1, March 2013.
7 Nicholas Apergis and James E. Payne, 'Renewable Energy Consumption and Economic Growth: Evidence from a Panel of OECD Countries', *Energy Policy*, Vol. 38, No. 1, 2010, 656–60.
8 Angie Austin, 'Energy and Power in China: Domestic Regulation and Foreign Policy', (London: The Foreign Policy Centre, April 2005). Available at: http://fpc.org.uk/fsblob/448.pdf.
9 T. J. Pempel, *The Economy-Security Nexus in Northeast Asia* (New York: Routledge, 2013).
10 Z. Wenmu, 'China's Energy Security and Policy Choices', *World Economics and Politics*, Vol. 5, 2003, 11–16.
11 Ian Storey, 'Slipping Away? A South China Sea Code of Conduct Eludes Diplomatic Efforts', East and South China Seas, Bulletin No. 11 (Washington, DC: Center for a New American Security, March 2013).
12 For related arguments, see: Zhao Hong, 'The South China Sea Dispute and China–ASEAN Relations', *Asian Affairs*, Vol. 44, No. 1, 2013, 27–43.
13 Brahma Chellaney, 'China's Hydro-Hegemony', *New York Times*, 7 February 2013. The author notes that China 'already boasts more large dams than the rest of the world put together and has unveiled a mammoth $635-billion fresh investment in water infrastructure over the next decade'.
14 Sigfrido Burgos Cáceres and Sophal Ear, 'China's Strategic Interests in Cambodia: Influence and Resources', *Asian Survey*, Vol. 50, No. 3, 2010, 615–39.
15 Poon Kim Shee, 'The Political Economy of China-Myanmar Relations: Strategic and Economic Dimensions', *Ritsumeikan Annual Review of International Studies*, Vol. 1, 2002, 33–53.
16 D. Brautigam, *The Dragon's Gift: The Real Story of China in Africa* (London: Oxford University Press, 2009).

142 *Conclusion*

17 John W. Garver, 'China's Push through the South China Sea: The Interaction of Bureaucratic and National Interests', *The China Quarterly*, Vol. 132, December 1992, 999–1028.

18 Denny Roy, 'Hegemon on the Horizon? China's Threat to East Asian Security', *International Security*, Vol. 19, No. 1, summer 1994, 149–68.

19 Jeffrey D. Wilson, 'Chinese Resource Security Policies and the Restructuring of the Asia-Pacific Iron Ore Market', *Resources Policy*, Vol. 37, No. 3, September 2012, 331–39.

20 Ross Garnaut, 'The Contemporary China Resources Boom', *Australian Journal of Agricultural and Resource Economics*, Vol. 56, No. 2, April 2012, 222–43.

21 Jeffrey D. Wilson, 'Resource Security: A New Motivation for Free Trade Agreements in the Asia-Pacific Region', *Pacific Review*, Vol. 25, No. 4, 2012, 429–53.

22 Alastair Iain Johnston, 'How New and Assertive Is China's New Assertiveness?' *International Security*, Vol. 37, No. 4, spring 2013, 7–48.

23 Michael Mandelbaum, *The Case for Goliath: How America Acts as the World Government in the 21st Century* (New York: Public Affairs, 2005); Robert D. Kaplan, 'America's Elegant Decline', *The Atlantic*, November 2007; Michael Mandelbaum, *The Frugal Superpower: America's Global Leadership in a Cash-Strapped Era* (New York: Public Affairs, 2010).

24 F. G. Hoffman, 'Forward Partnership: A Sustainable American Strategy', *Orbis*, Vol. 57, No. 1, 2013, 20–40.

25 John J. Mearsheimer, 'Imperial by Design', *National Interest*, January/February 2011, 31–34.

26 Nick A. Owen and Clive H. Schofield, 'Disputed South China Sea Hydrocarbons in Perspective', *Marine Policy*, Vol. 36, No. 3, May 2012, 809–22.

27 John Ravenhill, 'Economics and Security in the Asia-Pacific Region', *Pacific Review*, Vol. 26, No. 1, 2013, 1–15.

Bibliography

Alagappa, M., *Taiwan's Presidential Politics* (New York: M. E. Sharpe, 2001).

Albright, M., *Memo to the President Elect* (New York: Harper Collins, 2008).

Altman, R. C., 'The Great Crash, 2008: A Geopolitical Setback for the West', *Foreign Affairs*, Vol. 88, No. 1, January/February 2009, 2–14.

Anderlini, J., 'China's Growth Model Running Out of Steam', *Financial Times*, 5 March 2012.

Andrews-Speed, P. and R. Dannreuther, *China, Oil, and Global Politics* (New York and Oxford: Routledge, 2011).

Apergis, N. and J. E. Payne, 'Renewable Energy Consumption and Economic Growth: Evidence from a Panel of OECD Countries', *Energy Policy*, Vol. 38, No. 1, 2010, 656–60.

Austin, A., 'Energy and Power in China: Domestic Regulation and Foreign Policy', (London: The Foreign Policy Centre, April 2005).

Baker, P., 'Obama, in an Emerging Myanmar, Vows Support', *New York Times*, 18 November 2012.

Bandow, D., 'Strategic Restraint in the Near Seas', *Orbis*, Vol. 56, No. 3, summer 2012, 486–502.

Barbieri, K., 'Economic Interdependence: A Path to Peace or a Source of Interstate Conflict?', *Journal of Peace Research*, Vol. 33, No. 1, February 1996, 29–49.

Bardi, U., 'Peak Oil: The Four Stages of a New Idea', *Energy*, Vol. 34, No. 3, 2009, 323–26.

Bast, A., 'The Beginning of History,' *Newsweek*, 18 April 2011.

Bateman, S. and R. Emmers, *Security and International Politics in the South China Sea: Towards a Cooperative Management Regime* (New York: Routledge, 2009).

BBC News (London), 'Oil Markets Explained', 18 October 2007.

——, 'China's Premier Wen Jiabao Targets Social Stability', 5 March 2011.

——, 'Q&A: South China Sea Dispute', 27 June 2012.

Belfer, M., 'Editor's Policy Analysis: A Blueprint for EU Energy Security', *Central European Journal of International and Security Studies*, Vol. 6, No. 1, 2012.

Bernstein, R. and R. H. Munro, *The Coming Conflict with China* (New York: Alfred A. Knopf, 1997).

Betts, R. K., 'Wealth, Power, and Instability', *International Security*, Vol. 18, No. 3, 1993–94, 34–77.

Bloomberg News, 'China to Use Forex Reserves to Finance Overseas Investment Deals', *Bloomberg News*, 14 January 2013.

144 *Bibliography*

Bradsher, K., 'China's Focus on Aerospace Raises Security Questions', *New York Times*, 21 January 2013.

Brautigam, D., *The Dragon's Gift: The Real Story of China in Africa* (London: Oxford University Press, 2009).

Brown, L. R., *Eco-Economy: Building an Economy for the Earth* (Washington, DC: Earth Policy Institute, 2001).

Bumiller, E., 'U.S. Official Warns about China's Military Buildup', *New York Times*, 24 August 2012.

Burgess, P., 'The Politics of the South China Sea: Territoriality and International Law,' *Security Dialogue*, Vol. 34, No. 1, March 2003, 7–10.

Burgos-Cáceres, S., 'Understanding China's Global Search for Energy and Resources', *Central European Journal of International and Security Studies*, Vol. 7, No. 1, March 2013.

——, 'China, Japan, and the East China Sea', *Georgetown Journal of International Affairs*, 9 March 2013.

Burgos Cáceres, S. and S. Ear, 'China's Strategic Interests in Cambodia: Influence and Resources', *Asian Survey*, Vol. 50, No. 3, 2010, 615–39.

——, 'China's Natural Resource Appetite in Brazil', *Asian Journal of Latin American Studies*, Vol. 24, No. 2, 2011, 71–92.

——, 'The Geopolitics of China's Global Resources Quest', *Geopolitics*, Vol. 17, No. 1, 2012, 47–79.

——, 'China's Oil Hunger in Angola: History and Perspective', *Journal of Contemporary China*, Vol. 21, No. 74, 2012, 351–67.

——, *The Hungry Dragon: How China's Resource Quest Is Reshaping the World* (New York: Routledge, 2013).

Burgos Cáceres, S. and J. Otte, 'Linking Animal Health and International Affairs: Trade, Food, Security, and Global Health', *Yale Journal of International Affairs*, Vol. 6, No. 1, 2011, 108–09.

Bush, R., *The Perils of Proximity: China–Japan Security Relations* (Washington, DC: Brookings Institution Press, 2010).

Business Week, 'What America Must Do to Compete with China and India', 22 August 2005.

Buszynski, L., 'The South China Sea: Oil, Maritime Claims, and U.S.–China Strategic Rivalry,' *Washington Quarterly*, Vol. 35, No. 2, 2012, 139–56.

Callahan, W. A., 'National Insecurities: Humiliation, Salvation, and Chinese Nationalism', *Alternatives: Global, Local, Political*, Vol. 29, No. 2, 2004, 199–218.

CBS News, 'Clinton Seeks Chinese Accord on South China Sea', 4 September 2012.

——,'China's Real Estate Bubble', 3 March 2013. Available at: www.cbsnews.com/video/watch/?id=50142079n.

Center for a New American Security, 'Beijing Pushes the Diplomatic Envelop on South China Sea Dispute', Natural Security Blog: Post (Washington, DC: Center for a New American Security, November 2012).

Chan, S., *China, the US, and the Power-Transition Theory: A Critique* (New York: Routledge, 2007).

Chang, P. H., 'The Rise of Wang Tung-Hsing: Head of China's Security Apparatus', *China Quarterly*, Vol. 73, 1978, 122–37.

Chen, I. T. Y. and A. H. Yang, '"A Harmonized Southeast Asia? Explanatory Typologies of ASEAN Countries" Strategies to the Rise of China', *Pacific Review*, 26 February 2013, 1–24.

Chengyu, Y., 'Logistics Support for Regional Warfare', in *Chinese Views of Future Warfare*, ed. Michael Pillsbury (Washington, DC: National Defense University, 1997).

Chellaney, B., 'China's Hydro-Hegemony', *New York Times*, 7 February 2013.

Chernia, J. A. and J. Kentishb, 'Renewable Energy Policy and Electricity Market Reforms in China', *Energy Policy*, Vol. 35, No. 7, June 2007, 3616–29.

Chin, G. and R. Thakur, 'Will China Change the Rules of the Global Order?' *Washington Quarterly*, Vol. 33, No. 4, 2010, 119–38.

China Daily (Beijing), 'China the Largest FDI Recipient in First Half of 2012', 24 October 2012.

——, 'China's GDP Growth Eases to 7.8% in 2012', 18 January 2013.

Christensen, T. J., *Useful Adversaries: Grand Strategy, Domestic Mobilization, and Sino-American Conflict, 1947–1958* (Princeton, NJ: Princeton University Press, 1996).

——, 'China, the U.S.-Japan Alliance, and the Security Dilemma in East Asia', *International Security*, Vol. 23, No. 4, spring 1999, 49–80.

——, 'Fostering Stability or Creating a Monster? The Rise of China and U.S. Policy toward East Asia', *International Security*, Vol. 31, No. 1, 2006, 81–126.

Chu, Y., L. Diamond, A. Nathan, and D. C. Shin, *How East Asians View Democracy* (New York: Columbia University Press, 2008).

Click, A., 'Book Review: The Coming Conflict with China by Richard Bernstein and Ross H. Munro', *Tulsa Journal of Comparative and International Law*, Vol. 5, 1997–98, 413–17.

Clinton, B., *Back to Work: Why We Need Smart Government for a Strong Economy* (New York: Alfred A. Knopf, 2011).

Cohen, J. A., 'Chinese Law: At the Crossroads', *China Quarterly*, Vol. 53, 1973, 139–43.

Cole, B. D., *The Great Wall at Sea: China's Navy Enters the 21st Century* (Annapolis, MD: Naval Institute Press, 2001).

Collier, P., 'The Market for Civil War', *Foreign Policy*, May/June 2003, 38–45.

Collier, P. and A. Hoeffler, 'Greed and Grievance in Civil War', *Oxford Economic Papers*, Vol. 56, No. 4, 2004, 563–95.

——, 'Violent Conflict', in *Global Problems: Global Solutions*, ed. B. Lomberg, (Cambridge: Cambridge University Press, 2004).

Cordner, L., 'The Spratly Islands Dispute and the Law of the Sea', *Ocean Development and International Law*, Vol. 25, No. 1, 1994, 61–74.

Cronin, P., P. Dutton, R. Kaplan, W. Rogers, M. T. Fravel, J. Holmes, and I. Storey, *Cooperation from Strength: The United States, China, and the South China Sea* (Washington, DC: Center for a New American Security, 2012).

Cui, C. and T. Shumsky, 'China's Warning Signs for "Dr. Copper"', *Wall Street Journal*, 11 April 2011.

Das, G., 'The India Model', *Foreign Affairs*, Vol. 85, No. 4, 2006, 2–16.

Davis, B., 'In Fast-Growing China, Dangers Threaten to Hamper its Success', *Wall Street Journal*, 11 April 2011.

De Santis, H., 'The Dragon and the Tigers: China and Asian Regionalism', *World Policy Journal*, summer 2005, 23–36.

Dewey, C. 'Japanese Holiday 'Celebrating' Disputed Islands Sparks Backlash in South Korea', *Washington Post*, 23 February 2013.

Dobbins, J., 'War with China', *Survival: Global Politics and Strategy*, Vol. 54, No. 4, 2012, 7–24.

Dosch, J., 'The Spratly Islands Dispute: Order-Building on China's Terms?' *Harvard International Review*, 18 August 2011.

146 *Bibliography*

Dumbaugh, K., 'China–U.S. Relations: Current Issues and Implications for U.S. Policy', CRS Report for Congress No. RL33877 (Washington, DC: Congressional Research Service, March 2008).

Dupuy, F. and P. M. Dupuy, 'A Legal Analysis of China's Historic Rights Claim in the South China Sea', *American Journal of International Law*, Vol. 107, No. 1, January 2013, 124–41.

Economy, E., 'China's Rise in Southeast Asia: Implications for the United States', *Journal of Contemporary China*, Vol. 14, No. 44, 2005, 409–25.

Erickson, A. and G. Collins, 'Beijing's Energy Security Strategy: The Significance of a Chinese State-Owned Tanker Fleet', *Orbis*, Vol. 51, No. 4, 2007, 665–84.

Farley, R., 'The Future of U.S. Naval Power', in: *The Future of Maritime Security*, ed. Zachary Hosford, Abraham Denmark, Robert Farley and Mark J. Valencia (World Politics Review, 2010).

Federal Trade Commission Bureau of Economics, 'The Petroleum Industry: Mergers, Structural Change, and Antitrust Enforcement', FTC Staff Study, August 2004, 68.

Finnegan, W., 'Leasing the Rain: The World Is Running Out of Fresh Water, and the Fight to Control It Has Begun', *New Yorker*, Vol. 78, No. 7, April 2002, 43–52.

Friedberg, A. L., 'Ripe for Rivalry: Prospects for Peace in a Multipolar Asia', *International Security*, Vol. 18, No. 3, 1993–94, 5–33.

——, 'The Future of US–China Relations: Is Conflict Inevitable?' *International Security*, Vol. 30, No. 2, 2005, 7–45.

——, *A Contest for Supremacy: China, America, and the Struggle for Mastery in Asia* (New York: W. W. Norton & Company, 2011).

Friedman, G., 'The State of the World: Assessing China's Strategy', *Stratfor: Global Intelligence*, 6 March 2012.

Friedman, T. L., 'The Power of Green', *New York Times Magazine*, 15 April 2007.

——, *Hot, Flat, and Crowded: Why We Need a Green Revolution–And How It Can Renew America* (New York: Farrar, Straus and Giroux, 2008).

——, 'The Talk of China', *New York Times*, 15 September 2012.

Friedmann, S. J. and T. Homer-Dixon, 'Out of the Energy Box', *Foreign Affairs*, Vol. 83, No. 6, November/December 2004, 72–83.

Gallagher, M., 'China's Illusory Threat to the South China Sea', *International Security* Vol. 19, No. 1, summer 1994, 169–94.

Gao, Z., 'The South China Sea: From Conflict to Cooperation?' *Ocean Development and International Law*, Vol. 25, No. 3, 1994, 345–59.

Gao, Z. and B. B. Jia, 'The Nine-Dash Line in the South China Sea: History, Status, and Implications', *American Journal of International Law*, Vol. 107, No. 1, January 2013, 98–124.

Garnaut, R., 'The Contemporary China Resources Boom', *Australian Journal of Agricultural and Resource Economics*, Vol. 56, No. 2, April 2012, 222–43.

Garver, J. W., 'China's Push through the South China Sea: The Interaction of Bureaucratic and National Interests', *China Quarterly*, Vol. 132, December 1992, 999–1028.

——, 'The Diplomacy of a Rising China in South Asia', *Orbis*, Vol. 56, No. 3, summer 2012, 391–411.

Genba, K., 'Japan-China Relations at a Crossroads', *New York Times*, 20 November 2012.

Gholz, E. and D. G. Press, 'Enduring Resilience: How Oil Markets Handle Disruptions', *Security Studies*, Vol. 22, No. 1, 2013, 139–47.

Gilpin, R., *War and Change in World Politics* (New York: Cambridge University Press, 1981).

Glaser, B. S., 'Armed Clash in the South China Sea', *Contingency Planning Memorandum* No. 14 (New York and Washington, DC: Council on Foreign Relations, April 2012).

Godwin, P., *China's Defense Modernization: Aspirations and Capabilities* (Alexandria, VA: CNA Corporation, April 2001).

Goldgeier, J. and M. McFaul, 'A Tale of Two Worlds', *International Organization*, Vol. 46, No. 2, spring 1992, 467–92.

Greenwald, G. B., *Liquefied Natural Gas: Developing and Financing International Energy Projects* (Alphen aan den Rijn: Kluwer Law International, October 1998).

Guoxing, J., 'China versus South China Sea Security', *Security Dialogue*, Vol. 29, No. 1, 1998, 101–12.

Hara, K., '50 Years from San Francisco: Re-Examining the Peace Treaty and Japan's Territorial Problems,' *Pacific Affairs*, Vol. 74, No. 3, 2001, 361–82.

Hauser, C., 'Rising Gas and Food Prices Push U.S. Inflation Higher', *New York Times*, 13 May 2011.

He, D. and W. Zhang, 'How Dependent Is the Chinese Economy on Exports and in what Sense Has Its Growth Been Export-Led?' *Journal of Asian Economics*, Vol. 21, No. 1, 2010, 87–104.

Heinrichs, R., 'America's Dangerous Battle Plan', *The Diplomat*, 17 August 2011.

Helleiner, K. F., 'War and Human Progress', *Canadian Journal of Economics and Political Science*, Vol. 18, No. 2, May 1952, 205–08.

Herszenhorn, D. M. and C. Buckley, 'China's New Leader, Visiting Russia, Promotes Nations' Economic and Military Ties', *New York Times*, 22 March 2013.

——, 'China's Leader Argues for Cooperation with Russia', *New York Times*, 23 March 2013.

Hoffman, F. G., 'Forward Partnership: A Sustainable American Strategy', *Orbis*, Vol. 57, No. 1, 2013, 20–40.

Holmes, J., 'The South China Sea: Lake Beijing', *The Diplomat*, 7 January 2013.

Hong, N., *UNCLOS and Ocean Dispute Settlement: Law and Politics in the South China Sea* (New York and Oxford: Routledge, 2012).

Hong, Z., 'The South China Sea Dispute and China–ASEAN Relations', *Asian Affairs*, Vol. 44, No. 1, 2013, 27–43.

Hu, N. A., 'South China Sea: Troubled Waters or A Sea of Opportunity?' *Ocean Development and International Law*, Vol. 41, No. 3, 2010, 203–13.

Huang, Y., *Capitalism with Chinese Characteristics: Entrepreneurship and the State* (New York: Cambridge University Press, 2008).

——, 'Democratize or Die: Why China's Communists Face Reform or Revolution', *Foreign Affairs*, January/February 2013.

Hubbard, G. R. and P. Navarro, *Seeds of Destruction: Why the Path to Economic Ruin Runs through Washington and how to Reclaim American Prosperity* (Upper Saddle River, NJ: Pearson Education Ltd., 2011).

Hughes, C., *Japan's Remilitarization* (New York: Routledge, 2009).

Ikenberry, G. J., 'The Rise of China and the Future of the West', *Foreign Affairs*, Vol. 87, No. 1, 2008, 23–37.

Inkster, N., 'Chinese Intelligence in the Cyber Age', *Survival*, Vol. 55, No. 1, 2013, 45–66.

International Institute for Strategic Studies, 'China's Three-Point Naval Strategy', *IISS Strategic Comments*, Vol. 16, Comment 37 (London: International Institute for Strategic Studies, October 2010).

148　*Bibliography*

Indyk, M. S., K. G. Lieberthal and M. E. O'Hanlon, *Bending History: Barack Obama's Foreign Policy* (Washington, DC: Brookings Institution Press, March 2012).

Ito, S., 'Japan PM Quotes UK's Thatcher on Island Dispute', *Agence France-Presse*, 28 February 2013.

Jacobs, A., 'Tibetan Self-Immolations Rise as China Tightens Grip', *New York Times*, 22 March 2012.

Jacobs, A. and C. Buckley, 'China's Wen Warns of Inequality and Vows to Continue Military Buildup', *New York Times*, 4 March 2013.

Jakobson, L., 'China's Foreign Policy Dilemma', (Sydney: Lowy Institute for International Policy, 5 February 2013).

——, 'How Involved Is Xi Jinping in the Diaoyu Crisis?' *The Diplomat*, 8 February 2013.

Japan Research Institute (JRI), 'Asia Monthly—May 2013', report no. 146 (Tokyo and Osaka: JRI, 2013).

Jensen, N. and L. Wantchekon, 'Resource Wealth and Political Regimes in Africa', *Comparative Political Studies*, Vol. 37, No. 7, September 2004, 816–41.

Ji, Y., 'China and North Korea: A Fragile Relationship of Strategic Convenience', *Journal of Contemporary China*, Vol. 10, No. 28, 2001, 387–98.

Jianxin, Z., 'Oil Security Reshapes China's Foreign Policy', Center on China's Transnational Relations, Working Paper No. 9; The Hong Kong University of Science and Technology, n. d.

Johnston, A., 'Is China a Status Quo Power?' *International Security*, Vol. 27, No. 4, 2003, 5–56.

Johnston, A. I., 'How New and Assertive Is China's New Assertiveness?' *International Security*, Vol. 37, No. 4, spring 2013, 7–48.

Juhasz, A., *The Tyranny of Oil: The World's Most Powerful Industry—And What We Must Do to Stop It* (New York: HarperCollins, 2008).

Kang, D. C., 'Soft Power and Leadership in East Asia', *Asia Policy*, Vol. 15, 2013, 134–37.

Kaplan, R. D., 'America's Elegant Decline', *The Atlantic*, November 2007.

——, 'Center Stage for the Twenty-first Century: Power Plays in the Indian Ocean', *Foreign Affairs*, Vol. 88, No. 2, 2009, 16–32.

——, 'The South China Sea Is the Future of Conflict', *Foreign Policy*, Vol. 188, September/October 2011, 78–85.

Karim, M. A., 'The South China Sea Disputes: Is High Politics Overtaking?' *Pacific Focus*, Vol. 28, No. 1, April 2013, 99–119.

Keck, Z., 'Destined to Fail: China's Soft Power Push', *The Diplomat*, 7 January 2012.

Kennedy, A., 'China's New Energy-Security Debate', *Survival*, Vol. 52, No. 3, 2010, 137–58.

Kennedy, P., *The Rise and Fall of the Great Powers* (New York: Vintage Books, 1989).

Kim, S. S., *China and the World: Chinese Foreign Relations in the Post-Cold War Era* (New York: Perseus Books, 1998).

Kissinger, H., *On China* (New York: Penguin Books, 2012).

Kivimäki, T., *War or Peace in the South China Sea?* (Copenhagen: Nordic Institute of Asian Studies, 2002).

Klare, M., 'End of the Petroleum Age?' *Foreign Policy in Focus*, 26 June 2008.

——, 'We're On the Brink of Disaster,'*Salon.com*, 26 February 2009.

——, 'The United States Heads to the South China Sea: Why American Involvement Will Mean More Friction, Not Less', *Foreign Affairs*, Vol. 92, No. 1, January/February 2013.

Kripalani, M., D. Roberts and J. Bush, 'India and China: Oil Patch Partners?' *Business Week*, 7 February 2005.

Kristof, N. D., 'China's Rise', *Foreign Affairs*, Vol. 72, No. 5, November/December 1993, 59–74.

Krugman, P., *The Return of Depression Economics and the Crisis of 2008* (New York: W.W. Norton, 2009).

Kumar, H., 'India and China Deepen Economic Ties', *New York Times*, 27 November 2012.

Kurlantzick, J., *Charm Offensive: How China's Soft Power Is Transforming the World* (New Haven, CT: Yale University Press, 2007).

Lanteigne, M., 'China's Maritime Security and the Malacca Dilemma', *Asian Security*, Vol. 4, No. 2, 2008, 143–61.

——, *Chinese Foreign Policy: An Introduction* (New York: Routledge, 2009).

Lee, J., 'China's Geostrategic Search for Oil', *Washington Quarterly*, Vol. 35, No. 3, 2012, 75–92.

——, 'The 'Tragedy' of China's Energy Policy', *The Diplomat*, 4 October 2012.

Lee, M., 'Clinton Seeks Chinese Accord on South China Sea', *Washington Times*, 4 September 2012.

Leggett, K., 'China Flexes Economic Muscle throughout Burgeoning Africa', *Wall Street Journal*, 29 March 2005.

Leibo, S. A., *East Asia and the Western Pacific* (Washington, DC: Stryker-Post Publications, June 2000).

Lieberthal, K. G. and J. Wang, 'Addressing U.S.–China Strategic Distrust', John L. Thornton China Center, Monograph Series 4 (Washington, DC: The Brookings Institution, 2012).

Lieberthal, K. G., 'The 2013 People's Congress: A New Government, A New Direction?', Audio Interviews with Experts (Washington, DC: Brookings Institution, 28 March 2013).

Leifer, M., 'Chinese Economic Reform and Security Policy: The South China Sea Connection', *Survival*, Vol. 37, No. 2, 1995, 44–59.

Lo, B., *Axis of Convenience: Moscow, Beijing, and the New Geopolitics* (Washington, DC: Brookings Institution Press, 2008).

Looney, R., *Handbook of Oil Politics* (New York: Routledge, 2011).

Luttwak, E., *The Rise of China vs. the Logic of Strategy* (Cambridge, MA: Belknap Press, 2012).

Ma, L., 'Thinking of China's Grand Strategy: Chinese Perspectives', *International Relations of the Asia-Pacific*, Vol. 13, No. 1, 2013, 155–68.

Mabasa, R. C., 'Only Philippines, China Can Solve Territorial Row', *Manila Bulletin*, 3 April 2013.

McGregor, C., 'China, Vietnam, and the Cambodian Conflict: Beijing's End Game Strategy', *Asian Survey*, Vol. 30, No. 3, 1990, 266–83.

McKinsey Global Institute, 'Curbing Global Energy Demand Growth: The Energy Productivity Opportunity', McKinsey Global Institute Publication, May 2007.

Makower, J. and C. Pike, *Strategies for the Green Economy: Opportunities and Challenges in the New World of Business* (New York: McGraw-Hill, 2009).

Malik, J. M., 'China-India Relations in the Post-Soviet Era: The Continuing Rivalry', *China Quarterly*, Vol. 142, June 1995, 317–55.

Mallaby, S., 'NGOs: Fighting Poverty, Hurting the Poor', *Foreign Policy*, September/October 2004, 50–58.

150   *Bibliography*

Mandelbaum, M., *The Case for Goliath: How America Acts as the World Government in the 21st Century* (New York: Public Affairs, 2005).

——, *The Frugal Superpower: America's Global Leadership in a Cash-Strapped Era* (New York: Public Affairs, 2010).

Manning, R., 'The Oil We Eat: Following the Food Chain Back to Iraq', *Harper's*, Vol. 308, No. 1845, February 2004, 39–45.

Mattoo, A. and A. Subramanian, 'From Doha to the Next Bretton Woods: A New Multilateral Trade Agenda', *Foreign Affairs*, Vol. 88, No. 1, 2009, 15–26.

Mearsheimer, J. J., *The Tragedy of Great Power Politics* (New York: W.W. Norton & Company, 2001).

Meyer, C., *China or Japan: Which Will Lead Asia?* (New York: Oxford University Press, 2012).

Milivojevic, M., 'The Spratly and Paracel Islands Conflict', *Survival*, Vol. 31, No. 1, 1989, 70–78.

Miller, J. B. and T. Yokota, 'Japan Keeps Its Cool: Why Tokyo's New Government Is More Pragmatic than Hawkish', *Foreign Affairs*, 21 January 2013.

Milligan-Whyte, J. and D. Min, *US–China Relations in the Obama Administration: Facing Shared Challenges* (New York: New School Press Limited, 2011).

Mishra, K., *Rapprochement across the Himalayas: Emerging India–China Relations in Post-Cold War Period* (Delhi: Kalpaz Publications, 2004).

Motaal, D. A., 'Negotiating With Only One China on Climate Change: On Counting Ourselves Lucky', *Yale Journal of International Affairs*, Vol. 6, No. 1, Winter 2011, 74–84.

Mullen, J., 'Philippines Takes Territorial Fight with China to International Tribunal', *CNN* (Atlanta, GA), 22 January 2013.

Nathan, A. J., *China's Search for Security* (New York: Columbia University Press, 2012).

Nobrega, W., 'Why India Will Beat China', *Business Week,* 22 July 2008.

Norman, J., 'Wiki-Leaks: China Hiding Military Buildup, Intentions', *CBS News*, 6 January 2011.

Office of the Secretary of Defense, 'Military and Security Developments Involving the People's Republic of China 2011', Annual Report to Congress (Washington, DC: Department of Defense, 2012). Available at: www.defense.gov/pubs/pdfs/2011_cmpr_final.pdf.

Ogden, C. 'Beyond Succession: China's Internal Security Challenges', *Strategic Analysis*, Vol. 37, No. 2, 2013, 193–202.

O'Hanlon, M., 'Why China Cannot Conquer Taiwan', *International Security*, Vol. 25, No. 2, 2000, 51–86.

Organization for Economic Cooperation and Development (OECD), *Benchmark Definition of Foreign Direct Investment*; fourth edn. (Paris: OECD, 2008).

——, 'FDI in Figures', (Paris: OECD, January 2013).

Owen, N. A. and C. H. Schofield, 'Disputed South China Sea Hydrocarbons in Perspective', *Marine Policy*, Vol. 36, No. 3, May 2012, 809–22.

Pan, Z., 'Sino-Japanese Dispute Over the Diaoyu/Senkaku Islands: The Pending Controversy from the Chinese Perspective', *Journal of Chinese Political Science*, Vol. 12, No. 1, 2007, 71–92.

Papayoanou, P. A., *Power Ties: Economic Interdependence, Balancing, and War* (Ann Arbor: University of Michigan Press, 1999).

Pape, R. A., 'Soft Balancing Against the United States', *International Security*, Vol. 30, No. 1, 2005, 7–45.

Bibliography 151

Park, C., 'The South China Sea Disputes: Who Owns the Islands and the Natural Resources?' *Ocean Development and International Law*, Vol. 5, No. 1, 1978, 27–59.

Pempel, T. J., *The Economy–Security Nexus in Northeast Asia* (New York: Routledge, 2013).

Perlez, J., 'Vietnam Law on Contested Islands Draws China's Ire', *New York Times*, 21 June 2012.

Promyamyai, T., 'Myanmar President Visits Thailand', *Agence France-Presse*, 23 July 2012.

RAND Corporation, 'Asian Perceptions of a Rising China', Chapter 4 of Institutional Report # MR1170, in: *The Role of Southeast Asia in U.S. Strategy toward China* (Santa Monica, CA: RAND Corporation, 2001).

——, 'What's the Potential for Conflict with China, and How Can It Be Avoided?' Research Brief No. RB-9657-A (Santa Monica, CA: RAND Corporation, 2012).

Ravenhill, J., 'Economics and Security in the Asia-Pacific Region', *Pacific Review*, Vol. 26, No. 1, 2013, 1–15.

Reuters, 'China Military Build-Up Seems U.S.-Focused: Mullen', *Reuters*, 4 May 2009.

Rogers, W., 'India's South China Sea Gambit Redux', *Natural Security Blog* (Washington, DC: Center for a New American Security, December 2012).

Rohter, L., 'China Widens Economic Role in Latin America', *Washington Post*, 20 November 2004.

Ross, R. S., 'Beijing as a Conservative Power', *Foreign Affairs*, Vol. 76, No. 2, 1997, 33–44.

——, 'The Problem with the Pivot: Obama's New Asia Policy Is Unnecessary and Counterproductive', *Foreign Affairs*, November/December 2012.

Ross, R. S. and Z. Feng, *China's Ascent: Power, Security, and the Future of International Politics* (New York: Cornell University Press, 2008).

Roy, D., 'Hegemon on the Horizon? China's Threat to East Asian Security', *International Security*, Vol. 19, No. 1, summer 1994, 149–68.

Rudd, K., 'Beyond the Pivot: A New Road Map for U.S.–Chinese Relations', *Foreign Affairs*, March/April 2013.

Sachs, J. D., 'Welcome to the Asian Century', *Fortune*, Vol. 149, No. 1, 2004, 53–54.

Salameh, M. G., 'China, Oil, and the Risk of Regional Conflict', *Survival*, Vol. 37, No. 4, 1995, 133–46.

Samuels, M., *Contest for the South China Sea* (New York: Routledge, 2005).

Samuelson, R., 'The Sources of the Global Economic Stalemate', *Washington Post*, 24 June 2012.

Sandalow, D., *Freedom from Oil: How the President Can End the United States' Oil Addiction* (New York: McGraw-Hill, 2008).

Sang-Hun, C., 'North Korea Cuts Off the Remaining Military Hot Lines with South Korea', *New York Times*, 27 March 2013.

Schweller, R. L., 'Bandwagoning for Profit: Bringing the Revisionist State Back In', *International Security*, Vol. 19, No. 1, 1994, 72–107.

Scobell, A. and A. J. Nathan, 'China's Overstretched Military', *Washington Quarterly*, Vol. 35, No. 4, 2012, 135–48.

Shambaugh, D., 'China and the Korean Peninsula: Playing for the Long Term', *Washington Quarterly*, Vol. 26, No. 2, 2003, 43–56.

——, 'Coping with a Conflicted China', *Washington Quarterly*, Vol. 34, No. 1, 2011, 7–27.

——, *China Goes Global: The Partial Power* (New York: Oxford University Press, 2013).

152 *Bibliography*

Shee, P. K., 'The Political Economy of China-Myanmar Relations: Strategic and Economic Dimensions', *Ritsumeikan Annual Review of International Studies*, Vol. 1, 2002, 33–53.

Shirk, S., *China: Fragile Superpower* (New York: Oxford University Press, 2008).

Simon, S. W., 'China, Vietnam, and ASEAN: The Politics of Polarization', *Asian Survey*, Vol. 19, No. 12, 1979, 1171–88.

Slater, D. and P. J. Taylor, *The American Century: Consensus and Coercion in the Projection of American Power* (Malden, MA: Blackwell, 1999).

Smith, S. A., 'Japan and the East China Sea Dispute', *Orbis*, Vol. 56, No. 3, summer 2012, 370–90.

Song, Y. H., *United States and Territorial Disputes in the South China Sea: A Study of Ocean Law and Politics* (Baltimore, MD: University of Maryland School of Law, 2002).

Spegele, B., 'China Shops Around for Oil, Wary of Iran, Arab Spring', *Wall Street Journal*, 20 January 2012.

——, 'New Tensions Rise on South China Sea', *New York Times*, 5 August 2012.

Spence, J. D., *The Search for Modern China* (New York: W.W. Norton & Company, 1991).

Spero, J. E. and J. A. Hart, *The Politics of International Economic Relations* (Boston, MA: Wadsworth, 2010).

Storey, I. J., 'Creeping Assertiveness: China, the Philippines, and the South China Sea Dispute', *Contemporary Southeast Asia*, Vol. 21, No. 1, April 1999, 95–118.

——, 'Slipping Away? A South China Sea Code of Conduct Eludes Diplomatic Efforts', East and South China Seas, Bulletin No. 11 (Washington, DC: Center for a New American Security, March 2013).

Swaine, M. D., *The Role of the Chinese Military in National Security Policymaking* (Santa Monica, CA: RAND Corporation, 1998).

Tan, D., 'The Diaoyu/Senkaku Dispute: Bridging the Cold Divide', *Santa Clara Journal of International Law*, Vol. 5, No. 1, 2006, 134–68.

Tatlow, D. K., 'The Meaning of the China–Japan Island Dispute,' *International Herald Tribune*, 19 September 2012.

Teradaa, T., 'Forming an East Asian Community: A Site for Japan–China Power Struggles', *Japanese Studies*, Vol. 26, No. 1, 2006, 5–17.

Thao, N. H. and R. Amer, 'A New Legal Arrangement for the South China Sea?' *Ocean Development and International Law*, Vol. 40, No. 4, 2009, 333–49.

The Economist, 'A Job for China', 20 November 1993, 18.

——, 'Special Report: Beyond Doha', Vol. 389, No. 8601, 2008, 30–33.

——, 'Tibet and Xinjiang: Marking Time at the Fringes', 8 July 2010.

——, 'Indian, Pakistani, and Chinese Border Disputes: Fantasy Frontiers', 8 February 2012.

——, 'Military Spending in South-East Asia: Shopping Spree', 24 March 2012.

——, 'China's New Leadership: Vaunting the best, Fearing the worst', 27 October 2012.

——, 'China and Japan: Locked On: The Dangerous Dance around Disputed Islets Is Becoming Ever More Worrying', 9 February 2013.

——, 'China's Cyber-Hacking: Getting Ugly', 23 February 2013.

The Japan Times, 'Will ASEAN Step Up to Try to Bridge Japan-China Rift?', 7 September 2012.

The New York Times, 'Vietnam Defends Spratly Gas Project',12 April 2007.

——, 'Territorial Claims in South China Sea', May 2012.

The Wall Street Journal, 'China's Nationalist Wave: Beijing's Naval Aggression Is a Threat to Peace in the Pacific', 10 December 2012.

The Week, 'Canada: Beating the U.S. at its Own Game', 3 August 2012, 16.

Tian, W., 'Copper Giant Seeks Investment', *China Daily – Asia Pacific*, 15 March 2013.

Tønnesson, S., 'Vietnam's Objective in the South China Sea: National or Regional Security?' *Contemporary Southeast Asia*, Vol. 22, No. 1, April 2000, 199–220.

Tsui, M. and X. Li, 'Attitudes Regarding the Market Economy in Urban China', *Sociology Today*, Vol. 2, No. 2, 2012, 185–90.

U.S. Department of Defense, 'DoD Releases Fiscal 2010 Budget Proposal', News Release No. 304-09, 7 May 2009. Available at: www.defense.gov/releases/release. aspx?releaseid=12652.

U.S. Energy Information Administration, 'South China Sea', (Washington, DC: EIA, February 2013). Available at: www.eia.gov/countries/regions-topics.cfm?fips=SCS.

Valencia, M. J., 'The Spratly Islands: Dangerous Ground in the South China Sea', *Pacific Review*, Vol. 1, No. 4, 1988, 438–43.

Van Evera, S., 'Primed for Peace: Europe After the Cold War', *International Security*, Vol. 15, No. 3, 1990–91, 7–57.

Walt, S. M., 'Testing Theories of Alliance Formation: The Case of Southwest Asia', *International Organization*, Vol. 42, No. 2, spring 1988, 275–316.

Wang, J., 'China's Search for a Grand Strategy: A Rising Great Power Finds Its Way', *Foreign Affairs*, Vol. 90, No. 2, 2011, 68–79.

Warnock, F. E., 'Doubts About Capital Controls', (New York: Council on Foreign Relations Press, 2011).

Weagley, R. O., 'One Big Difference between Chinese and American Households: Debt', *Forbes*, 24 June 2010.

Webb, J., 'The South China Sea's Gathering Storms', *Wall Street Journal*, 20 August 2012.

Wenmu, Z., 'China's Energy Security and Policy Choices', *World Economics and Politics*, Vol. 5, 2003, 11–16.

Wesley, M., 'What's at Stake in the South China Sea?' Snapshot 11 (Sydney: Lowy Institute for International Policy, July 2012).

White, H., 'Power Shift: Australia's Future between Washington and Beijing', *Quarterly Essay*, No. 39, 2010.

Whitlock, C., 'U.S. Eyes Return to some Southeast Asia Military Bases', *Washington Post*, 22 June 2012.

Wilson, J. D., 'Resource Security: A New Motivation for Free Trade Agreements in the Asia-Pacific Region', *Pacific Review*, Vol. 25, No. 4, 2012, 429–53.

——, 'Chinese Resource Security Policies and the Restructuring of the Asia-Pacific Iron Ore Market', *Resources Policy*, Vol. 37, No. 3, September 2012, 331–39.

Wong, E. 'Thousands of Dead Pigs Found in River Flowing Into Shanghai', *New York Times*, 11 March 2013.

——,'As Pollution Worsens in China, Solutions Succumb to Infighting', *New York Times*, 21 March 2013.

World Bank, 'Clear Skies, Blue Water: China's Environment in the New Century', (Washington, DC: The World Bank, 1997).

Xinhua, 'China Keeps 2013 GDP Growth Target Unchanged at 7.5%', 5 March 2013.

Yahuda, M., *The International Politics of the Asia Pacific* (New York: Routledge, 2012).

Yan, X., *Ancient Chinese Thought, Modern Chinese Power*, trans. D. Bell, Z. Sun and E. Ryden (Princeton, NJ: Princeton University Press, 2011).

154 *Bibliography*

Yao, K. and A. Wang, 'China Bets on Consumer-led Growth to Cure Social Ills', *Reuters*, 5 March 2013.

Zha, D. and M. J. Valencia, 'Mischief Reef: Geopolitics and Implications', *Journal of Contemporary Asia*, Vol. 31, No.1, 2001, 86–103.

Zhai, Q., *China and the Vietnam Wars, 1950–1975* (Chapel Hill, NC: University of North Carolina Press, 2000).

Zhao, S., 'China's Global Search for Energy Security: Cooperation and Competition in the Asia-Pacific', *Journal of Contemporary China*, Vol. 17, No. 55, 2008, 207–27.

——, *China–US Relations Transformed: Perspectives and Strategic Interactions* (New York: Routledge, 2008).

——, *China's Search for Energy Security: Domestic Sources and International Implications* (New York: Routledge, 2012).

Zhang, Y., 'China's Evolution toward an Authoritarian Market Economy: A Predator–Prey Evolutionary Model with Intelligent Design', *Public Choice*, Vol. 151, No. 1–2, 2012, 271–87.

Zhou, F., 'China, India Forming Strategic Ties', *China Daily*, 18 February 2005.

Zweig, D. and B. Jianhai, 'China's Global Hunt for Energy', *Foreign Affairs*, Vol. 84, No. 5, September/October 2005, 25–38.

Index

Abe, Shinzo 63, 64, 65, 66–67, 69–70
Afghanistan, military intervention in 83–84
Africa 25, 26, 28, 35, 37, 46, 49, 59, 75, 83, 108, 129, 132–33, 136; China-Africa Cooperation Forum 34, 42n43; *see also* North Africa; South Africa
agriculture, energy utilization for food production 31–32
Alagappa, Muthiah 102n25
Albright, Madeleine 55n14
Algeria 48
Altman, Roger C. 43n51
Amnesty International 7
analogical thinking 121
Anderlini, Jamil 55n19
Andrews-Speed, P. and Dannreuther, R. 100–101n5
Angola 27, 41n12, 41n17, 45, 48, 55n21
Apergis, N. and Payne, J.E. 141n7
Aquino, Benigno 76
Arab Spring 3
artificial resources 132
Arunachal Pradesh 8, 59
ASEAN (Association of South-East Asian Nations) 13, 17, 18, 20, 22n27, 34; Concert of Powers 99; international politics 17; powerful 'others' and 65–67; Sino-Philippine relations and 75–76, 78; South China Sea, US and 98; United States and 87, 88, 93–94, 97, 99; Vietnam and 105, 106, 107, 108, 110, 111, 115, 116n14
Asia: financial crisis (1997–98), defence spending reductions and 93; power balance in, United States and 38; *see also* Central Asia; East Asia; North-East Asia; South-East Asia 38

Asia-Pacific, United States and 36, 39–40, 61
Asian Development Bank 131n21
Asia's Democratic Security Diamond (Shinzo Abe initiative, 2013) 66
assertiveness: in China Seas, power projection and 17–18; confidence and 26; growth and 36–37; resource security and 138–39
Austin, Angie 141n8
Australia 29, 34, 39, 66; Lowy Institute 69; security dynamics and 96
autocratic capitalism 8–9, 39, 77, 87, 92, 127; authoritarian growth, admiration for system of 49
Azerbaijan 48

Baker, Peter 22n26
Bandow, Doug 103n44
Bangladesh 12, 37
Barbieri, Katherine 103n34
Bardi, Ugo 41n4
Bast, Andrew 44n62
Bateman, S. and Emmers, R. 101n19
Bateman, Sam 27
BBC (British Broadcasting Corporation) 41n2, 54n3, 101n16
Belfer, Mitchell 55n24
Berkshire Miller, J. and Yokota, T. 73n18
Bernstein, R. and Munro, R.H. 101n13, 103n39
Betts, Richard K. 130n5
bilateral trade with oil-rich states 26
biomass fuels 32
Bloomberg News 116n7
Bolivia 3, 26, 33
Borneo 10, 88
Bradsher, Keith 22n34

156 *Index*

Brautigam, D. 141n16
Brazil 24, 27, 29, 32, 35, 36, 46, 48, 104;
  energy insecurity and demand from
  36; oil and gas production in 32;
  resource security and 132, 133;
  vibrant economy of 27
Breslin, Shawn 27
British Petroleum 48, 111
Brown, Lester R. 42n27
Brunei 74, 81, 88
Bumiller, Elisabeth 103n37
Burgess, Peter 103n45
Burgos Cáceres, S. and Ear, S. 41n5,
  41n10, 41n12, 41n13, 41n17, 42n42,
  43n55, 54n1, 54n5, 55n21, 55n23,
  72n7, 100n4, 103n49, 116n10, 117n23,
  141n1, 141n2, 141n14
Burgos Cáceres, S. and Otte, J. 43n58
Burgos Cáceres, Sigfrido 100–101n5,
  141n6
Bush, Richard 73n14
Business Week 44n60
Buszynski, Leszek 117n32

Callahan, William A. 20n5
Camago, Philippines 113
Cambodia 12, 34, 86, 87, 111, 113, 136
Canada 48, 51, 52, 132
capitalism 34–35, 86, 102n32; autocratic
  capitalism 8–9, 39, 77, 87, 92, 127;
  catalyst for contention 94–95
Caspian Sea 32, 36
CBS News 72n6
Center for a New American Security
  103n43
Central Asia 26, 28, 36
Central Bank of China 104, 116n6
*Central European Journal of
  International Security Studies* 41n1
Central Military Commission 89
central planning 5, 133
Chamdo, Battle of (1950) 13
Chan, Steve 130n1
Chang, P.H. 22n31
Chellaney, Brahma 141n13
Chen, I.T.-Y. and Yang, A.H. 22n27
Cherni, J.A. and Kentish, J. 41n9
Chevron 48
Chile 24, 133
Chin, G. and Thakur, R. 55n15
China: aid targeted to interior 8; anti-
  China sentiments among population
  127; assertiveness, confidence and 26;
  assertiveness, growth and 36–37;

autocratic capitalism 8–9, 39, 77, 87,
  92, 127; border with India, problems
  concerning 7–8; buffer territories 5–6,
  7; Central Bank of China 104, 116n6;
  Central Military Commission 89;
  central planning 5, 133; China Seas,
  strategic vulnerability of 5, 6;
  Communist Party (CCP) 4–5, 6–7, 13,
  30, 45–46, 49, 76–77, 82, 84, 104–5;
  complexity of issues facing
  government 9, 15, 20; Concert of
  Powers 99; construction projects 4, 12,
  31, 135; corruption and cronyism 52,
  76, 126, 128–29, 130n15, 131n17;
  currency revaluation, calls for 25;
  cyber warfare 11, 62; decision-making
  proclivities of CCP leadership 89–90;
  democratic modernization, barriers to
  39; destabilization effects, challenges
  of 38–39; domestic politics,
  interlocking rationales of 14–15;
  domestic security and stability,
  importance for Government of 3, 8;
  economic growth, rate of 25;
  economic growth, security and 4;
  energy consumption 24, 27–28, 133;
  energy cooperation talks with India
  35; energy imports from developing
  countries 27; energy insecurity and
  demand from 36; exports, pressures
  for 5; Finance Ministry 9–10; fiscal
  deficit target, rise in 7; foreign
  exchange reserves, investment of 51–
  52; foreign imports, dependence on
  99; foreign oil operations, control of
  45–46, 52; foreign policy objectives of
  CCP leadership 76–77; foreign policy
  towards Philippines 76–78;
  geographical contours and orientation
  of 89; 'Grand Strategy' for future 19;
  Great Proletarian Cultural Revolution
  (1966–76) 94; gross domestic product
  (GDP) 6–7, 20n9, 27, 31, 39, 45, 52,
  55n18, 116n2, 133, 135, 138; growth
  and assertiveness of 36–37; growth
  and prosperity, importance for
  Government of 3–4; hard power and
  Japan 61–63; household income 3–4;
  incursion into Vietnam (1979) 13;
  industrial expansion, funding for 4;
  inequality and divisiveness, risks of 3–4;
  infighting within CCP 17; inflation
  rates 9; infrastructure projects 4;
  interconnectedness with rest of world

6; internal transfers, inflows and outflows, challenge of 8–9; international politics, national policy-making and 16–18; investment-driven, export-dependent growth model 51; job security, weakening of 6; Law on the Territorial Sea and the Contiguous Zone (1992) 59–60; major power, emergence as 17; Manchuria, interests in 5–6; manufacturing output, need for paradigm shift in 9; military modernization, new leaders' push for 15–16; military power, build-up of 8, 96; military power, misconceptions about 16; Mongolia, interests in 5–6; National Bureau of Statistics 31, 42n31; National Energy Administration (NEAC) 25; National People's Congress (2013) 70; National Space Administration 11; nationalism, popular loyalty and 4–5; non-interference principles of 98; passive behind-the-scenes diplomacy 18–19; People's Armed Police (PAP) 14, 15; People's Liberation Army (PLA) 7–8, 14, 15, 45, 62, 103n36, 105; Politburo Standing Committee of CCP 4; politics and power projection 126–28; popular trust, security and 4; power aspirations, United States and 82; power projection, Vietnam and 104–5; pragmatic internationalism 5; proactive stage-managing diplomacy 18–19; Public Security Bureau 127; Qing dynasty 84, 91; rapprochement with rogue and unstable countries 12; reformists' hopes for new CCP leadership 19; regional participation 36; resource security, policy and maneuvers on 137–38; sea-based targeting, vulnerability to 11; sea-routes, focus on protection for 8; security apparatus 14; Shanghai uprising (1927), effects of 3–4; social unrest, triggers of 6–7; socialist market economy 8–9; South China Sea, claims to 99–100; South China Sea, national interest and 99–100; South China Sea, potential for balanced approach on 98–99; sovereignty issue 9–10, 17, 19, 21n12; State Oceanic Administration 63, 73n12; Strategic and Defence Studies Centre 15; strategic reorientation,

need for 9; structural limitations 11; territorial losses to great powers 91; Tibet, interests in 5–6, 7; trade-dependence of 5; trade promotion, focus on 8; United States and China Seas 4–5; vibrant economy of 27; warfare strategy 11–12; West and, historical perspective 91–94; Western economic problems, effects on 6–7; Western perspectives on emergent power of 17–18; Xinjiang, interests in 5–6, 7; *see also* oil security; power projection; resource security

China-Africa Cooperation Forum (CACF) 42n43

China Daily 116n2, 116n4

China Geology Newspaper 110

China Ocean's Development (China State Oceanic Administration) 63

China Seas, strategic vulnerability of 5, 6; *see also* East China Sea; South China Sea

Christensen, Thomas J. 23n42, 130n6

Chu Y.-h., Diamond, L. *et al.* 131n16

Chung Hong-Won 125

clean energy 53

Click, Amy 103n39

climate negotiations 33

Clinton, Bill 53, 55n25

Clinton, Hillary 61, 98

Code for Unalerted Encounters at Sea (CUES) 99

Cohen, Jerone Alan 22n31

Cole, Bernard D. 42n41

Collier, P. and Hoeffler, A. 43n44, 43n45

Collier, Paul 44n59

Communist Party (CCP) of China 4–5, 6–7, 13, 30, 45–46, 49, 76–77, 82, 84, 104–5

Concert of Powers 99

ConocoPhillips 48

construction projects 4, 12, 31, 135

consumer-led growth in US 50–51

containment of China 122–23, 129

control, exertion of outright influence and 139–40

conventional oil 47–48

copper, benchmarking on 28

Cordner, Lee 114, 117n36

corruption: checks on 128–29; cronyism and 52, 76, 126, 128–29, 130n15, 131n17

Cronin, Patrick M. 82, 100n3

Cui, C. and Shumsky, T. 41n19

158 *Index*

currency revaluation 25
cyber warfare 11, 62

Dalai Lama 22n28
Das, Gurcharan 28, 41n18
Davis, Bob 41n7
De Santis, Hugh 43n55
demand management 46
democracy: democratic modernization, barriers to 39; transparency and 128–29
Deng Xiaoping 5, 94
Denmark 37
Dewey, C. 73n17
Diaoyu/Senkaku Islands, disputes over 59–60, 61, 67, 71, 72n3, 73n22, 73n26, 74
diplomacy: diplomatic overtures on oil security 48–50; geostrategic diplomacy 61; maritime and territorial disputes, diplomacy on 78–79; North Korea, Chinese diplomacy and 50; oil security, diplomatic overtures on 48–50; passive behind-the-scenes diplomacy 18–19; proactive stage-managing diplomacy 18–19; soft power and 110–12; tact in diplomacy with calculated outcomes 48–50; Taiwan and Chinese diplomacy 49–50
discovery deficit, oil security and 47
Dobbins, James 101n20
Dosch, Jorn 117n26
Dow Chemical 31
Downs, Erica 27
Dumbaugh, Kerry 43n50
Dupuy, F. and Dupuy, P.-M. 117n34
Dutton, Peter 82, 100n3

Earth Policy Institute 30
East Asia 22n36, 34, 62, 64, 68, 70, 81, 82, 83, 84–85, 86, 88, 89–90; hegemony, imposition on 85; peaceful coexistence in 85; power politics in Western Pacific and 92; threats to harmony and stability of 59; Western Pacific and, power struggle epicentre 84–86, 92–93
East China Sea 4–5, 6, 10, 12, 15, 37, 64, 66, 70–71; Chinese assertiveness in 17–18; deep-water ports in, Chinese plans for 12; disputed delimitations in 40; infrastructure projects on shores of 13; maritime surveillance of 74–75
economic growth 6, 8–9, 12, 18, 20, 33, 34, 35, 45, 51, 71, 87, 95–96, 104–5, 109, 124, 133; accelerated growth,

pattern of 14–15, 27, 112, 137; assertiveness of China and 36–37; demand for resources and 24, 25, 81–82; economic models, oil security and 50–52; economic policies, oil security and 45, 52–53, 94–95; inputs for rapidity in Philippines 74; investment-driven, export-dependent growth model 51; prosperity and, importance for China 3–4; rate in China of 25; security and 4, 36, 52, 63, 88; sustainability and oil security 53, 135; Western with Eastern styles 27–30
The Economist 21n13, 21n16, 22n33, 42n22, 68, 73n20, 73n25, 102n29, 116n8
Economy, Elizabeth 103n40
Ecuador 26
Emmers, Ralf 27
energy conservation 37; technologies for 53
energy consumption in China 27–28
energy cooperation talks between China and India 35
energy imports: China from developing countries 27; energy insecurity and demand 36; global relations and energy requirements of China 81–82; Japan 88; Philippines 74–75; security challenges for United States 99
environmental considerations 31–33
Erickson, A. and Collins, G. 21n25
European Union (EU) 5, 6, 19, 25, 26, 35, 36, 37, 140; Asian power balance and 38; consumer-led growth in 50–51; energy security, challenges for 99; regional struggles in Asia, interference in 68
exclusive economic zone (EEZ) in Vietnam 109, 111
exploration technology 47
external power projection 14–16
Extractive Industries Transparency Initiative 43n46
ExxonMobil 48

Falklands War (1982) 69
Farley, Robert 103n37
Federal Trade Commission Bureau of Economics 54n9
Finance Ministry in China 9–10
Finnegan, William 33, 42n38
fiscal deficit target 7
Forbes magazine 3

Index

foreign direct investment (FDI) 104, 116n3
foreign exchange reserves, investment of 51–52
foreign policies: objectives of CCP leadership 76–77; oil security and 45; policy paradigm in Japan 64–65
fossil fuel consumption 32
Fravel, M. Taylor 100n3
Friedberg, Aaron L. 73n19, 82, 130n3, 130n5
Friedman, George 20n3
Friedman, Thomas L. 41n3, 42n32, 42n34, 73n24
Friedmann, S.J. and Homer-Dixon, T. 41n8, 43n57

Gallagher, Michael 116n9
Gao Z. and Bing B.J. 117n33
Gao Zhiguo 103n50, 107, 116n16
Garnaut, Ross 142n20
Garver, John W. 80n11, 96, 103n42, 142n17
Gates, Robert 62
Genba, Koichiro 72n4
geopolitics: geopolitical turmoil in East Asia, potential for 59; of oil and power 33–34; resource security and 33–35
Georgetown Journal of International Affairs 72n1
geostrategic diplomacy 61
Germany 37
Gholza, E. and Pressb, D.G. 41n5
Gilpin, Robert 130n7
Glaser, Bonnie S. 101n8
Global Corruption Report 131n20
global hunt for vital resources 132–33
global interdependence 47, 53–54, 95, 101n11, 123
global order, China and transformation of 36
global search for resources 24–41, 52
Godwin, Paul 42n41
Goldgeier, J. and McFaul, M. 130n5
Great Proletarian Cultural Revolution (1966–76) 94
green economies, aims for development of 33
Greenwald, Gerald B. 42n36
gross domestic product (GDP) 6–7, 20n9, 27, 31, 39, 45, 52, 55n18, 116n2, 133, 135, 138
Gulf War (1991) 34

Hainan Island 88, 108
Han Chinese 5, 7, 22n28
Hara, Kimie 72n2
Hauser, Christine 41n16
He, D. and Zhang, W. 20n6
hegemonic powers 75, 90, 95, 99
Heinrichs, Raoul 22n32
Helleiner, Karl F. 102n27
Herszenhorn, D.M. and Buckley, C. 22n40, 43n48
Ho Chi Minh 106
Hoffman, F.G. 139, 142n24
Holmes, James 73n13, 100n3
Hong Kong 84
Hong Nong 100n2
Hong Zhao 141n12
household income 3–4
How East Asians View Democracy (Chu, Y., Diamond, L., Nathan, A. and Shin, D.C.) 126, 131n16
Hu, Nien-Tsu Alfred 117n38
Hu Jintao 20n4, 60, 63, 126
Huang Yasheng 54n6, 131n22
Hubbard, G.R. and Navarro, P. 42n24
Hughes, Christopher 73n11
human and civil rights considerations 26, 93, 123

Ikenberry, G. John 42n40, 102n28
India 5, 24, 32, 35, 48, 66, 81; China and problems concerning border with 7–8; Concert of Powers 99; energy cooperation talks with China 35; energy insecurity and demand from 36; Sino-Indian rapprochement 8; vibrant economy of 27
Indian Ocean 12, 15, 21n24, 37, 46, 81, 88, 90
Indonesia 24, 37, 61, 66, 67, 87, 88, 93, 113, 115, 128, 133
Industrial Revolution 38
Indyk, M.S., Lieberthal, K.G. and O'Hanlon, M.E. 80n14
inequalities: and divisiveness in China, risks of 3–4; in wealth and income distributions 46–47
inflation rates 9
infrastructure projects 4, 7, 12, 13, 32, 37, 52, 53, 106, 141n13; oil-for-infrastructure deals 28–29, 46
Inkster, Nigel 22n29
interconnectedness 6, 35–36, 70, 84, 123
intergovernmental organizations 112–13

160 *Index*

internal security targets, external power projection and 14–16
internal transfers, inflows and outflows, challenge of 8–9
International Court of Justice (ICJ) 59–60
International Crisis Group (ICG) 116n11
International Institute for Security Studies (IISS) 21n22
international oil markets 35, 45, 46
international politics 16–17, 19, 26, 49, 121; national policy-making and 16–18, 19
International Security and Defense Policy Center at RAND Corporation 90–91
interstate reciprocity, need for 129
investment-driven, export-dependent growth model 51
Iran 19, 34, 45, 46, 48
Iraq 19, 48; US military intervention in 83–84
Ito, Shingo 73n21

Jacobs, A, and Buckley, C. 21n12, 22n30
Jacobs, Andrew 22n28
Jaffe, Amy 27
Jakobson, Linda 73n22, 79n4
Japan 6, 10, 18, 24, 35, 37, 40, 59–72, 81, 84, 86; ASEAN, powerful 'others' and 65–67; Chinese hard power and 61–63; co-existence without defiance, Sino-Japanese tensions and 67–69; Concert of Powers 99; counterbalancing Chinese power 65–67; Diaoyu/Senkaku Islands, dispute over 59–60, 61, 67, 71, 72n3, 73n22, 73n26, 74; energy imports 88; foreign policy paradigm 64–65; geopolitical turmoil in East Asia, potential for 59; global security concerns 59; high-stakes politics, China and new figures in 69–70, 71–72; International Court of Justice (ICJ) 59–60; international politics 16–17; interstate relations with China, normalization efforts 71; maritime dispute with China, core issues 70–71; North Korea, China and 98; Philippines and 75; pragmatic approach to interstate issues 66; purchase of Diaoyu/Senkaku Islands by 60; reaction to Chinese expressions of hard power 63–65; San Francisco

Peace Treaty (1951) 59; Sino-Japanese maritime activities 98; Sino-Japanese relationship 67–69, 70; Sino-Japanese relationship, encouraging signs of change in 71–72; Sino-Japanese War (1895) 59; South China Sea as 'Lake Beijing' for 63; strategic interests shared with China 71; territorial dispute with China, core issues 70–71; two-way conversation with China, prospects for 71–72; United States and neighbours, issues and options for 60–61; US largest export market for 71; win-win scenarios between China and 70
Japan Times 102n31
Jensen, N. and Wantchekon, L. 41n17
Ji Guoxing 20n8
Ji You 130n14
Jian Chen 116n12
Jianxin Zhang 54n12
job creation 53
job security 6
Johnston, Alastair Iain 130n9, 138, 142n22
Juhasz, Antonia 54n8

Kang, David C. 22n36
Kaplan, Robert D. 21n24, 82, 100n3, 101n10, 142n23
Karim, M. Aminul 117n39
Kashmir 8
Kazakhstan 45, 48; oil and gas production in 32
Keck, Zachary 43n53
Kennedy, Andrew 54n11
Kennedy, Paul 102n21
Kerry, John 79, 100
Kim, Samuel S. 41n14
Kim Jong Un 125
Kissinger, Henry 103n42
Kivimäki, Timo 82, 100n1
Klare, Michael T. 42n26, 42n35, 80n13
Koizumi, Junichiro 66
Kōno, Yōhei 73n16
Koo, M. 27
Korean Peninsula 21n21, 86, 100, 123, 130n11; potential for crisis on, effect on China 125–26; *see also* North Korea; South Korea
Korean War (1950–53) 13
Kreft, Heinrich 27
Kripalani, M., Roberts, D. and Bush, J. 43n47

Kristof, Nicholas D. 104, 116n1
Krugman, Paul 102n33
Kumar, Hari 43n48
Kurlantzick, Joshua 43n53
Kuwait 27, 48; oil and gas production in 32

Lanteigne, Marc 36, 43n52, 101n14
Laos 86
Latin America 34
Law on the Territorial Sea and the
  Contiguous Zone (1992) 59–60
Lee, John 54n2, 54n5
Lee, Matthew 103n48
Leggett, Korby 42n41
Leibo, Stevan A. 101n9
Leifer, Michael 107, 116n18
Li Keqiang 70, 76
Libya 45, 48
Lieberthal, Kenneth G. 79–80n6
Lieberthal, K.G. and Wang, J. 23n43
liquid fuels consumption 74
literature reviews: resource security 26–
  27; Sino-Chinese relations 82; South
  China Sea, China, US and 81–82
Lo, Bobo 27, 43n48
Lombok Strait 87
London Metal Exchange 28
Looney, Robert 41n2
Luttwak, Edward 73n23

Ma Lian 22n37
Mabasa, Roy C. 80n7
Macau 84
Macclesfield Bank 111
McGregor, Charles 106, 116n15
McKinsey Global Institute 26, 41n15
Makassar Strait 87
Makower, J. and Pike, C. 42n37
Malacca, Strait of 37, 46, 87, 88
Malampaya, Philippines 113
Malaysia 10, 81, 87, 88
Malik, J. Mohan 21n15
Mallaby, Sebastian 42n25
Manchuria 91; Chinese interests in 5–6
Mandelbaum, Michael 142n23
Manning, Richard 42n33
Manning, Robert 54n7
Mao Zedong 3–4, 30, 105–6
Marcos, Ferdinand 128
maritime and territorial disputes: core
  issues for China and Japan 70–71; US
  diplomacy on 78–79; Vietnam and
  border delineations and 112–13; *see
  also* East China Sea; South China Sea

Marxism 94, 102n32
Mattoo, A. and Subramanian, A. 43n49
Mearsheimer, John J. 130n7, 142n25
Mexico 48, 133; oil and gas production
  in 32
Meyer, Claude 72n5
Middle East 3, 25, 28, 29, 59, 75, 90, 91,
  99, 128; oil security and 35, 37, 39,
  46; resource security and 133, 134,
  137; supplies from, volatility
  of 47–48
militariness: build-up of military in
  China 8, 96; military power in China,
  misconceptions about 16; military
  technology 15; modernization, new
  leaders' push for 15–16; oil security
  and military strategy 45; power
  projection and military build-up 9–14;
  South China Sea, militarization and
  134–36; US military interventions 83–
  84; US military presence in Asia 97
*Military and Security Developments
  Involving the People's Republic of
  China 2011* (US Defence Dept.) 62
Milivojevic, Marko 117n35
Milligan-Whyte, J. and Min, D. 103n47
Mischief Reef, naval stand-off between
  China and Philippines over 75–76,
  77–78
Mishra, Keshav 21n15
Mobutu Sese Seko 128
Monaghan, Andrew 27
Mongolia 84; Chinese interests in 5–6
Motaal, Doaa Abdel 42n39
Mullen, Jethro 80n9
Murayama, Tomiichi 73n16
Myanmar 12, 15, 22n26, 34, 37, 45, 53,
  55n22, 72, 113, 136, 141n15

Nanking, Treaty of (1842) 102n23
Nansha Islands 111
Napoleonic Wars (1803–15) 82–83
Nathan, Andrew J. 103n49
National Bureau of Statistics, China 31,
  42n31
National Energy Administration
  (NEAC), China 25
national interest, defence of 19, 45, 50,
  61, 92, 99, 108–9, 112–13, 129
National Offshore Oil Corporation
  (CNOOC), China 29, 110
National People's Congress (2013) 70
National Space Administration in China
  11

162 *Index*

nationalism 18, 63, 92, 105, 109, 122–23; muscular nationalism 72; popular loyalty and 4–5

Natuna Islands 113

natural gas, appetites for 29–30

natural resources 25–26, 28, 34, 35–36, 37, 38, 40, 46, 74, 87, 92, 105, 108, 109; power projection and 5, 12, 20, 124, 128–29; resource security and 132, 134

Natural Security Blog 21n20

naval power 17, 21n25, 37, 67, 84, 91–92, 95, 105

New York Times 30, 79n1, 117n31

Nguyen Van Tho 111

Nicaragua 34

Nigeria 27, 48

Nobrega, William 42n28, 44n61

Noda, Yoshihiko 65

non-renewable energy 17, 100, 132

non-renewable energy resources 132

Norman, Joshua 43n56

North Africa 3, 37, 39, 59, 91, 128

North-East Asia 64; United States and 86

North Korea 10, 19, 29, 30, 34, 64, 84, 85, 86; China and 98; Chinese diplomacy and 50

Norway 37, 48

Obama, Barack (and administration of) 12, 62, 72, 78

Ogden, Chris 22n31, 27

O'Hanlon, Michael 130n3

oil-for-infrastructure deals 28–29, 46

oil security 45–54; actions beyond national borders, effects of 53; authoritarian growth, admiration for system of 49; clean energy 53; conventional oil 47–48; demand management 46; diplomatic overtures 48–50; discovery deficit 47; economic growth, sustainability in 53; economic models 50–52; economic policies and 45, 52–53; energy conservation technologies 53; exploration technology 47; export promotion 53; foreign oil operations, control of 45–46, 52; foreign policies and 45; inelasticity of demand 29; inequalities in wealth and income distributions 46–47; international oil markets 46; job creation in China 53; manufacturing improvements 53; Middle East supplies, volatility in 47–48; military strategy and 45; multi-pronged approach to 53–54; national interest and 45; oil and gas deposits, scramble for 109–10; political legitimacy and 45; privileged access, aim of 46; prosperity, CCP formula for 52–53; renewable energy production 53; reserve exhaustion 48; scarcity 133–34; search for sources overseas 25–26, 40–41; shale oil 48; social stability and 45, 52–53; strategic priorities, China's reshaping of 53; sustainability 46, 47; tact in diplomacy with calculated outcomes 48–50; unconventional oil 47; US imports 29

Organization for Economic Cooperation and Development (OECD) 74, 116n3, 116n5, 141n7

Owen, N. and Schofield, C. 139, 142n26

Pacific Ocean 74, 84–85

Pakistan 8, 12, 37, 98, 102n29; US military intervention in 83–84

Pan, Zhongqi 72n3

Panama Canal 88, 90

Papayoanou, Paul A. 102n28

Pape, R.A. 23n41

Paracel archipelago 10, 40, 88–89, 90, 101n15, 105, 108, 111, 113, 114–15, 116n11, 117n20, 137

Park, Choon-ho 117n21

Park Geun-Hye 125

Pempel, T.J. 141n9

People's Armed Police (PAP) 14, 15

People's Liberation Army (PLA) 7–8, 14, 15, 45, 62, 103n36, 105

Perlez, Jane 80n10, 117n29

Peru 29

Philippines 6, 10, 24, 26, 59, 60, 74–79, 81, 88; ASEAN and Sino-Philippine relations 75–76, 78; Chinese foreign policy towards 76–78; economic growth, inputs for rapidity in 74; energy demands 74–75; indisputable sovereignty over South China Sea, Chinese claims of 74–75; Japan and 75; liquid fuels consumption 74; Mischief Reef, naval stand-off with China over 75–76, 77–78; Sino-Philippine relations 75–76, 78–79; South China Sea, Chinese challenge to legality of claims on 77; South China Sea, claims to 74, 79; UN Convention on the Law of the Sea

Index 163

(UNCLOS) 75; United States, indifference to Sino-Philippine relations 78–79; United States and 75

Pillsbury, Michael 130n10

Politburo Standing Committee of CCP 4

political geography, spatial structures and 84

political legitimacy, oil security and 45, 63, 133, 135

power projections 9–19, 121–29, 140–41; analogical thinking 121; assertiveness in South China Sea 17–18; Chinese politics and 126–28; containment of China 122–23, 129; corruption, checks on 128–29; democracy, need for transparency and 128–29; engagement with China 122–23, 129; external projection 14–16; internal security targets and external projection of power 14–16; international politics, national policy-making and 16–18, 19; interstate reciprocity, need for 129; Korean Peninsula, China and 125–26; military build-up 9–14; naval fleets and 17, 21n25, 37, 67, 84, 91–92, 95, 105; power and uses of, Chinese conceptualization of 106–8; power as tool 123–25; power competitions 107; power transition theory 121; problem-finding, solution-fitting and 121–22; regional perception and 107; security, sovereignty and 124; South China Sea, critical sea routes of 129; Spratley Islands, Chinese power projection and 122; Transparency International 128; weapon, power as 123–25

power transition theory 121

pragmatic internationalism 5, 66

productive inputs, demand for 25–26, 27–30, 40–41

Promyamyai, Thanaporn 55n22

prosperity, CCP formula for 52–53

Public Security Bureau in China 127

Putin, Vladimir 22n39

Qatar 48

Qian, Nancy 128

Qing dynasty 84, 91

RAND Corporation 22n35, 23n44, 90, 102n21

Ravenhill, John 142n27

Reed Bank 40

renewable energy 25–26, 37, 47, 53, 99; non-renewable energy 17, 100, 132

reserves of crude oil and natural gas 140; reserve exhaustion 48

resource competition 40

resource depletion 25–26

resource needs 132

resource security 24–41, 132–41; analysis, reflections from afar and 38–40; artificial resources 132; assertiveness and 138–39; balance and 139; bilateral trade relation with oil-rich states 26; challenges of, East and South-East Asia and 140; Chinese policy and maneuvers 137–38; civil and human rights considerations 26; consensus and search for 136–37; control, exertion of outright influence and 139–40; economic growth, demand for resources and 24, 25; economic growth, Western with Eastern style 27–30; environmental considerations 31–33; geopolitics 33–35; global hunt for vital resources 132–33; global search for resources 24–41, 52; hunger for energy, problems caused by 132; literature review 26–27; National Offshore Oil Corporation (CNOOC) 29, 110; natural gas, appetites for 29–30; natural resources 132; non-renewable energy resources 132; oil, inelasticity of demand for 29; oil, scarce input 133–34; oil and gas, search for sources overseas 25–26, 40–41; oil-for-infrastructure deals 28–29, 46; oil trading 24; productive inputs, demand for 25–26, 27–30, 40–41; raw material resources 132; renewable energy resources 132; reserves of crude oil and natural gas 140; resource competition, optimism on 40; resource depletion, recognition of 25–26; resource needs 132; South China Sea, China's strategic interests in 140–41; South China Sea, growth, oil, militarization and 134–36; South China Sea, militarization and 134–36; South China Sea, oil and 134–36; South China Sea, petroleum geology in 24–25; state sovereignty, fundamental basis for 140; strategic

164 *Index*

considerations 35–37; world energy demand, growth in 26
Rogers, Will 79n5, 100n3
Rohter, Larry 42n41
Ross, Robert S. 39–40, 43n56, 44n63, 130n4
Ross, R.S. and Feng Z. 130n8
Roy, Denny 137, 142n18
Rudd, Kevin 39, 43n56, 44n63
Russia 5–6, 24, 29, 34–35, 45, 48, 64, 81, 86; oil and gas production in 32; vibrant economy of 27

Sachs, Jeffrey D. 43n54
Salameh, Mamdouh G. 117n25
Samuels, Marwyn 101n15
Samuelson, Robert 55n17
San Francisco Peace Treaty (1951) 59
Sandalow, D. 42n29
Sang-Hun Choe 130n12
Sarawak 113
Saudi Arabia 27, 48; oil and gas production in 32
Scarborough Shoal 76
Schweller, Randall L. 116n17
Scobell, A. and Nathan, A.J. 72n7
Sea Of Japan 6, 17, 73
sea-routes: focus on protection for 8; surveillance of 108–9; *see also* East China Sea; maritime and territorial disputes; South China Sea
security: security apparatus in China 14; sovereignty and 124; US security dynamics 95–97; *see also* resource security
Security Treaty between Japan and US 68
Senkaku Islands 40, 59, 70; *see also* Diaoyu/Senkaku Islands
shale oil 48
Shambaugh, David 54n13, 100n1, 130n11
Shandong Peninsula 91
Shanghai Cooperation Organization 49
Shanghai uprising (1927), effects of 3–4
Shee Poon Kim 141n15
Shell 48
Siberia 5–6
Simon, Sheldon W. 116n14
Singapore 10, 87, 88
Singapore Strait 124
Sinh Ton Island 109, 110–11
Sino-Indian rapprochment 8
Sino-Japanese maritime activities 98

Sino-Japanese relations 67–69, 70, 71–72
Sino-Japanese War (1895) 59
Sino-Philippine relations 75–76, 78–79
Sino-US collaboration 100
SIPRI (Stockholm International Peace Research Institute) 102n29
60 Minutes (CBS TV) 4
Slater, D. and Taylor, P.J. 130n7
Smith, Sheila A. 98, 103n47
social stability, oil security and 45, 52–53
socialist market economy 8–9
Song Yann-Huei 101n7
South Africa 24, 35, 133; vibrant economy of 27
South America 26, 29
South China Sea 4–5, 6, 15, 37, 46, 111; Asia's power dynamics in 10–12; challenges for regional relations 81, 87–91; China's strategic interests in 140–41; Chinese assertiveness in 17–18; Chinese challenge to legality of claims on 77; claims and counterclaims in connection with 89, 99–100, 112–14; critical sea routes of 129; disputed delimitations in 40; disturbances in 112; energy frontier 24–25; exploitable resources in 81; freedom of navigation in 81–82; geopolitical importance of 81–82, 91–92; geostrategic relevance of 88–89; growth, oil, militarization and 134–36; indisputable sovereignty over, Chinese claims of 74–75; infrastructure projects on shores of 13; 'Lake Beijing' for Japan 63; literature review, China, US and 81–82; maritime surveillance of 74–75; militarization and 134–36; mineral exploration in 29; misconceptions on, potential for 98; national interest and 99–100; naval experience and China's defence of 10–11; oil, resource security and 134–36; petroleum geology in 24–25; Philippines claims to 74, 79; potential for balanced approach on 98–99; power politics and 114–15; security dynamics emergent in 92–93; security dynamics of 92–93, 97–98; strategic vulnerability of China and 74–75; transit through, contentions issue of 81–82; US stability guarantees for 93–94; Vietnamese strategic interests in 108–9

Index 165

South-East Asia 18, 26, 34, 35, 40, 49, 66–67; South China Sea and 86–88; United States and 86–87, 98
South Korea 6, 10, 63–64, 65, 71, 84, 86; energy imports 88
South Kuril Islands 66
sovereignty: humanity, warfare and 83; issue for China 9–10, 17, 19, 21n12; *see also* state sovereignty
Soviet Union 34, 90, 92, 94, 95, 106
Spain 37
Spegele, Brian 43n53, 54n1
Spence, Jonathan D. 102n24
Spero, J.E. and Hart, J.A. 41n6
Spratly archipelago 10, 40, 76, 88, 90, 101n15, 105, 107, 108, 109–12, 113, 114–15, 116n11, 117n28, 122
Sri Lanka 12
State Oceanic Administration in China 63, 73n12
state sovereignty: defensive rights and 83; fundamental basis for 140
Storey, Ian James 77, 80n12, 82, 100n3, 141n11
Strategic and Defence Studies Centre in China 15
Sudan 34, 45, 46
Sunda Strait 87
Swaine, Michael D. 22n35
Syria 29

Taiping Dao, naval bases on 110
Taiwan 6, 10, 59, 74, 81, 84, 93, 102n22; Chinese diplomacy and 49–50; Chinese military focus on 72n8; energy imports 88
Taiwan Strait 37
Takeshima Day 65, 73n17
Tan, Dai 73n26
Tatlow, Kirsten 73n26
Taylor, Ian 27
Teradaa, Takashi 103n46
territorial disputes 21n21, 59, 60, 65, 78, 79n2, 105–6, 108, 109, 123, 134, 139; border delineations (China-Vietnam) 112–13; Japan-China 70–71
Thailand 53, 67, 87, 96, 98, 133
Thao, N.H. and Amer, R. 117n37
Thatcher, Margaret 69
Thirty Years' War (1618–48) 82–83
Tian Wei 41n20
Tibet 21n13, 22n28, 59, 112–13; Chinese interests in 5–6, 7; Chinese invasion of 13; unrest in 17

Tonkin, Gulf of 35, 112
Tønnesson, Stein 108–9, 117n22
trade 16, 38, 85–86, 87, 88, 91, 112, 126, 133; bilateral trade relation with oil-rich states 26; Chinese trade surplus 25, 52; expansion 31; Federal Trade Commission (US) 34, 54n8; free trade arrangements 65, 94, 127, 138; globalized trade 134; investment and, importance of 61, 127; Japan-China trade, decline in 67; liberalization of 138; maritime trade 66, 81, 95, 108, 113, 132, 134, 135, 137; oil trading, resource security and 24; openness 3, 30, 86, 139; preferential trade agreements 34, 98; promotion 34, 100; promotion of, Chinese focus on 8; technology and 106; trade-critical sea lanes in South China Sea 108, 132, 134, 137, 141; trade-dependence of China 5; trade protection 81, 132; trade-relevant infrastructure 13; UN Conference on Trade and Development (UNCTAD) 104; US trade deficit 29
Transparency International 128
Tsui, M. and Li, X. 21n18
Turkey 24, 133

United Arab Emirates (UAE) 48
United Nations (UN): Conference on Trade and Development (UNCTAD) 104; Convention on the Law of the Sea (UNCLOS) 75, 113–14, 115; Security Council 14, 46, 113
United States 5, 6, 10, 18–19, 25, 26, 35, 36, 48, 66, 81–100, 140; Afghanistan, military intervention in 83–84; ASEAN, South China Sea and 98; ASEAN and 87, 88, 93–94, 97, 99; Asia-Pacific and 36, 39–40, 61; Asian financial crisis (1997–98), defence spending reductions and 93; Asian power balance and 38; capitalism, catalyst for contention 94–95; Census Bureau 54n10; China and West, historical perspective 91–94; China Seas and 4–5; Chinese power aspirations and 82; Code for Unalerted Encounters at Sea (CUES) 99; Concert of Powers 99; consumer-led growth in 50–51; defence and security treaties 76; Defence Department 62, 72n9; Office of

166   *Index*

Secretary of Defence 72–73n10; East Asia and Western Pacific, power struggle epicentre 84–86, 92–93; Energy Department 54n10; Energy Information Administration (EIA) 54n10, 79n2, 79n3, 117n27; energy requirements of China, global relations and 81–82; energy security, challenges for 99; Federal Reserve 55n16; Geological Survey (USGS) 110, 117n28; geopolitics of oil and power 33–34; geostrategic diplomacy 61; hegemonic power of 99; indifference to Sino-Philippine relations 78–79; international politics 16–17; Iraq, military intervention in 83–84; Japan and neighbours, issues and options 60–61; Japan's largest export market 71; literature review, Sino-Chinese relations 82; Malacca, Strait of 88; maritime and territorial disputes, diplomacy on 78–79; military interventions 83–84; military presence in Asia 97; military technology 15; nationalism 92; North-East Asia and 86; North Korea, China and 98; oil imports 29; Pakistan, military intervention in 83–84; Panama Canal and 88, 90; partnerships with Japan and Philippines 75; political geography, spatial structures and 84; power projection, naval fleets and 84, 91–92; regional struggles in Asia, interference in 68; security dynamics 95–97; Security Treaty between Japan and 68; Sino-US collaboration 100; South China Sea, challenges for regional relations 81, 87–91; South China Sea, claims and counterclaims concerning 89; South China Sea, freedom of navigation in 81–82; South China Sea, geopolitical importance of 81–82, 91–92; South China Sea, geostrategic relevance of 88–89; South China Sea, literature review, China, US and 81–82; South China Sea, potential for misconceptions on 98; South China Sea, security dynamics in 92–93, 97–98; South China Sea, stability guarantees in 93–94; South-East Asia and 86–87, 98; sovereignty, humanity, warfare and 83; states' defensive rights 83; strategic interests 82; trade deficit

29; US Mexican War (1846–48) 90; US Spanish War (1898) 90; warfare strategy 11; wars, security and global geography 82–83; world-wide reputation, decline of 49
US Steel 31

Valencia, Mark J. 117n24
Van Evera, Stephen 130n5
Venezuela 34, 45, 46, 48
Vietnam 6, 10, 24, 35, 59, 74, 81, 86, 88, 93, 104–15; ASEAN and 105, 106, 107, 108, 110, 111, 115, 116n14; buffer between hegemons 108–9; Chinese incursion into (1979) 13; Chinese power projection and 104–5; diplomacy, soft power and 110–12; exclusive economic zone (EEZ) 109, 111; historical perspective on China and 105–6; intergovernmental organizations, border disputes and 112–13; maritime disputes, border delineations and 112–13; national security, energy supplies and 108–9; oil and gas deposits, scramble for 109–10; power and uses of, Chinese conceptualization of 106–8; sea routes, surveillance of 108–9; South China Sea, power politics and 114–15; South China Sea, strategic interests in 108–9; supremacy over resources, struggle for 111–12; territorial disputes, border delineations and 112–13; UN Convention on the Law of the Sea (UNCLOS) 113–14, 115; Zone of Peace, Freedom and Neutrality Declaration (Kuala Lumpur, 1971) 106

Walt, Stephen M. 116n17
Wang, J. 22n38
warfare: ethical predicaments and moral quandries on 85; security, global geography and 82–83; strategies of China and US 11–12
Warnock, Francis E. 42n23
Washington Post 73n17
Weagley, Robert O. 20n2
Webb, James 92, 102n26
The Week 55n20
Wen Jiabao 20n4, 21n12, 54n3
Wenmu, Z. 141n10
Wesley, Michael 10, 21n21

West: economic problems of, effects on China 6–7; perspectives on emergent power of China 17–18
White, Hugh 103n41
Whitlock, Craig 102n30
WHO (World Health Organization) 31
Wilson, Jeffrey D. 138, 142n19, 142n21
Wong, Edward 30
Woody Island 89
World Bank 31, 42n30
world energy demand, growth in 26
WTO (World Trade Organization) 30, 126

Xi Jinping 5, 17, 21n17, 69–70, 71, 76, 126–27
Xinhua news agency 20n9, 89
Xinjiang, Chinese interests in 5–6, 7
Xisha Islands 111, 117n20

Yahuda, Michael 41n6
Yan, X. 21n23
Yang Chengyu, Major General 130n10
Yao, K. and Wang, A. 21n11
Yasukuni Shrine 64, 73n15

Zha, D. and Valencia, M.J. 80n8
Zhai Qiang 116n13
Zhang Yongjing (Eugene) 21n19
Zhao Hong 20n10
Zhao Suisheng 54n4, 101n6, 103n40
Zhongsha Islands 111
Zhou Fang 43n47
Zone of Peace, Freedom and Neutrality Declaration (Kuala Lumpur, 1971) 106
Zweig, D. and Jianhai, B. 26, 41n11, 132, 141n5
Zweig, David 27